WORLD WAR II
REFLECTIONS

WORLD WAR II
REFLECTIONS

AN ORAL HISTORY OF
PENNSYLVANIA'S VETERANS

BRIAN LOCKMAN

With additional text by Dan Cupper
Introduction by Kenneth C. Wolensky

STACKPOLE
BOOKS

⊓PCN

Published by
STACKPOLE BOOKS
5067 Ritter Road
Mechanicsburg, PA 17055
www.stackpolebooks.com

Printed in the United States of America

10 9 8 7 6 5 4 3 2 1

FIRST EDITION

Cover design by Tessa J. Sweigert

Library of Congress Cataloging-in-Publication Data

World War II reflections : an oral history of Pennsylvania's veterans / [edited by] Brian Lockman ; with additional text by Dan Cupper ; introduction by Kenneth C. Wolensky.
    p.   cm.
    "Part of a project started in 2002 by the Pennsylvania Cable Network"—Foreword.
    Includes bibliographical references and index.
    ISBN-13: 978-0-8117-3608-4 (pbk. : alk. paper)
    ISBN-10: 0-8117-3608-3 (pbk. : alk. paper)
    1. World War, 1939–1945—Personal narratives, American. 2. World War, 1939–1945—Veterans—Pennsylvania—Biography. 3. Veterans—Pennsylvania—Interviews. 4. Veterans—United States—Interviews. 5. Oral history—Pennsylvania. 6. Interviews—Pennsylvania. I. Lockman, Brian. II. Cupper, Dan. III. Pennsylvania Cable Network. IV. Title: World War 2 reflections. V. Title: World War Two reflections.
D769.2.W65   2009
940.54'81748—dc22
                                                                    2009020508

☆ CONTENTS ☆

☆ FOREWORD ☆

Today, Ed Halluska travels the world teaching bridge on cruise ships. When Ed invited us into his home, he showed us souvenirs from all over the globe. He is one of the few who have visited the Antarctic. He is also one of the few to have worked on the Manhattan Project. This tool-and-die maker from Westinghouse was drafted in 1945 to machine the uranium used in the atomic bomb. Our crew listened in rapt attention as he described the process. His only protection on the job: rubber gloves, a mask, and overalls. He saved every little chip of the precious metal; he was told it was worth $1,000 a gram, which meant he held millions of dollars in his hand.

Ed's job during the war was unique, but he and his wife were typical of the people we met while working on this project. Many of the veterans we interviewed invited us into their homes. These homes were mostly modest, built shortly after the war. When the veterans saw our crew coming in with large equipment bags, they wanted to help. And they always wanted to feed us.

While working on this project we came to realize how lucky we are. My grandparents and great aunts and uncles told us stories of the Great Depression and World War II, two monumental events requiring great sacrifice from the majority of Americans. I was born in 1966 and have a vague recollection of the Vietnam War and gas lines in the 1970s. As I sit here in 2009, the country is in a recession, yet in my lifetime I've known relative stability and peace. For better or worse, my generation as a whole has not had to sacrifice for that prosperity.

The original producer of this series of interviews was twenty-three-year-old Jolene Risser. She found it difficult to fathom "parting with a loved one and the uncertainty of his return," as she wrote in her introduction to the first book, *World War II: In Their Own Words*. I'm a bit older and have a son and daughter. I can't imagine the anxiety of sending them to war, not knowing where they were, hoping to get a letter—and praying that the knock on the door is just a neighbor.

The men and women we interviewed were all Pennsylvanians but they could have been from any city, town, or borough in the country. They came from all walks of life and all ethnic groups. Many volunteered for the service and some were drafted. They were forced by circumstance to put their lives on hold and to fight a war thousands of miles away from the places they called home. Most were young, but some, like Ezekiel Dorsey, were more seasoned.

Dorsey was thirty-six when he enlisted after Pearl Harbor; when I met him he was one hundred. Never having met anyone more than one hundred years old, I didn't know what to expect when we arrived at his Pittsburgh home. We were greeted by a spry man who—we later found out from his son—was on the roof of his garage making some repairs just days before our interview. A one-hundred-year-old being on a garage roof is a feat in itself, but even more so if you know anything about the topography of Pittsburgh and its hills and valleys. While the front of the garage was the typical one story above the ground, the nearest ground to the rear was three to four stories down.

Dorsey had his own business, an auto garage that he had to close when he enlisted. He became interested in radios when he was a boy; he was an amateur radio operator, and during the war it was his job to repair radio transmitters. When Mr. Dorsey gave us a tour of his house we could tell by the equipment packed in the second floor that it was still a passion of his.

I listened in awe as he described his childhood in Pittsburgh, before automobiles, with horse-drawn wagons delivering ice. He spoke of early memories of Armistice Day (the end of World War I), the beginning of aviation (he got his pilot's licenses), and the early automobile industry. He laughed when he talked about his trip overseas and his aching joints, joking that he was the old man of the group. I was struck by just how much change this man had seen in his life.

This book is filled with fascinating and sometimes death-defying stories. Conducting the interviews was an enlightening and inspiring experience. My eleven-year-old daughter read the first book in one sitting; she was in awe of these people. All of the interviews in that book and this one came from the PCN television series *World War II: In Their Own Words*. The experience was profound for everyone who had an opportunity to work on the production. My thoughts as I recount the interviews are of sacrifice. These men and women are here to tell us their stories; we should listen. It struck me that after several of the interviews, some of the veterans' sons and daughters said that this was the first time they had heard their fathers or mothers talk so openly about the war. These veterans are the survivors, and they speak not only for themselves but for the fallen comrades who made the ultimate sacrifice.

William J. Bova
Vice President of Programming
Pennsylvania Cable Network

☆ ACKNOWLEDGMENTS ☆

This book is part of a project started in 2002 by the Pennsylvania Cable Network, a non-profit, public affairs cable television network. The project has so far consisted of more than 250 interviews with Pennsylvania's World War II veterans, nearly all of which aired without editing; one book prior to this one, *World War II: In Their Own Words*, published by Stackpole Books in 2005; an audio version of that book, published by PCN in 2009; and this volume.

We owe thanks first to the veterans who were willing to share their stories. They gave their recollections with remarkable accuracy and were able to describe not only the big events, many of which were difficult for them to relive, but also the very small events, like the discovery of a deck of cards in a foxhole or the taste of a pint of milk.

In addition to the veterans, dozens of people have lent us valuable assistance. Rick Cochran, PCN's Vice President of Marketing, called upon his years in the print media to help with the editing and proofreading. Rick also researched and wrote all of the "After the War . . ." pieces that add so much to the book. In addition, he spent countless hours assembling and selecting photos, some from the veterans and others from the National Archives. Rick also made arrangements with the Army Heritage Center Foundation for the fact-checking of the veterans' stories.

The job of producer was, at times, all-consuming. It involved locating the veterans willing and able to tell their stories, gathering pre-interview information for the person conducting the interview, selecting an interviewer, finding a location for the interview, scheduling the interview, assigning a production crew, accumulating photographs that illustrate the veterans' stories, spending countless hours in the editing room preparing the tapes for airing, and then, when everything was in place, arranging for an air time for the interviews. Jolene Risser served as producer for three years. She was succeeded first by Theresa Elliot, who held the position from 2005 until 2008, and then by Kat Prickett, who is currently the series producer.

The interviewers' job was to read the background material assembled by the producer, prepare a wide range of questions to ask, and then, as much as possible, to keep his or her mouth shut. The interviewers would try to make the veterans feel comfortable, get them started with a few simple questions, and then stay out of the way. Usually the best interviews have been the ones in which the host has said very little. Our interviewers for the series have been Bill Bova, Corey Clarke, Theresa Elliot, Larry Kaspar, Brian Lockman, Kevin Love, Kat Prickett, Jolene Risser, Francine Schertzer, and Doug Sicchitano.

Bill Bova, PCN's Vice President of Programming, oversaw the entire television series from its inception to the present. His guidance and enthusiasm were essential in making this project happen.

Roseann Mazzella is PCN's post-interview liaison with the veterans. Her friendly approach has helped PCN establish wonderful relationships with the veterans. Pam Wert spent many hours transcribing interviews and putting them in a form that could be edited for this book.

The entire PCN staff is involved in this project in one way or another, whether it be research, camera operation, audio, editing, graphics, scheduling, tape playback, logistics, promotion, or any of the other jobs that keep a television network on the air. In addition to the people mentioned above, they are Erik Appleyard, Jeremy Baker, Debbie Eckstine, Dave Emenheiser, John Fox, Steve Grassa, Michelle Harter, Alicia Higby, Melissa Hiler, Tucker Knerr, Dave Koch, Robert Krout, Brian McCarty, Shawn McLain, Paul Padelsky, Matt Popecki, Diana Robinson, Debra Sheppard, Dean Vaccher, Jeremie Vu, and Jonathan Whaley.

Kyle Weaver of Stackpole Books has given us his support and encouragement throughout. And thanks to Stackpole Books, an outstanding publisher of military history and Pennsylvania history titles, for their willingness to work with us on this book.

Thanks also to Congressman Joseph Sestak; Tina Raybold and Kandace Wertz of the Masonic Homes, Elizabethtown; Roger Sands of the Lebanon

VA Medical Center, Lebanon; Linda Schyleske from the Citizen Standard newspaper, Schuylkill, Dauphin, and Northumberland counties; Kevin Craft from the Columbia VFW, Lancaster County; Dick Tyler of the Purple Heart, Rydal; Joanna Murphy, Suzanne Swain, and Ed Buffman of the Pennsylvania Veterans Museum, Media; the Borough of Media; the Berks County Department of Veteran Affairs; Scott Shugart from the Dillsburg Senior Center, York County; the Hershey Library, Hershey; the Northampton Township Building, Richboro; Pete Palenstina, Northampton Township Supervisor; and Lisa Russo, Northampton Township Administrative Assistant.

Thanks to Hank Heim and Frank Lashinsky, whose stories were told in our first volume, *World War II: In Their Own Words*, and to Frank's charming wife, Dorothy. They have volunteered many hours of their time to appear on behalf of PCN to sign books and give more of their recollections of the war.

Thanks to Dan Cupper and Ken Wolensky, who unlike me are real historians. Dan did an outstanding job researching and writing the sidebars, the short background pieces that appear throughout the book; they help put the veterans' stories in context and give the reader an opportunity to better understand the situations the veterans faced. Ken Wolensky authored the Introduction, on Pennsylvania's contributions to the Second World War. Both Dan and Ken have written very interesting books about Pennsylvania history that deserve your attention.

Allowing that, through the passage of time, some of the veterans might not have remembered events with historical precision, we received essential help with fact-checking from Lorraine Luciano, Education Director at the Army Heritage Center Foundation; Shawn Connery of the Shippensburg University Public History Program; Matthew Pollart of the Shippensburg University Undergraduate History Program; and Scott Orris, who graduated with a B.A. in History from Messiah College. Their work made us appreciate how accurate the veterans' memories were.

The Pennsylvania Cable Network is the creation of Pennsylvania cable television operators, who founded the network in 1979 as a public service to the people of Pennsylvania. The cable companies represented on PCN's Board of Directors are Armstrong Cable, Atlantic Broadband, Blue Ridge Communications, Comcast, and the Service Electric Companies. PCN's Board also includes World War II veterans Joseph Gans and our chairman, Jim Duratz, whose story is told in this book. Since its inception, PCN has been funded entirely by the cable television companies who carry the network on their channel lineup and make it available to more than 10 million Pennsyl-vanians. Because of their financial support, PCN been able to operate and grow with private funding and without receiving any taxpayer dollars.

My contributions to the book—editing the veterans' transcripts and pulling together its various elements—are relatively minor, especially compared to the contributions made by the brave, humble, and patriotic Pennsylvanians fea-tured here.

Brian Lockman

☆ INTRODUCTION ☆

Kenneth C. Wolensky

Pennsylvanians contributed mightily to the Second World War. Remarkably, one and a quarter million residents—out of the Commonwealth's population of nearly seven million—served directly in various branches of the U.S. armed forces. One out of every seven members of the U.S. armed forces was a Pennsylvanian. Some service members returned to the homelands of their ancestors—places such as Italy, Germany, and Poland—to bring an end to the threat of totalitarianism. Others ventured to the Pacific to avenge the Japanese attack on Pearl Harbor. Hundreds of thousands who didn't serve in the military supported the war effort at home through their work, volunteerism, and patriotism. Indeed, at no other time in state history have so many been engaged in sustaining such a far-off effort; the survival and future of millions depended upon their success.

When it comes to those who managed the war, the roster of Pennsylvanians is most impressive. These include Army general and Chief of Staff George C. Marshall, a native of Uniontown; Gen. Matthew Ridgway of western Pennsylvania, Commander of the 82nd Airborne Division; Gen. Jacob L. Devers of York, Commander of the Sixth Army Group; Gen. Joseph T. McNarney of Emporium, Deputy Allied Commander in the Mediterranean; and Gen. Carl Spaatz of Boyertown, Commander of the American Strategic Air Forces in Europe. The U.S. Navy also had its Pennsylvania-bred leaders, including Chief of Naval Operations Adm. Harold R. Stark of Wilkes-Barre, who was also appointed Commander of American Naval Forces in Europe; Adm. Richard S. Edwards of Philadelphia, Deputy Chief of Naval Operations; and another Philadelphian, Adm. Thomas C. Kinkaid, Commander of the Seventh Fleet in the South Pacific.

In addition to these noteworthy individuals, Pennsylvania produced more than 125 generals and admirals, plus many other leaders. Consider, for example, McKeesport native Helen Richey. In 1934, she became the first woman to pilot a commercial airliner and the first to be licensed by the Civil Aeronautics Board. During World War II, she served as Commandant of the American Wing, British Air Transport Auxiliary, and held the rank of major. In addition to Michael Musmanno's military service during the war, he was also the presiding judge at the War Crimes Tribunal at Nuremberg in 1947–48 and became a justice on the Pennsylvania Supreme Court. Of course some veterans went on to greater fame; Indiana native and actor Jimmy Stewart, who flew twenty combat missions during the war, rose to the rank of brigadier general in the Air Force and, later in life, received the Presidential Medal of Freedom.

Strategic military encampments, depots, and reservations, forty in all, dotted the Keystone State. These included Fort Indiantown Gap, Camp Reynolds, Johnsville Naval Air Development Center, Carlisle Barracks, Middletown Air Depot, Philadelphia Navy Yard, Mechanicsburg Naval Supply Depot, Letterkenny Ordnance Depot, Frankford Arsenal, and the Philadelphia Quartermaster Depot. At these locales, tens of thousands of people left behind civilian life for military service, supplying the needs of the war effort. The Connellsville Canteen in southwestern Pennsylvania made its own mark on history, as more than 600,000 troops passed through its doors going to or returning from service. A major stop on the Baltimore & Ohio Railroad, many servicemen said goodbye to loved ones at the Canteen. Some never returned. Many others were joyously reunited with wives, girlfriends, and families at the Canteen.

Any history of Pennsylvania's contributions to World War II is incomplete without mentioning its industrial prowess and the importance of its natural resources. The Keystone State's rich reserves of fossil fuels—coal, oil, and their byproducts—were essential to victory. For example, in 1944, mineworkers produced 64 million tons of anthracite coal and more than 144 million tons of bituminous coal. Consider as well the remarkable role of Standard Oil's Pittsburgh Grease Plant, which produced more than five million pounds of "Eisenhower Grease" used in military vehicles, ships, planes, and other transports. Likewise, Allegheny County's inland Dravo Corporation Shipyard and its sixteen thousand workers manufactured more than one thousand Navy Landing Ship Tanks (LSTs) in addition to munitions, hardware, vehicles, and other supplies. Many of the workers lived in nearby Mooncrest, a community of planned industrial housing built by the federal government. The Sun Shipbuilding and Dry Dock Company, along the Delaware River in eastern Pennsylvania, was the largest shipyard in the world during the war. Thirty-five thousand workers built and repaired nearly two thousand ships at this single location. In central Pennsylvania, factory workers produced a special version of Hershey's famed chocolate bar by the tens of thousands for military food rations.

Industrial giant Bethlehem Steel stands out for its many contributions to the Allied cause. The company had seen its work slow during the Great Depression, but Bethlehem Steel emerged as indispensable following the passage of President Franklin Roosevelt's Lend-Lease Program (initiated prior to U.S. entry into the conflict to assist Great Britain and other Allies with equipment and supplies) and the Japanese attack on Pearl Harbor. The company's mills in Bethlehem, Steelton, Johnstown, and elsewhere worked day and night and constructed hundreds of ships, including the famed aircraft carrier *Lexington* and the battleship *Massachusetts*. Bethlehem Steel was the nation's largest maker of ordnance, shells, armor plate, components for aircraft engines, and air systems for submarines. Incredibly, the company employed 300,000 workers and, in 1945, had assets of nearly one billion dollars, revenues of $1.3 billion, and net income of $35 million.

The company recruited workers from distant areas in order to ensure a sufficient supply of workers at its Bethlehem plant. Company buses transported workers daily from the anthracite region. More workers carpooled from New Jersey, Delaware, and Philadelphia, while others rented rooms in boardinghouses, returning home only on weekends. Employees at "the Steel" (the term workers used to refer to the company) weren't always docile and compliant, however. Under the leadership of the Steel Workers' Organizing Committee (SWOC), Bethlehem's rank-and-file staged a strike in 1941 and demanded higher wages, workplace safety rules, and union recognition. SWOC argued that workers had the right to be fairly compensated for their essential role in building U.S. defenses and military might. At times the strike was violent, pitting state police and company security against workers and the community. Workers won many of their demands and SWOC emerged not long after as the United Steelworkers of America.

Important innovations came out of the Keystone State during the World War II era. In Butler, the American Bantam Car Company developed the pro-

SERVICE ON THE HOME FRONT

★ CITIZENS DEFENSE CORPS
★ CITIZENS SERVICE CORPS
★ AMERICAN UNITY
★ SALVAGE PROGRAM
★ VICTORY GARDENS

WPA

There's a job for every Pennsylvanian in these CIVILIAN DEFENSE EFFORTS

PENNSYLVANIA STATE COUNCIL OF DEFENSE
CAPITOL BUILDING,   HARRISBURG, PENNA.

WIKIMEDIA COMMONS

totype for the jeep and, during the war, produced nearly 3,000 of these light and easily maneuverable vehicles for the U.S. Army. Besides serving an important military role for the better part of the twentieth century, the jeep went on to become America's first mass-marketed, multi-purpose vehicle (today commonly referred to as a sport-utility vehicle). Adequate medical care and medicine was critical to saving lives of the sick and wounded. By the early

1940s, G. Raymond Rettew of West Chester had pioneered the mass production of penicillin, the world's first antibiotic. Working with Wyeth Laboratories, his laboratory—a converted car repair shop—produced and shipped more penicillin to the Allied forces than any other lab in the world.

It is no small accomplishment that more Congressional Medals of Honor were awarded to Pennsylvanians than to citizens of any other state, or that commonwealth residents ranked among the top purchasers of war bonds. Throughout the war years, citizens continued to turn out to vote in large numbers, ensuring that this fundamental right of democracy was exercised to its fullest extent, especially during difficult times. As the potential for war loomed during the 1940 presidential election, Franklin Roosevelt secured more than two million votes in the Keystone State; his opponent, Wendell Willkie, earned nearly 1.9 million. During the height of the war in 1944, Roosevelt again tallied two million Pennsylvania votes, while Thomas E. Dewey secured 1.8 million. U.S. senatorial elections in 1940 and 1944 were equally important to Pennsylvanians, and electoral turnout was similarly high in the gubernatorial election of 1942. Pennsylvanians remained fiercely loyal to the state, the nation, and to political leaders who strongly advocated Allied victory.

The important and patriotic contributions of so many Pennsylvanians during World War II are retained and captured by the memories and stories of those who lived in that era. Especially valuable are the stories of ordinary persons, hundreds of thousands in number, who worked, fought, voted, sacrificed, and raised families. Probably every Pennsylvanian alive today could discover a story in their family or community relating to World War II. And there are Pennsylvanians alive today who can recount the stories first-hand, because they experienced the times and events. The stories are countless. Those who can give first-hand accounts are rapidly dwindling in number, however.

The most prominent story in my family is of my dad's brother, Mike. He was assigned to an army combat group in Czechoslovakia in 1944. When his unit encountered heavy German fire, Mike was severely wounded in the right hip. As the Germans advanced, Mike, bleeding heavily, lay on the snow-covered ground and played dead for several hours. After the enemy vacated the area, some in Mike's group returned looking for wounded, found him, and secured medical help. Mike later received the Purple Heart, but he never recovered from the wound that left a gaping hole in his side. The wound often became infected, required regular attention and dressing for the remainder of his life, and was a constant source of pain. Uncle Mike died at a veteran's hospital in October 1969 when he was in his early fifties. My dad and his brothers—five in all, each of whom served in World War II and, remarkably, returned unscathed except for Mike—said that Uncle Mike died young because of the wound, shell shock (later termed post-traumatic stress disorder), and addiction to pain medication.

I remember Uncle Mike very well from my childhood. He was a friendly guy who always had a few coins or dollar bills in his pocket for his nieces and nephews (he never married and had no children). He would frequently buy us ice cream and make us laugh. He walked very slowly with a severe limp and had to use a cane. He usually grimaced with each step. Though my father and his siblings are all deceased, I can always count on the story of Uncle Mike coming up at a gathering of Wolensky relatives.

History shows us that, during times of war, the human impact is often overshadowed by the desire to win—as well as the lure of might and dominance. Yet history also shows that the human impact of war is deep and wide. From the World War II era we need only look at the Holocaust or Hiroshima and Nagasaki to measure the human impact of the conflict, to say nothing of the lives lost, areas destroyed, dollars spent, and mental anguish that resulted. As people in Western societies live longer now than at any other time in human history, the World War II generation may be the first American cohort to have the advantage of ample time to reflect on their contributions and sacrifices. And the wide-scale collection of oral histories of World War II veterans across the nation is the most comprehensive first-person documentation of war veterans ever undertaken. The combination of reflective time and an ample collection of oral histories bears out the significance of the World War II generation.

The Pennsylvania Cable Network deserves much credit for its vision and work to collect, save, publish, and air the oral histories of many Pennsylvania veterans of World War II. In the pages that follow, we witness the noteworthy contributions of people whose modesty dictates that what they did wasn't so astonishing, and that their stories were not even really worthy of being recorded in the pages of history. As Americans grow each day to value this generation—and to appreciate the physical, psychological, and emotional contributions they made—we also grow to recognize how extraordinary they were in doing what they thought was ordinary. We have also come to highly value their stories. Their words tell the stories best.

☆ Albert DeFazio ☆

Verona, Pennsylvania

Albert DeFazio served under Gen. Mark Clark in Italy,
near the birthplace of his parents. At age nineteen he
was involved in the assault on Monte Cassino
and the landing at Anzio, where he was wounded.

I quit school when I was sixteen and went to work in a steel mill. Then,
right after I turned eighteen, I was drafted into the service. I went to
Camp Shelby, Mississippi, for basic training. It was rigorous, tough, but it
didn't hurt you. It made a man out of you.

When I went to Aberdeen training grounds in Maryland they asked me
what I wanted to be, and I told them, "I'd like to be in the Marines," and
they said no. I said, "Well, how about the Navy?" and they said no. They said,
"We're going to put you in the infantry, because you don't have a high
school education."

After thirteen weeks of basic training, they sent us home for two weeks.
When I came back they called us all together and started reading names off,
saying, "These people are going overseas." They went down the list in alpha-
betical order, and they passed up my name. When they got through they said

there was another list which they called the "supernumerary list." My name was on that. After it was over I went up and said, "What is this super list that you got me on?" They said, "In case somebody on the first list cannot go, they'll pick somebody out of this super list."

That didn't go good with me. I went to the company commander and said, "I want to go overseas with my friends." He said, "This came from headquarters; there's nothing I can do about it." So I left. I was really distraught. I really wanted to go. The next day the lieutenant came to me and said, "DeFazio, I don't know what you did, but you're on the list to go." I was elated, believe me.

They shipped us to Newport News, Virginia, and put us with five hundred men on a Liberty ship that was controlled by the merchant marines, and we took off overseas. They nearly starved us. They called for chow call and would give us a round cracker. I was waiting for something else, but there was nothing else. I said, "Maybe in the evening they'll give us something." But there was nothing else.

We were on that ship zigzagging across the ocean for thirty days when we landed in Oran, Africa. From there they shipped us off by train. They put us in cattle cars, eighty of us to one car. You couldn't lie down to sleep; you had to sit down with your knees up to go to sleep. Then after three days we found ourselves in Algiers. They almost starved us there, too. We only got one meal a day. There was a place where you could buy big, beautiful oranges, and if you got there in time in the morning, you got your share. If you didn't, you got nothing.

From there they took us back down to the port and put us on an English transport ship. That thing was rusted and it was leaning. I thought it was the *Merrimack* from the Civil War. We took off at night, and when we sighted land it was Italy. That left me with a funny feeling, because my mother and dad were born in a town outside of Naples. I said, "They must have taken off from here to come to America."

Then they came around and gave us our divisional badges, and said, "Sew them on. You're going to be in the 36th Infantry Division, which is in the Fifth Army under Gen. Mark Clark." Again they shipped us out at night. We couldn't travel during the daytime because we were close to the front lines, near the abbey at Monte Cassino. Our objective was to capture Monte Cassino because the Germans were dug in there. It was like a fort. They didn't want to bomb it, because there were monks there and it was a historic religious building.

They took us as far as they could to the mountain, then we had to unload. In the morning we joined the rest of the guys in the 36th and climbed on the top of this mountain where we pitched our tent. It was January and it was cold. It snowed about four inches that night. The next morning was January 14, my birthday. I had just turned nineteen.

Our commanding officer was a redhead. We called him Lieutenant Spike. He got us all together and told us, "I'm your new company commander. Most of you guys will be killed before I even know your name." That didn't go down too good with the guys. I don't think he should have said that, but he said it and he was right. Periodically the Germans would lob a shell at us. There was a direct hit on one guy in our foxhole. He was twenty or twenty-five feet from me. It got him right in the heart. He looked up at the guys and said, "Can you help me?" and he died right there.

Orders came down that we would be making the attack on Monte Cassino; we were going to cross the Rapido River and head towards the abbey. They said, "We're going to put smoke pots out so they won't be able to see, and when they go off, everybody get close, bunched in like bananas, because you ain't going to be able to see nothing." Which you couldn't. You couldn't see your hand in front of your face. We were holding onto other guys' backpacks to make sure we didn't drift off.

We hit the smoke and started going through when, all of a sudden, everything broke loose: mortars, machine-gun fire, small-arms fire, everything. A shell hit to my right, and it blew the smoke away, lit up the sky, and oh my God, I saw bodies, three and four piled up. Within a second, another one

The ruins of the abbey at Monte Cassino following Allied bombing in February 1944. WIKIMEDIA COMMONS

Monte Cassino

The Allied bombing of Monte Cassino, an ancient monastery on a hill in southern Italy, represented one of the stickiest ethical dilemmas—and one of the most controversial attacks—of World War II.

After the Allies began their invasion of Axis-held Italy from the Mediterranean on September 3, 1943, they pushed northward toward at least two important targets. One was the militarily strategic port city of Naples, and the other was the psychologically important Rome. If the Allies could recapture Rome, it would be the first Axis capital to fall in World War II.

Hitler had earlier ordered German troops to occupy Italy in order to forestall the possibility that the Axis-aligned Italian government would capitulate to the Allies and give the latter a clear northward path toward Germany. Despite the German efforts, Italy had done just that following the overthrow of Benito Mussolini in July 1943. To block the Allied advance, the Germans erected a coast-to-coast defense called the Winter Line, also called the Gustav Line. From these fortifications in the mountainous heights, they blocked the Allies during an unusually harsh winter that made battle conditions even worse.

About eighty miles southeast of Rome lay the town of Cassino, population 25,000, crowned by a monastery, Monte Cassino, on a 1,500-foot-high ridge overlooking it. The monastery had been founded by St. Benedict in about AD 529, and the fortress-like collection of stone buildings housing it measured four stories high by a city block in area. The ridge overlooked the junction of the Rapido and Liri rivers; the Liri Valley offered a straight shot to Rome—the obvious route for any Allied invasion.

Although the monastery had become a national monument in 1866 and housed priceless antiquities and works of art, the Benedictine monks continued to live, study, and teach there as administrators of the property. At risk during the battle were the monastery's library of 70,000 books and archives containing 80,000 documents, including

Ruins in the city of Cassino following fighting in spring 1944.
WIKIMEDIA COMMONS

manuscripts of St. Gregory the Great, St. Thomas Aquinas, Cicero, Horace, Virgil, and Seneca. Paintings by Titian, Raphael, and Leonardo da Vinci, among other masterpieces, also were held there. When the Germans occupied the area, they removed most of these treasures to the Vatican in Rome for safekeeping, capitalizing on the public-relations value of doing so. Accompanying them were sixty-nine of the eighty monks who lived at the abbey.

The Allies mounted the first of four attacks on Cassino beginning on January 4, 1944, but it was unsuccessful. The ethical dilemma centered on whether the Germans were using the monastery as either a fortress or a lookout point. Allied generals debated the merits and drawbacks of bombing the monastery. On one hand were those who believed that Germans were in fact occupying the spot and that to prevent further casualties and push the battle toward Rome, it was necessary to destroy it. One Allied officer, Lt. Gen. Bernard Freyberg of New Zealand, insisted on bombing, saying that he wouldn't risk his men's lives with a German-occupied fortification above them; he threatened to withdraw his troops if his demand wasn't met. This would have proven to be an embarrassment and a blow to the morale of the 105,000-strong Allied coalition, which comprised forces from the United States, Great Britain, France (the Free French), Canada, India, Poland, South Africa, and New Zealand.

On the other hand were those who were both unconvinced that the Germans were there (they did occupy many surrounding locations

(continued on page 12)

(continued from page 11)

on the mountain) and hesitant to obliterate a historic and, many believed, sacred monument. In addition, not only were some of the monks still living there, but many townspeople had sought refuge in what they perceived to be a safe haven.

American general Mark Clark opposed bombing, but agreed to authorize it if given a direct order by Gen. Sir Harold Alexander, commander-in-chief of Allied Armies in Italy. Alexander did give the order, and on the morning of February 15, the Allies launched their second attack, code-named Operation Avenger. An aerial and artillery assault was led by 142 B-17 Flying Fortress bombers, 47 B-25 Mitchell bombers, and 40 Marauder bombers. Although the 1,150 tons of explosives smashed the monastery to rubble, the Allies were unable to take the mountain, and the Germans quickly occupied the ruins, which of course still overlooked the valleys below.

A third assault, carried out on March 15–20, was similarly unsuccessful. By this point, the Americans had lost 54,000 men, yet still did not hold the town of Cassino or the Rapido Valley. The final battle—code-named Operation Diadem—began on May 11. Alexander's goal was to force Germany to commit major resources to Italy at the same time the D-Day invasion of Normandy was about to begin. Polish troops, who at great cost attacked the Germans on the mountains surrounding Monte Cassino, finally entered the ruins of the monastery to find it evacuated and deserted. The capture of the summit enabled the Allied push for Rome to proceed.

Allied troops changed directions, moving northwest up the coast and the Liri Valley. By using decoy maneuvers, the Allies tricked the Germans into thinking that they were advancing on Rome from the north with a seaborne invasion. Rome fell to the Allies on June 4, but the news and the celebration were overshadowed by the Normandy invasion two days later.

In the aftermath of the war, nobody could definitely prove that Germans had ever directly occupied the monastery, and the official U.S. record of the battles eventually was changed to reflect this point. The monastery was rebuilt after the war. ★

would hit and I'd see the same thing: another pile of bodies, shattered. I said, "I don't want to see any more," so I hit the ground and covered my head. The noise was terrific. You couldn't hear any orders or anything, so I said, "I've got to get out of here."

I proceeded forward and got to the river. It wasn't a wide river but it was high, and the current was very swift because of the snow they had up in the mountains. I saw guys falling into the river with all their equipment on, and God, they could never come up to swim. There was a bridge there, and we were among the first ones at the river, so I hit that bridge and by God, it didn't take me too much time to get on the other side. When I hit the bank I put my head down and heard orders, "Fall back!" I took off and got across the river again and went back up the mountain.

I was wet, I was cold, and I was tired. I just put my head on my knees. I couldn't get it out of my mind what I had seen. When I got home after the war I had nightmares. I couldn't sleep. I was afraid to go to sleep for fear the nightmares would come on. It took me a long time before they started to go away.

As I sat there with my head on my knees, the lieutenant came by and said, "Put some dry socks on and get some rest. We're going back again tonight." I couldn't rest all day. I didn't eat anything. Then orders came that we were going to start back down again. "This time," he said, "we're not going to have the smoke pots out." I said, "Thank God. I don't know who the idiot was who ordered it, because the Germans knew where we were the whole time."

So the second time we got down to the spot where all hell had broken loose the first time. I wanted to brace myself for it, but how can you brace yourself for something like that? So we got down to that spot, and nothing happened. Not a shot was fired. We got down to the riverbank again, but this time somebody came up with another bright idea. Instead of the footbridges, they had a rubber pontoon raft anchored on each side. So again, our company was the lead for the attack, and our platoon was the first one down there to cross the river.

The second lieutenant made his rounds, and he came up to me and my buddy who I went through training with and said, "You two guys look so much alike I can't tell you apart." We crossed the river on the rubber raft, got on the bank and looked across. You could just see the shadow of the abbey. There were only a few of us across the river when the lieutenant said, "All right, let's go." So I got up and started across. I was out there fifty or sixty feet and I looked to my left and there was my look-alike, about five feet to my left and a few feet behind me. I didn't see anybody else. Everybody was back at the river, still crossing, and so far the Germans had not fired a shot. I said to myself, "They must have taken off."

No sooner had I said that than a shell hit behind me. The concussion blew me about two feet into a drainage ditch with water in it. I was stunned. I didn't know where I was. I felt a pain behind me, stuck my hand back there and my finger went into a hole, and I was bleeding. Part of my backpack was shattered; my shirt was all torn up. I put my hand back there again and my finger went into another hole. I was hit in two places. I looked over to the left to my look-alike. His whole back was shot. I knew he was gone. We went through boot camp and everything together.

Then the lieutenant hollered over, "Are you guys all right?" I said, "No, lieutenant, I'm hit two places, but I think my buddy's gone." He said, "You get back to the river and get some help." I was fifty or sixty feet away from anybody. I thought, "How in the world am I going to get back there?" All this small-arms fire, machine guns, everything was coming in heavy. I had to make a decision; either try to get some help or stay there in the water and freeze and bleed to death. If I'm alive in the morning, the Germans are going to get me. So I opted to take a chance and go back. I started limping back and I could hear gunfire whizzing past me, through my legs, all around me. How in the world I didn't get hit I'll never know.

I was headed toward the pontoon boat so I could get back across and get some help when a shell hit to my left. I saw one of the GIs bounce about an inch or two off of the ground. So instead of going to the boat and getting across the river I detoured to him, because there was nobody else around. I went over and leaned down and who do you think it was? It was Lieutenant Spike, the same one who said, "Most of you guys will be killed before I even know your name," and here he was, laying there. He was shot up pretty bad. He must have had a direct hit, but he wasn't dead.

I spotted another guy there, getting ready to go back across the river, and I said, "Come here, it's Lieutenant Spike, and he's hurt pretty bad. We have to get him out of here. He's going to die here." So we took him down to the river and put him in a rubber raft and shimmied across the river. The rubber raft had handles on the side, and we started to walk along the riverbank with him in the raft. I was hurting, but when you're scared you can do anything.

The field hospital was way back from the front lines. When we got there, there were guys lying all over the place. They were packed inside and out-side. I caught the orderly and said, "I got the lieutenant here. He's shot up pretty bad." The orderly looked at him and said, "We're loaded inside, but we'll take him. How about you?" I said, "I'm hit in two places." He said,

"Will you be all right for a few minutes?" I said, "Sure." Before long he came out to get me, put me on the stretcher, brought me in on the operating table and the next thing I knew I woke up in a hospital in Naples, Italy. I still don't know whether Lieutenant Spike ever made it or not.

From there they shipped me back to my outfit that was in the rest area, and everybody was new. Out of our original platoon, there were only six of us who came back alive. The rest of them were either dead or wounded so bad that they weren't able to come back.

One day I got a pass to go into a town called Avellino. I had heard my mother and dad talk about that town many a time when I was a kid. I went into a canteen they had there and heard a GI say, "Is anybody here from around Pittsburgh?" I said, "Yeah, I am, why?" He said, "An Italian fella over there is asking if there's anybody from around Pittsburgh." I started to talk to him and, believe it or not, as God made green apples, that man was my mother's first cousin. He said, "I'm going to call the town where your mother and dad were born. I have to let them know you're here."

So I went back to camp and saw the captain, because he owed me a favor. I said, "Captain, not far from here is the town where my mother and father were born. I have uncles and aunts and cousins there. Could I possibly get a leave of absence to go and see them?" He said, "I'll give you a pass for two days, nothing more than that, because we're going to be shipping out soon, and nobody knows where to." So I went to the train station—the trains were running—and took a train to a town called Foggia, then I started walking to the town my mom and dad came from.

I ran into one gentleman there, and asked him if he knew anyone with my name or my mother's maiden name. He said, "I'm sorry, I don't, but you see that farmhouse down there? Go there and ask him. He probably knows." So I went down and knocked on the door and a little short Italian fella came out. I started talking to him and, so help me God, that man was my mother's brother. He gave me a meal and then took me up the mountain to the town, where he introduced me to my mother's sister and my dad's brother. I also met my godfather who had baptized me when I was born. I missed my grandmother by six months. She had died.

When I got back to camp they said, "We're shipping out. We're going to Anzio." The 3rd Division went in first at Anzio, and they had no resistance. Maybe a shot or two was fired, that's it. When we came in there was no resistance. But then we stopped and dug in, which was the worst thing we could have done, because ahead of us was a mountain, and on the other side of the mountain was Rome. If we had kept going we would have had the high ground

A Warning from Aloft

On February 14, 1944, a day before the Allies bombed Monte Cassino, they dropped leaflets urging evacuation. The text read:

Italian friends, ATTENTION! Up until now we have tried to avoid bombing the monastery of Montecassino. The Germans have taken advantage of this. But now the fighting has gotten even closer to this Holy area. The time has come where, unfortunately, we have positioned our arms against the Monastery itself.

We are telling you this so that you have the possibility of saving yourselves. Our warning is urgent: Leave the Monastery. Go away immediately. Respect this warning. It is being given to you for your own good.

—THE FIFTH ARMY

at the mountain, but we stopped for a couple nights. In the meantime, the Germans had time to move their Panzer Division from Monte Cassino over to stop our coming in, because if we'd have gotten to Rome, it would have been over.

We were lying there, and all at once we heard a big noise. We looked up in the sky and there was a shell that came by that was as big as a small car. That thing whizzed right by, and when it hit it left a hole big enough to build a foundation of a house.

They sent some patrols out to try to contact the Germans and I went out with a couple of guys. We didn't run into anybody so we bivouacked that night—dug our foxhole. When we were on the march again the sergeant said to me, "DeFazio, you're going to take the point." The point was one guy out there by himself, which was me. The guy behind me was about fifty yards back, and behind him was the rest of the division. I said, "They should change that name to the sacrificial lamb."

I got out there all by myself. Along the side of the road I saw a German soldier lying there dead, and I felt so sorry for him. The Germans were moving so fast that they didn't have a chance to pick the poor soul up. Even though he was the enemy I felt bad, because he had a family back home. He didn't want to be here, the same as everybody else.

So I was out there, and I was scared. Well, thank God we didn't run into anybody until later when we ran into the main German force, and that's where we dug our foxholes. There was some scattered small fire coming in when all of a sudden one of our tanks came up alongside my foxhole and the Germans started shooting a 37-millimeter antitank gun at our tank. We were hollering, "Get that tank out of here!" because it was drawing all the fire. They hit it so many times the noise was just tremendous.

So we fell back, and all of a sudden everything came in. Artillery was coming in and shaking the ground, the trees were going, and my head was just ringing. I was lying on the ground and they were hitting all around me. I must have been shell-shocked. A medic happened to be there and he took me back to a farmhouse where there were wounded guys lying around. One guy, his belly was split and his bladder was sticking out. They tried to push it back in and it wouldn't go. Finally they gave me a pill that knocked me out, and the next thing I knew I was back at the field hospital, and from there I was on my way home.

When I got home I was going to reenlist to go over to the Pacific, but the Army guy said "You're eligible to get out on the point system." So that's what I did. I saw a lot of sadness over there, but it was a very good experience. You couldn't buy that education for $100,000, so I don't regret it. I just feel sorry that a lot of them didn't come back.

As far as I'm concerned, I would rather sleep in a gutter in this country than live in any other country in the world. We may be the peacekeepers of the world, but if it wasn't for this country, the countries over in Europe wouldn't be living the lifestyle that they're living today. So those boys that died over there didn't die for nothing. They died to make us live free and eat well and live a good life and sleep at night.

AFTER THE WAR . . .

Two weeks after Albert DeFazio left the service, he went back to work for the water company. He married and became the father of a son and daughter. After fifty-two years of marriage, Mrs. DeFazio passed away in July 2007. Mr. DeFazio has said that he has lived his life with no regrets. "I served my country and they owe me nothing," he said. "God bless America."

☆ Marlin Groft ☆

Lancaster, Pennsylvania

• •

**Marlin Groft joined the Marine Corps at age eighteen
and received his training at Parris Island and Quantico.
He saw action in the South Pacific at Tulagi, New Georgia,
Okinawa, and Bloody Ridge on Guadalcanal.**

• •

When I left school, I went into the Civilian Conservation Corps, the CCCs. It was a gathering of young boys between the ages of seventeen and nineteen, and it was designed to take kids off the street during the Depression. I went in because my family was rather unfortunate. They couldn't provide for me going through school; I left in the tenth grade. I made up for it later, but at the time I went in to help the family out. We got $30 a month from the government when we were in these camps, and out of that $30 we got $5 for ourselves and $25 was sent home. It was quite handy for some families, particularly mine, because my father had been disabled since 1928 and the Depression found us in pretty dire straits.

After the CCC, I was eighteen and I secured a job in silkscreen printing in Lebanon. That Sunday I was down at the William Penn Hotel in Lebanon, having breakfast with some of my friends. We finished our breakfast, went out and sat on an old Ford running board on our car, and somebody came running out and hollered that the Japanese had bombed Pearl Harbor. The immediate reaction was, "Where's Pearl Harbor? What is that all about?" We had no idea where it was, but it dawned on us a little later. And that's the thing that changed my whole life.

I came in to Lancaster and went to the recruiting office. I reported to the Army recruiting officer and told him that I'd like to go in the Army, but I wanted to go into the cavalry, since I was familiar with horses and my father was very active in that regard in the Spanish-American War. He was a bugler in the cavalry and had taught me to blow a bugle. They informed me that there was no longer a horse cavalry. They only had one unit in the whole Army, and the chances of me getting in it were pretty slim. He said, "But we have mechanized." I said, "What's mechanized?" He said, "They're tanks." I didn't want anything to do with that. I happened to look down the hallway, and a fellow was sitting in a blue uniform with a beautiful gold stripe on his trousers, and he looked really good to me. So I went down there and found out he was a marine. I had never seen a marine before in my life; I didn't even know what they did. In three weeks, I was on my way.

I took my basic training in Parris Island, South Carolina. That's that mysterious place where they make men out of boys. My training involved getting ready for combat, which was the firing range, doing health exercises, swimming—all those things that prepare you to be an infantryman in the Marine Corps. You see, in the Marine Corps everybody, even though you might be a specialist, you are first and always a rifleman.

I went from there to Quantico, Virginia, to fire at the rifle range there. While I was there, just before we broke boot camp, I heard about a raider battalion that was being formed by a Colonel [Merritt] Edson. He was running around scalping all the other outfits, getting the best men he could get a hold of, and that didn't include me. But I was given permission to go over and be interviewed by him. I reported to this room, and there sat Colonel Edson, all by himself. He had red hair and blue eyes that would actually penetrate you. And me being just a raw recruit, this was the biggest thing I ever saw, a lieutenant colonel.

We did an awful lot of extensive training in Quantico, and then in April we got aboard a train and went to San Diego, California, and from there we transferred to a ship and headed for Pago Pago, Samoa. It seemed like it took forever. We stopped on the equator and had to go through an initiation. Those who were polliwogs got the treatment. King Neptune came aboard and took his throne, then he elected the sheriff to go out and get all the polliwogs; that was me, because that was the first time I'd ever been across the equator. A shellback is a guy who had been across the equator before.

Once we arrived, we established a camp and got our assignments and began to do some very extensive training. The hills in Pago Pago are very high with a lot of bush. You can cut a trail there in the morning and by the following morning it would be grown over. It really grows fast down there, and rains a lot. I was a rifleman at that time. In fact, I was an assistant BAR man. A BAR is a Browning automatic rifle, and it was a weapon that was extremely helpful for us in the war. The difference between a raider battalion and another regular infantry unit is that we had fire teams. We had three fire teams made up of four men each; a BAR man, assistant BAR man, and two riflemen, with just a rifle. We achieved a high standard of mobility, a sense that we were now part of a very important unit. All of us were brothers together. I think that was one of the big things that came across to all of us, and it has lasted for over sixty years, because we're still together, what's left of us.

On August 7, 1942, we left Pago Pago and went to New Caledonia. We were there 'till the end of July when we boarded destroyers that took us to the fighting on Tulagi. When we left New Caledonia a British coast watcher was with us. He was familiar with Tulagi and had been there when the English were still in command, before the Japanese took over. We went down there because the Japanese had advanced all the way from Buka, in the islands north of us, and were about ready to take New Caledonia, which would have been bad news for our country. So that's why we went to Tulagi. I landed on Tulagi with the Raiders, and the 1st Division landed on Guadalcanal. This was the first offensive of the United States in World War II. We had not fought on the offensive anywhere in the world, and we take a lot of pride in that.

The night before we were to land, our ship pulled into Tulagi. The following morning we heard a lot of strafing and bombing and shelling, and we all ran up topside and got along the rail to see what was going on. We saw the little island of Tulagi, a half a mile wide and a mile long, and the Navy ships were shelling it. The bombing was so severe it seemed like the island itself was going to explode right out of the water. My impression was that there wouldn't be anybody left in there for us to fight. They'd all be killed; they couldn't live through anything like that. Well, they did. A lot of them did. There was a big cut through the islands, almost like a loaf of bread, with about half a dozen slices out of the middle. That's the way Tulagi was. They had caves in each side, and I suspect quite a few of them went in there during this hellish bombing. You must remember that we were only eighteen or nineteen years old, and none of us were prepared to look upon something like that. It just seemed like the island was going to be blown apart and sink into the ocean. So we had our breakfast, and they gave us steak and eggs. Now, that's a big breakfast in the Marine Corps, especially aboard an old leftover World War I destroyer. They gave us this big breakfast, and it was almost like it was going to be our last breakfast, but it was really great.

There was no beach on Tulagi; it dropped right off into the water. The landing craft at that time were called Higgins boats. The bow was round and there wasn't any ramp. You just had to vault over the side with all your equipment, your BAR, which is twenty pounds, your ammunition, and everything else. As we jumped, we went right over our heads in water. My thought was, "Did I come nine thousand miles to drown?" That was the impression that hit me when I saw other guys ahead of me going under. I was pretty short, but by the grace of God, I guess I came down on a bunch of coral, so when I jumped in, it only came up to my neck and I made it into the bush. It wasn't but a couple more minutes and we were starting to get fired upon. And it got pretty severe. I don't know what happened to my BAR man, but he lost himself. He threw himself on the ground and swore we were all going to get killed, because by that time the fire was pretty intense and people were getting hit. So my squad leader hollered at me, and he said, "Grab that BAR." And I had to grab it, and I became a BAR man at that moment until we got up top on the ridge.

I had no feeling except getting to my destination, doing what I came to do. I had no thought about "This is terrible, I'm going to die," and all that kind of stuff. The thought never occurred to me, nor did it for most of us, except my BAR man. We landed there with three days' rations in our packs. We were supposed to take the place, and then the Navy would pick us up and take us over to Guadalcanal to help out the 1st Division. That never happened. We took the island in three days. The only water that was on Tulagi was on a big cistern-type tank, and they shot holes through it, assuming it might be poisoned by the Japanese. After we took the island we had no water, but we had three days' rations of food, and that's all we had. And we were there for three weeks. The Navy never came to pick us up. On that second night after we landed, there was a huge naval battle, the battle of Savo. I could see it from up on top of my hill on Tulagi. I had to duck a couple times because a Japanese machine gunner was really pouring that lead at us. So after the beating they got on Savo, the Navy pulled out. The ships that the Japanese didn't sink at

Bougainville Island

Bougainville Island, largest of the Solomon Islands, was another in a string of strategically important positions that the Allies and Japan fought over in the western Pacific. Beginning in 1942, the Japanese had occupied the 3,600-square-mile island, using it as a refueling and resupply base for their aerial and naval offensive against the Allies on Guadalcanal, four hundred miles to the southeast. That campaign lasted from August 1942 to February 1943 (see page 78) and ended with the Japanese being forced to abandon Guadalcanal to the Allies.

One of the Allies' main objectives was to isolate and neutralize the major Japanese stronghold of Rabaul, which was a naval and air base on the island of New Britain, lying about three hundred miles northwest of Bougainville. By knocking out that strategic center, the Allies hoped to turn back Japanese aggression and influence, while at the same time advancing toward retaking the Philippines, and ultimately, attacking the home islands of Japan.

As a diversionary tactic, Allied troops landed in the nearby Treasury Islands on October 25–27, 1943, sixty-five miles off the southeast coast of Bougainville, and on Choiseul Island, about the same

Pearl Harbor, they almost sunk on Savo. So the admiral and the fleet along with his carrier just left. And we were absolutely deserted; left there to die.

There were just about seven hundred of us. We ate every coconut on the island until there was none left. The Japanese did not have very good supplies because they hadn't intended to stay there that long. They were going to move over to Guadalcanal. So we starved. After a couple days a Japanese cruiser and a destroyer came into the channel and they felt free to come right over to Tulagi. They trained their guns over and started firing on us. There was nobody to disturb them; our Navy was all gone. They did that for three days in a row. Finally, the fourth morning, they came into the channel to do their bit again, but a B-17 of ours appeared in the sky. The destroyer got away, but the B-17 hit the cruiser. The cruiser then ran ashore on Guadalcanal, and the 1st Marines over there got them.

distance east of Bougainville, on October 28. Then, U.S. Marines landed at Cape Torokina on Bougainville on November 1.

Japanese naval and ground forces attacked the Allies without success. The Allies did not intend to occupy the entire island, only enough of it to build several airstrips for fighters and bombers. From these locations, the Allies flew missions against Rabaul and other targets. They also attacked the Japanese airfields on Bougainville, and naval and air forces isolated the Japanese garrison, cutting off food and supply lines. In December 1943 and January 1944, Army forces replaced the Marines. The enemy did not give up easily, and often clashed with the Allies, frequently in close jungle warfare. The Allies repeatedly repulsed them, and the Japanese then concentrated on survival.

Among the units that reinforced the Americans was the 93rd Infantry Division, the first African-American infantry unit to see combat in World War II. Late in 1944, American forces were replaced by those from Australia and Fiji, who contained the Japanese until the end of the war in September 1945.

In all, the Allies landed 126,000 troops and maintained a fleet of 728 aircraft, compared to 40,000 Japanese and 154 aircraft. The Allies suffered 1,243 deaths compared to at least 17,500 Japanese, many of whom died of malaria or malnutrition. Despite being wracked by so many fatalities, the remaining Japanese on Bougainville were among the last to surrender. ★

Then after three weeks the Navy finally came back and picked us up. By that time we were all sick with dysentery, our clothes were falling off of us, and we were in bad shape. But that didn't stop old Edson from taking us over to Guadalcanal. At that time the Canal was being bombed every day by the Japanese from up in Bougainville. As we landed in Guadalcanal, the destroyer I was on got hit and it went down within three minutes. I was still on the cargo net when we were coming down. Everybody else in my company was in the Higgins boats and I was coming down last. The ship got hit, exploded, the bow went right up into the air, and was out of sight within about three minutes. I dropped off from the cargo net into the Higgins boat and made it ashore to Guadalcanal.

We made patrols over to Florida Island—Florida was the big island behind Tulagi—and picked up some survivors from the battle of Savo; some sailors and some Marines. Some of them were dead and floated ashore over on Florida. Then on Guadalcanal they took us out to Coconut Grove where we set up camp in a coconut grove. We dug holes and got ready for whatever was going to come next. This was the last part of August, the first week of September 1942. We weren't there but a couple days and we had our first decent food in three weeks. We had been eating coconuts and anything else we could get, but this was our first food; I remember it was called Corn Willy. It was corned beef with a lot of barley in it, and they cut open a gasoline drum to make a pot. Of course, they washed it out first. It was pouring rain, and we had our ponchos on. They would just throw the food in your pan and give you a cup of coffee. The water from the rain ran down off your poncho into your Corn Willy, and pretty soon you had soup. That was our first food in over three weeks.

We then went on a raid, the only raid we ever made, to a place called Tasimboko. That was twenty miles down from Henderson Field, which was in the process of being built. We went down to Tasimboko because we had discovered that the Japanese had been sending lots of ships through at night, and they were bringing in troops, a lot of troops. At that time, there was less than eight hundred of us, and about eleven thousand of 1st Marine Division men. That's all we had on the island. So a fellow by the name of General [Kiyotaki] Kawaguchi was landing down there and building up a big base to attack us south of Henderson Field at a place which later became known as Bloody Ridge.

We went down there one morning to destroy his supplies. We were fortunate, because as we went ashore to attack this village of Tasimboko, a bunch of our ships were coming up to the Canal, from where I do not know. It looked to the Japanese like it was a big invasion and they took off. That gave us enough time to go in, capture the village, blow up all the cannons that were in there, and destroy all their food. They had a big warehouse full of food, and I would have loved to have eaten some of it. But we destroyed it all.

By that time, somebody from the Japanese command came to the conclusion that we were only a raiding party, that there were only about four hundred of us on this raid, and they started coming back. Of course, when they started coming back we tangled with them and lost a few men. But then it was determined that we had done our duty; our mission was completed, and we had to get back aboard ship as best as we could. We all ran out into the ocean where folks were coming in and picking us up. I can remember running to a boat, and the Japanese bullets were flying all around the water before I got on. So we got out of there and went back up to Coconut Grove.

It wasn't too many days after that that Edson and his staff went up to what would become Bloody Ridge, and I was one of the scouts that went up there. This was about 1,900 yards from Henderson Field, and Edson determined exactly where the Japanese were going to hit us from. He knew exactly. While we were there he came over to me. I was sitting there with a 1903 Springfield rifle; that was the same rifle we used in World War I. We were still using it then. He came over to me, and I was looking very alert—that's my job—because Edson was there with his staff. And he said to me, "What do you think about this place, son? Have a good fight." Well, coming from a private to a colonel, what do you say? I said, "I think it will be swell." Something like that. But he had that look I saw in his eyes that I remembered back in Quantico when he signed us up. When you talked to him you got the impression you were talking to Saint Peter. Only I found out later on that Edson stood about two rungs higher, he was just that kind of man.

Anyway, we came back from this reconnoitering situation and went back into camp on Coconut Grove, and I was told to go and sleep with the paratroopers that night. I was going to be their scout to take them back out to the Ridge, because none of them had been there. So here I was, a PFC now by this time, and I'm sleeping with these paratroopers.

Paratroopers are the boys that landed at Gavutu and Tanamboga, and they got hit pretty bad over there. I think they probably lost about half their command on Gavutu and Tanamboga. So they were going to help us out on the ridge. I slept with them that night, and the following morning I woke up, and Captain Harry Torgerson, who was in command of the paratroopers at that time, asked me to come out front and center. I stepped out of ranks and he said, "PFC Groft, take us to the ridge." And boy, I felt like MacArthur. I got myself a whole company of Marines here, and I'm going to lead them out to the ridge, which I did. We got out there, and after I got them up to the ridge I reported back to my unit. In the meantime, my unit had also gone out there, and we all assembled together and got ready for what we knew was coming, the Japanese.

For a couple days we patrolled. I guess I was a member of the last patrol that went off of what was at that time called Edson's Ridge. It later became known as Bloody Ridge. I took the last patrol off the ridge and ran into a Japanese unit that was coming to attack us. They had to come through a dense jungle to get there. They fired upon us, we hit the deck and started

Invasion of Tulagi

As the Japanese planned to consolidate their hold over the western Pacific following their attack on Pearl Harbor and other targets in December 1941, they pinpointed various of the British Solomon Islands—nine hundred miles northeast of Australia and about the same distance northwest of Fiji—as being strategically necessary to capture. By seizing control of New Guinea and the Solomons, they hoped to establish bases and build airfields, while at the same time disrupting the 3,425-mile-long Allied supply and communications link between the U.S. and Australia.

One of these was the tiny island and town of Tulagi in the southern Solomons. Measuring two miles long by several hundred yards wide, it was situated just off the much larger Florida Island and twenty-two miles north of, and across the Sealark Channel from, Guadalcanal. Tulagi was favored for its good harbor facilities and its freedom from tropical diseases. Since the 1890s, Tulagi had been the seat of government for the British Solomon Islands protectorate. Early in 1942, the British colonial government and a cohort of Australian troops fled just before the Japanese seized the island, unchallenged, on May 3. The Japanese intended to establish a seaplane base on nearby Gavutu to support their further thrust southward toward Australia.

Early the next day, officers on the aircraft carriers *Lexington* and *Yorktown*—acting on intelligence from Australian aircraft observers—launched an offensive action comprising fifty-eight planes. Making three consecutive attacks, they launched twenty-two torpedoes and dropped seventy-six 1,000-pound bombs. They hit and sank the Japanese destroyer *Kikutzuki*, three minesweepers, and four barges, and destroyed several Kawanishi reconaissance seaplanes. Three Allied

crawling to a dry riverbed and my patrol leader said, "You're on your own. Get back to our lines the best way you can." I remember running into a paratrooper that had his rifle right pointed at my head. I came through the bush and ran smack into this rifle pointed right in between my eyes. He had good fire control; he didn't squeeze it off.

U.S. Marines wade ashore at Tulagi Island during the August 1942 landings. NAVAL HISTORY AND HERITAGE COMMAND

planes were lost in the action. *Yorktown* then cruised west toward the Battle of the Coral Sea on May 7–8.

Tulagi remained under Japanese occupation for several months. On August 7, 1942, U.S. forces launched Operation Watchtower to secure Guadalcanal and Tulagi. While the battle for Guadalcanal raged on for four months, Tulagi fell to the Allies relatively quickly. About 8:00 A.M., raiders of the U.S. 1st Marine Division arrived on the southwestern shore and began to drive eastward toward the Japanese Special Naval Landing Force troops who had been holding the island. Supported by aerial bombardment, U.S. forces had recaptured Tulagi, at the cost of forty-five Marines' lives; very few of the five hundred Japanese defenders survived.

The island and adjacent Purvis Bay then became a minor naval center for repair and resupply of damaged warships, including those that supported the continuing fight to secure Guadalcanal. Short-range motor torpedo boats also were based there for about a year, including the PT-109 of Lieutenant (and future U.S. president) John F. Kennedy, which sank in 1943 after being struck by a Japanese destroyer.

When the war ended, the capital of the Solomons was reestablished at Honiara, a new town built on Guadalcanal. ★

We got back and organized ourselves on the ridge. That following night they hit us. Down there it got so dark that you could not see your finger in front of your nose. Just before the night fell on us we were all lined up and my company commanding officer, a fellow by the name of Capt. Edwin Wheeler, came down through and touched each one of us and looked at us and told us what the conditions were. That we were going to have to hold here at all cost, as Henderson Field was in jeopardy. If we lost that, we lost the island. So I said to him, "Captain Wheeler, how many men do you think are coming?" He said, "Between four thousand and five thousand. That's estimated." I knew we had no more than eight hundred men at the most. I looked over to a friend of mine, old Stuart, and I said, "Stu, I'll see you in the morning." Then night came.

We hadn't dug in. There was too much coral; the ground wasn't suitable for digging holes. So we pretty much were on top. Then you prayed. You prayed for your family, you prayed to the Lord that you would have the courage to stand up and do the job that you were supposed to do. And then, of course, above all, you prayed for the Corps. You always did that. And they came. They didn't come quietly, you really heard them coming. They were screaming. Finally, they made contact with us. It was quite a nasty affair, but we got through the night. The following morning, the Japanese left. They didn't stay there in their positions, they just left, which was a great thing for us.

There was another night coming, but we could lay there and get some food, eat some crackers, drink some water, and go to sleep and wait for the following night, because Colonel Edson announced to all of us that that was just the first time; they would come back. And they did. When they came back a second night it was for all the marbles. That second night was the most horrific night I guess I ever spent in my life, except maybe up in Okinawa. It was a bad, bad night, but we held out. We lost, I think, 79 killed and 119 wounded out of our less than seven hundred men up there. That's a big percentage, but the Japanese left eight hundred dead up there on that ridge. And they never threatened us again.

The time came for us to pull off. We had been going at it for quite a while. We were all tired and hungry and your mind gets lost when you walk off a ridge after a fight like that. And this was all hand-to-hand stuff. You got body and body together, that's all there was to it. When I walked off that ridge the following morning I thought for a couple moments that we had lost, that we were walking away. Your mind got mixed up, but what saved us that night was the 11th Marines, with their artillery, the 105s. They started firing at the time the Japanese began to attack. Our forward observers dropped their shells right in among us. I don't think it was twenty feet in front of us those shells were landing. And the Japanese were coming in to us at the same time. So between the artillery and the Japanese making contact with us, it was pretty much of a nightmare.

We walked off the ridge, went through the 11th Marines who were still firing, and I think it was the first time I ever saw men, especially servicemen, hugging each other. We knew they had pretty much saved us. We would have been destroyed up there had it not been for the 11th Marines.

After that battle we went to Wellington, New Zealand, for a little bit of R and R. We spent a month there, then we went back to New Caledonia and got ready for the Battle of New Georgia. The Army was fighting in the southern end and we landed on the northern end to close the back door. That was July 4, 1943, a night that I'll never forget, because it rained so hard. We went ashore at Rice Anchorage and were told to lay down and sleep wherever we were. I remember covering up with my poncho and water just running over my body. Then we went twenty-five miles through the most horrific jungle I have ever seen to get to a village we wanted to attack, which was Enogai Inlet. They never even knew we were coming.

Then I went to Okinawa, fought through the campaign of Okinawa, and then I came back to Guam. In that time, they dropped the bomb on Japan. We had one big party. We weren't going to Japan. Instead, they sent me to China as part of our regiment to accept the surrender of the 8th Japanese Army in Tsingtao, China. I returned back to the States in January 1946.

Americans today should know that there was an awful, great, horrendous, heroic effort made so they could live free in this country today. They should never forget that we have white crosses across the country and in every part of the world, and they all signify one thing—that they paid the price so we can enjoy the country that we have today.

AFTER THE WAR . . .

• •

After serving as an overseer in the Naval Retraining Command in Norfolk, Virginia, Marlin Groft married his hometown sweetheart in 1951 and returned to Lancaster, Pennsylvania. He was employed by RCA for thirty-four years. While in the RCA engineering department, he worked on the largest tube and the smallest camera tube that were sent into space on the moon lander. The Grofts are the parents of three children.

• •

☆ Frank Yarosh ☆

Glen Mills, Pennsylvania

• •

Frank Yarosh was offered the opportunity to train at West
Point, but he chose to remain with his infantry unit and was
the lead man in many attacks. At age twenty, while serving on
the Maginot Line, he was taken prisoner by the Germans.

• •

I came from Lopez, a small town in Sullivan County, which is in the north-eastern section of Pennsylvania. My father was a coal miner and was not educated. When he arrived in this country, he could not read or write the English language. I went to Lopez High School for three years, and I finished at Dushore High School in Dushore, Pennsylvania, the home of the only newspaper in the county—the great *Sullivan Review*.

At the time the state of the war was a bit mixed. You couldn't figure out who was winning or who was losing, and there was a lot of intensity in the United States because of people going into the service. A lot of my buddies were enlisting. I was about to enlist in early '43, and my dad, who was a World War I veteran, urged me to wait my turn to be drafted. He said, "They'll take you in time." And he was right; in March of 1943, soon after I had registered for the draft, I was inducted into the service. I went to

Wilkes-Barre by bus, which is about forty miles away from Lopez, and then from Lopez a large group of us were sent to New Cumberland and we were there for a couple of days. From there we went by rail to Fort Lewis, Washington, a trip that took about five days on a train.

For the first three months of Army life, I was a trainee in the combat infantry in Fort Lewis. At the end of that training, I was called into the company commander's office and told that because of my Army intelligence scores and my deportment as a soldier, I was offered two opportunities: I could go to Fort Belvoir, Virginia, to become a second lieutenant as a combat engineer or to go to college and become a graduate engineer. Naturally I took the college route, and I was sent to Utah. And after being at the University of Utah for a few days, I was sent to Brigham Young University and the ASTP program there, which stands for "Army Specialized Training Program." In other words, in 1943, during World War II, there was a shortage of college graduates. People were poor and couldn't go to college, so there were not too many highly educated people in the Army. That's why the Army needed college-educated people to perform whatever duties were necessary. So I wound up at Brigham Young for over a year, and really enjoyed it. It was a great experience. I was like a sponge, I absorbed everything in all the courses I took. Things were going along fine for over a year, and I was almost into the middle of my sophomore year when Ike [Gen. Dwight D. Eisenhower] needed troops in England for the invasion, at least that's what we were told. So the ASTP program was abandoned and most of us wound up in the infantry; two of us wound up in Company C, 274th Infantry Regiment of the 70th Division, in Camp Adair, Oregon.

I got another three months of infantry training, and this was on top of my previous three months basic training as a combat engineer, so you might say I was a pretty well-trained soldier. At the end of the training in the infantry, which was quite tough, I was called in to the battalion colonel's office and he informed me that he had a request to send one person from the battalion to West Point, and that there were three of us in the battalion who had most of the qualifications, except that our IQ was a bit low. You needed 130 points to go to West Point and mine was 128. I'm not bragging, but I was two points short. He said, "Retake the test," which I did, and a few days later I was called in and told that I was the candidate for West Point, that I had met the qualifications, except that I had to go through a strict physical exam and a board of inquiry of West Point officers. Well, I was accepted.

The morning I was to leave I didn't tell anyone, not even my parents, that I had been accepted for West Point. I had a lot of apprehension about going there because I felt I was not really cut out to be a warrior; I was not cut out to be a military man; I was not trained to kill. I didn't have a mind-set of that type and to spend the rest of my life, if I had committed myself to West Point, would have been a big decision. I thought it over for about two days. In fact, I had a 3.2 percent beer the night before I went; it was a very weak alcohol, and when I went to bed I was going to go to West Point, but when I woke up in the morning, something said, "Don't go." The colonel was very unhappy, and he told me I was going to become the battalion scout and that I was to lead all attacks in the future, if there were any. Sure enough, when I did wind up in combat—and during training—I was always the lead man.

A short time later our battalion, the 274th Infantry Division, was moved to Fort Leonard Wood, Missouri, where we got all our ducks in order for combat. Then we moved to Camp Miles Standish, Massachusetts, and on December 1, 1944, we boarded the luxury liner *Mariposa* in the Boston Harbor for Europe. After ten days of a rough trip, which I will never forget—the stormy Atlantic in December—we wound up through the Straits of Gibraltar into Marseilles, the battered city in France.

On January 4, 1945, after serving some time on the Rhine River in a defensive position, we were moved into combat—an attack on the town of Phillipsburg, France, a town smaller than Lopez, Pennsylvania; a town filled with chickens and cows and a few people, but a lot of German soldiers. I remember my first day of combat as plainly as looking at your face. I was a nervous chicken. I had a cigarette in my mouth, a helmet on, my gun in a ready position, and snow up to my rear end. The temperature was 15 or 20 degrees—cold, biting, eight o'clock in the morning. It was a very scary situation. A lot of artillery was going on and a lot of shells were exploding. But from the 1,500 troops in back of me, the whole 274th Battalion, there was not a peep from anyone except for my scout Rob.

He and I were up front, waiting for the command for the attack. Then it finally came and I moved very cautiously. That's one thing from my background in Lopez: I did a lot of hunting and fishing and spent a lot of time in the woods; that type of background helped me considerably in the Army. As we moved up into that valley towards the town of Phillipsburg, the Germans didn't shoot at me. I thought, "Hey, maybe they won't shoot at me." As I got up into the town, they still did not shoot at me; they waited for the main body of the troops to come up and then all hell broke loose. There I was, up on the side of a hill on the West Bank of the Rhine unharmed but with a lot of activity around me—a lot of things hitting my helmet and my body—but I was never wounded in combat. The next couple of weeks of combat I wasn't afraid, but it was a spooky-type affair with people getting hurt, buddies being killed, and the snow being drenched in red blood. It was a terrible sight. I don't recommend infantry combat for anyone.

The first casualty I witnessed was our lieutenant. He was hit, and Rob and I worked on him and ripped up his clothes and put some sulfa powder on him and called for the medics, and on we went. Whether he lived or died I don't know, I never heard and I never inquired.

I don't usually talk too much about combat, but I was in one battle where the colonel asked for me to be in front of a tank on an approach to an upper road in the town of Phillipsburg where I encountered a Tiger tank. That was scary.

We eventually captured the town. Several of my buddies got killed or wounded. One guy in particular, I spent a whole night with him in a foxhole. His name was John and he was a sergeant. It happened to be Russian Christmas Eve, and I belonged to the Russian Orthodox Church as a youngster. We talked about Christmas all night long in that foxhole as we peered out, looking for Germans in the darkness. In the morning we got the order to advance and John got out first. He took a few steps and the 88s came in through the treetops and John was killed. That was a very tough moment for me. I went out to him and discovered that he was gone. That's one thing about the Army: You leave the dead and the wounded and you go on to your objective, whatever it may be.

On January 20 our squad went off in a truck to a location, and then we walked up a mountain all afternoon and all night. During the middle of the night while going up through this snow in the bitter cold, I fell down the side of a mountain. I went down fifty or seventy-five feet, and two of my buddies went down and dragged me back up with my rifle and my full field pack. I found that I had sprained my left ankle. We were on our way to a position at the Maginot line to relieve some Company G men in a concrete bunker. The bunker had thick walls, a big heavy steel door, and was entirely covered with snow three or four feet deep. There were three rooms and there was a tower with iron steps that you could walk up, and from the tower you could see the Germans about three hundred yards away on the nearby hillside. The sergeant said that he would be over the hillside and would check with us at dark.

Around eight o'clock at night we realized that the sergeant did not come calling as he said he would. He said he'd be back by dark, but he did not show up. So two other guys went out and scoured the hillside, came back in about an hour, and said they could not see any sign of anyone. Incidentally, I was the ranking officer; I was private first class. My ankle was very sore, but I got all my stuff together and took the other guy with me to go look for the sergeant or any of Company G. We went into all the foxholes that I presumed the men would have occupied and there was no sign. Then a blizzard came up. It was blinding and very cold, so after about an hour we went back to the bunker. We had a meeting and decided we were going to leave about four o'clock in the morning, before dawn so the Germans would not see us or our tracks in the snow. I took the first turn around midnight. I lit up a cigarette and all of a sudden there was a blinding noise and a flash, and the light went out. I remember seeing stars and hearing music just like in the movies. I guess we were knocked out because of the force of whatever caused the light to go out. It must have been a shell or dynamite or something of that type. Then we heard a voice shout out, "You are our prisoners. Come out."

I volunteered to go out first, and as soon as I went out, a gun was rammed into my stomach, and I was moved over to the wall of the pillbox and searched. Then the others came out and soon all four of us were standing there with our hands up. In the background, I could see the outline of various hooded soldiers. The Germans wore white parka uniforms to blend in with the snow. Then the officer went into the pillbox, looked it over, came back out with the interpreter, and invited us back in. There we sat for the next ten or fifteen minutes while the officer looked us over. We were scared. We thought we were going to be questioned and then be killed. Why would they want to save us? From what? We were out there in the boondocks and there was nobody around in the mountainous territory, in the deep snow.

We were taken to an isolated farmhouse. I was asked to salute the German officer and I refused, I don't know why. To this day I always ask myself why I didn't, but I did not salute that officer. That's one thing about the Army: They never told us how to be a prisoner of war, how to conduct ourselves, none of that stuff. I remained stoic, frozen, and they finally gave up asking me to salute. Then I was put in a room with a couple of wounded Germans, and one of the Germans—he could speak very good English— said, "Do you remember your President Roosevelt said that no soldier would be sent to European soil? What are you doing here tonight?" I couldn't answer that question; I still can't answer that question.

We were moved to another farmhouse, and they got the interpreter—Captain Otto, he called himself—out of bed. I was placed in the dining room of this farmhouse. The other three disappeared; I don't know where they went. Captain Otto looked me over; he was a man about thirty-five, handsome-looking fellow. Then he made me strip off all my clothes including my socks. He went over every item of clothing, through my backpack, and all the items I had in it. He read the labels. He read the rations. He read everything. He read the letter in my wallet that I got from my mother and he just said, "Good mother."

Then Captain Otto said, "Put on all your clothes again, one at a time, except for your overcoat." He led me into the kitchen and set me down opposite a kitchen table and he started to question me. He asked me a ton of questions, besides my name, rank, serial number, where I was from, and what I did in the Army. He thought I was an officer.

I did not answer any of the questions. I remained stoic; I was frozen. I wonder today how I ever had the nerve to do this because of the circumstance I was in. There was one window, and a guard would walk by the window every now and then and he had his bayonet flashing in the light from the lamp. Captain Otto played with a revolver and took out his bullets and shined them with his handkerchief and put them back in and loaded it back up again. Can you imagine what's going through a twenty-year-old kid's mind at this point?

And at one point during the interrogation, there were three shots fired, and I thought, "One for each of my three buddies." And then he started questioning me again. He said, "Nobody knows you're here tonight. Your mother and father don't know you're here, your company commander doesn't know you're here. No one knows you're here except your three buddies upstairs and me and my fellow officer." He came around the back of my chair at one point and hit me so hard on the side of my face it practically spun me right out of the chair. Tears came out of my eyes, I was hit so hard. A couple minutes later, he walked around the table again and hit me from the other side.

This went on until about six o'clock in the morning. He finally then complimented me about my deportment and wished that all his buddies in the German Army acted the same way as I did. He vigorously shook my limp, wet hand, looked me in the eye, and said, "You're a damn good soldier, and I wish you good luck." I was shocked. After all I went through, to have him say that. Then he took me out to the porch, and there stood my three buddies; they were alive.

We wound up in a church for a day or so. That was where I had my first encounter with German people. A German lady came out of a store with an apron on and with rosy cheeks, a nice-looking lady, and she spit on me and hit me right in the side of the face. I couldn't wipe it off because the guard was hollering at me, "Achtung! Achtung! Achtung!" They hated us, even the kids. I got hit with an icy snowball that hit the back of my neck and produced a big welt. So there I was with my swollen ankle and a welt on the back of my neck and my two swollen cheeks; I wasn't in very good shape.

We were then taken by truck; it was the first time I was ever on a truck that burned wood for fuel. We were taken to a camp called "Stalag 12A" in Limburg, across the Rhine. The next day we were placed in a train with about ten cars with fifty men per car and the sliding doors were bolted shut and away we went. For five days and five long nights we traveled in that unheated car on our way north.

All we got to eat was one slice of bread and maybe two little potatoes, and that was it. During that train ride we were strafed by American aircraft fighter planes. The shells ripped right down through the roof of the car we were in, and two guys in the front of the car were killed. We figured it was American planes. They did their job and they went back to their warm bunk, not knowing that they killed a couple of Americans. Things happen in a war with friendly fire; people get killed.

Conditions on the train were horrible. People had the flu, or pneumonia, and they died from it, or whatever it was. The next morning they were removed from the car along with the bucket that was used as a latrine. It was terrible.

After five days we made it to "Stalag 11B." The camp was said to have between 12,000 and 20,000 prisoners of war of all nationalities. I was placed in a barracks on the third bunk. The conditions were very bad; there was no heat, there were only two electric light bulbs in the whole barracks, it was very cold, and the only toilet facility was a trough for urine. If you had to make a number two you had to go outside to an open pit and sit on a rail with searchlights and guards watching what you were doing. I occupied a bunk where a guy had died the night before. A fellow named Taylor lived in the middle bunk and he became a friend of mine during my POW life. I attribute my survival to him.

An average day involved getting up at six in the morning and going out for roll call. Then we were divided up into groups, with twenty-five people to a work detail. Since I was an infantry soldier and not an officer, I was treated like scum. We were dirt in the Germans' mentality. Taylor and I and a few others walked about four miles every morning without breakfast to a site that was full of stumps, and old picks and old shovels and ropes were there. It was very cold. We picked in the snow, and pulled stumps out and dragged them to the side. The site we were working on was to be a V-2 rocket site for firing rockets to England. We worked all day with no lunch, nothing to drink except snow that we ate. Then about four o'clock we'd walk back and get one slice of bread and two little potatoes if we were lucky, and a cup of boiled barley. No breakfast, no lunch, and that was dinner. And that was it for the rest of my time until I was liberated. I lost sixty-five pounds. I was a well-developed kid when I went into the Army, but I came out a pretty scrawny-looking guy.

Lice were a problem in a prisoner-of-war camp; they would bite you all night long in your sleep. They would crawl into your eardrums, crawl up into your nostrils, and if you snored and had a mouth open, they'd crawl inside your mouth. One day we were told we were going to get deloused, that the lice were going to be killed by chemicals. We were marched out of our barracks up to another building and we were told to strip. We were given a little towel and off we went down a ramp, naked with that little towel, whole gang of us. It was a concrete building and had a couple pipes sticking out of it, but no sign of any water anywhere. After the door was shut and we were crammed in there body to body, rear end to rear end, with no sign of any water, somebody said, "Are we going to be gassed?"

This put a lot of fright in us; it was dark in there except for two little lights burning, and everybody started to say the Lord's Prayer, including me. Nothing came out for a long, long time. It was dead silence except for a humming sound. People were crossing themselves and others were just standing there. Then the water came out and everybody said, "Hooray!" Then we went back up to our place, shivering cold.

One morning we heard rumbling that got louder and louder and louder. We went outside, and a British tank came up and stopped. They hollered, "Where are we?" I hollered out, "You're in Stalag 11B!" He said, "You're free, get back in your barracks." We went back into the barracks but everybody was very quiet. We were liberated.

That was April 16, 1945. I had been there less than three months and I'd lost sixty-five pounds through all this horrible experience. We went back to the barracks and were there for a short time, and Taylor said, "I'm not going to stay here any longer, I'm starving." The guards had left, they had run away. So Taylor and I went down the road, and Taylor went into a farmhouse, and robbed a lady of six eggs while I stood guard at the kitchen door. Then a British guard came up and rammed a tommy gun in my stomach and said, "Who are you?" I told him I was an American prisoner of war. He said, "You better get back there quick before you get shot. This is dangerous out here. We've only been here an hour."

We were there for four or five more days and then we were taken to an airfield and C-47s were there waiting. Taylor and I and a couple of the other guys got on those planes, and I was the last guy on. The belly of the plane was full of holes from machine-gun fire, and I could see out the holes. When we got to England ambulances came for us. They were four-tiered ambulances and I was put on the fourth tier. What a ride we had through London to Oxford, England, to Winston Churchill General Hospital! We were told to strip and take off all our clothes. Two nurses had to bathe me because I was so weak. I was in the hospital for six or seven weeks recuperating. I was drinking a lot of white-chalk fluid because I couldn't eat, and because we had all these diseases. I weighed ninety-eight pounds.

They wouldn't let us go home early because they didn't want the American people to see how thin we were, how the Germans had treated us. Then we were taken to Swansea, Wales, and got on an ammunition ship. A couple hundred miles from New York, the ship's engine broke down and we had to wait out in the ocean for a few days until an oceangoing tug came and pulled us into Fort Hamilton, New York. Taylor said, "There's not going to be any bands waiting for us." And sure enough, there was one Red Cross lady there, bless her soul; she had some coffee and a doughnut for us to eat.

When I got home there was a little celebration, and everybody was glad to see me back.

There must have been a couple dozen people there. My mother had some soft drinks and cookies and cake and people came around and gave me a hug and "Welcome home." It was nice of them; it was a small-town atmosphere.

In the prison camp it was a constant battle of thinking positively. If there's one thing I'd like to let people understand is that there is a will to live, and regardless of what your circumstances are, what type of sickness you're going through, or what type of tragedy you're experiencing, you must have the will to live. Otherwise, you're not going to make it. It's all in the mind. It is a power; I cannot explain it. But if you want to live, you must think positively. I promised my parents that I would come back alive and that's what I tried to do. To uphold a promise I made.

AFTER THE WAR . . .

In 1946 Frank Yarosh entered Bucknell University to pursue a degree in chemical engineering. Upon graduation he went to work for the Philadelphia Gas Works and retired in 1987 after thirty-seven years of service. Mr. Yarosh married Margaret McHutchinson in 1954 and they settled in Erdenheim, Pennsylvania, and raised two sons. In 1992, Mr. Yarosh published his own book, *World War II is Not Over.* Today he continues to talk to school groups about his experiences.

☆ Glenn Bowers ☆
Dillsburg, Pennsylvania

• •

After finishing Naval Aviation Flight Training, Glenn Bowers was assigned to serve in the South Pacific in the "Black Sheep Squadron" under Col. Gregory "Pappy" Boyington. He flew eighty-six missions as a fighter pilot.

• •

Before the war I was a college student at Penn State. I learned to fly there in the old cow pasture, which was called the State College Air Depot, out by Boalsburg. I soloed on March 27, 1941, and that summer I tried to enlist in the Army Air Corps, but they didn't take me. And I guess I've always been very thankful that they didn't take me.

When World War II broke out in December 1941, I immediately took steps to try to get into naval aviation. I finally passed the physical and enlisted in April. I began active duty after my junior year in college on May 28, 1942. I went into naval aviation flight training. The Navy had initiated a new program when we enlisted, in that you went to three months of pre-flight training. This was strenuous physical activity. We did all kind of exercises, we had to run track, we played football, and all that kind of business. But one of the main things we did was swimming. We had to jump off a tower that was quite high, down into the water, and then swim so far underwater, like you were abandoning a ship. Or if your plane went down and it was burning on the surface, to swim underwater far enough to get away from the flames. It was tough.

I went from there to Grand Prairie, Texas, for primary training. Even though I had learned to fly, that meant nothing to the Navy. You had to start from scratch. I had been being tutored by an ensign named Irwin, but one day when I went out to the flight line I had a new instructor. I asked, "What happened to my instructor, Ensign Irwin?" He laughed and said, "He had a slight mishap. He took a student out and forgot to strap himself in and did a loop and fell out of the airplane. The student had never soloed, but he brought the plane down safely."

From there I went down to Corpus Christi, where I got most of my training. That's where I won my wings, on April 17, 1943. But when the time came to be commissioned and get our wings most of us were commissioned as second lieutenants in the Marine Corps instead of the Navy, because they wanted more Marine Corps pilots, and Marine Corps pilots were trained the same way naval aviators were.

From there I went to gunnery training in the F6F fighter over at Jacksonville, and I also qualified on the carrier in the F4F fighter, the Wildcat. To qualify on a carrier you've got to make six landings and six takeoffs on the carrier. I qualified, but I never used that in combat, because when I went overseas they put us in the Corsairs. At the time they didn't have Corsairs on carriers, so we were land-based.

After I finished qualifying on the carrier in July 1943 I was shipped out to the West Coast and awaited transportation over to the South Pacific. That transportation didn't come until in late August. We went on a huge Navy transport, carrying eighteen thousand troops from San Diego to Nouméa, New Caledonia. It took fourteen days, just zigzagging across the Pacific to avoid submarines and enemy ships. From New Caledonia we went up to an island in the New Hebrides called Espiritu Santo. That's where the airstrip was located where we joined the Black Sheep Squad. There were about twenty of us that filled in to bring the complement of the squadron up to the normal forty pilots. The Black Sheep got its name because the squadron was formed over in the islands. Most squadrons were formed here in the United States, then shipped overseas, but this squadron was put together from people from other squadrons, and replacements coming from the states like the twenty-odd of us that joined them.

Our commanding officer, "Pappy" Boyington, wanted to have a name for this squadron, and the one that he originally suggested was "Boyington's Bastards." But a war correspondent said that wouldn't fly in the press, and he suggested "Black Sheep." So that's how the Black Sheep got its name. Contrary to what was depicted on the TV show, we were not a bunch of misfits and no-goods. In reality, the only person who ever got into trouble in the squadron was Boyington. He was a wrestler in college, and he liked his moves. The first thing he'd always want to say is, "Well, let's wrestle, let's wrestle!" That's really how he came to be the leader of the squadron. He broke his ankle on the assignment he was on, and when the time came for a leader of the Black Sheep Squadron, he was available because his ankle had healed. He was confined to quarters one time for going over the head of his immediate superior. While he was in there, we'd sneak around the back with a Coke bottle with whiskey in it, rap on the shutter, and he'd take the bottle of Coke in and have a snort. And the guard—he wasn't paying that much attention because, hell, Boyington was a major. He wasn't going to create a big fuss anyhow.

The first mission was a ground-support mission. The Marines on Bougainville were in a bad situation because of the Japanese mortar fire along their perimeter. So during the night the Marines went out on the beach and put in big white muslin-cloth arrows to show us where we were to come in off the ocean and strafe that part of the jungle. We made our strafing runs until we had exhausted our ammunition supply. We later learned that we killed 106 of the enemy. I don't know how they knew that we'd killed 106 of the enemy but we got credit for 106.

We were flying off an island called Vella Lavella, which is in the South Pacific between Munda and Bougainville. On December 12, 1943, the Seabees finally got the airstrip they were building ready for use at Cape Torokina on Bougainville. We'd take off from Vella Lavella, fly to Torokina on Bougainville where they would top off the fuel tanks, and from that point we would take off on the big mission to Rabaul, which was several hours away over the Pacific. Rabaul was the Japanese bastion in that area, and it was subdued entirely by air power, and a little bit of sea power. There were never any ground troops that went in to take it. There were five airfields at Rabaul, and there was a wonderful natural harbor, Simpson Harbor, so the Japanese knew what they were doing when they picked that place to make a big base out of it.

The plane I was flying was a Corsair. It had a Pratt and Whitney R-2800 engine in it, which was the biggest at the time. They used a thirteen-foot-diameter prop to harness the two thousand horsepower that was generated by the engine. It was unusual because it had what they call an inverted gull wing. They built it that way so they could put the wheels at the bottom to get the clearance for the big prop it had up front. It had a forty-one-foot wingspan. It was thirty-three feet long, and fifteen feet high when it sat on the runway. It was a sleek plane. It was a good plane. We had excellent ground crews who did amazing work with little. And planes were very hard to come by, so they tried to keep them in repair. We had some clunkers that we had to deal with that didn't work too well, but it was an excellent airplane, the Corsair.

It was hot and humid all the time, and we wore as little clothes as we had to. We lived in huts, and we had to sleep under mosquito netting to keep from getting malaria, but the living conditions were pretty good.

On New Year's Day 1944 we were assigned to escort the B-24 bombers up over Rabaul. I don't know why my flight leader got so high, but we were up at 36,000 feet. The bombers were probably about 17,000 when the enemy just put up a solid cloud of flak at those bombers. I don't know how any of them got through. They all did get through, but some of them were crippled.

We were at 36,000 feet, flying in a four-plane formation. I didn't think that they had antiaircraft fire that would get up that far, but the first thing you know there was a burst of antiaircraft fire right behind our four planes. Then the next one was out ahead of us. Well, then you know where the next one's going to be. We were bracketed. So we dove out. In the process of diving out there were some clouds and the four planes got separated. I finally found one Corsair, but the bombers were straggling back because they had been hit by the antiaircraft fire. That's when the Japs came out and wanted to try to finish off those planes.

Well, this other Corsair pilot and I would scissor so we could see each other at all times and make sure we didn't get anyone on our tail, and whenever we would get close enough to those Jap fighters who were trying to finish off the bombers, they would just turn tail and go. So we didn't get a chance to shoot any of them down. But at least we protected the bombers as long as we could to try to get them out to the place they called the "ditch area" where they could put the plane down in the ocean and they'd get a Dumbo, or a seaplane, there to pick up the crew.

I never had the good fortune of shooting down an enemy plane. There was one time I might have gotten one. I was diving on one, trying to get in

Black Sheep Squadron

U.S. Marine Corps Fighter Squadron 214, the "Black Sheep Squadron," achieved fame in World War II by shooting down a large number of Japanese planes. Its lore includes the story of one of its commanding officers, Maj. Gregory Boyington (1912–88), a fighter ace whose record of twenty-six enemy kills equaled those of another marine flier, Maj. Joe Foss, and also Capt. Eddie Rickenbacker in World War I.

Boyington assembled the group from an unassigned band of twenty-seven pilots—some of them seasoned veterans with combat experience, others who were green replacement pilots.

The squadron was organized in 1942 under a different name, but did not gain the Black Sheep distinction until Boyington and another Marine major got permission in the summer of 1943 to form a new squadron from a group of pilots who did not fit into other assignments in the military; hence the name Black Sheep.

Boyington acquired the nickname "Pappy" because he was thirty-one at the time, a full decade older than most of the men he commanded; thus, he was considered to be an "old man." An aeronautical engineering graduate of the University of Washington, he worked as a draftsman for the Boeing aircraft company, and soon thereafter he held a series of posts with the Marine Corps Reserve and Marine Corps, eventually serving as a flight instructor.

A signature tactic of the Black Sheep squadron was to taunt the enemy into fighting. The United Press reported on Boyington at the time: "The Marine ace's 'Dare You to Come Up and Fight' forays over Japanese airfields sometimes goaded the enemy to come up for battle. And sometimes the Japanese would get on his fighter frequency and ask where he was. Then Boyington would give his position, curse at the Japanese and dare them to send up fighters."

Flying F-4U Corsairs, the Solomon Islands-based squadron accumulated a record of 203 enemy planes destroyed or damaged during its eighty-four-day deployment. The unit accumulated a record of ninety-seven verified air-to-air kills.

NATIONAL ARCHIVES

Boyington was shot down over Rabaul on January 3, 1944, the same day he registered his twenty-sixth kill, and initially was reported missing. Pilots in the squadron spent most of that day searching for him, but were unsuccessful. He was not killed, but rather picked up by a Japanese submarine. He spent the rest of the war in a POW camp.

The squadron was disbanded five days after the January 3 air battle in which Boyington was declared missing, and the pilots of the Black Sheep Squadron were dispersed to other units. Eventually, Boyington was awarded the Medal of Honor and the Navy Cross, and the squadron was awarded the Presidential Unit Citation.

The squadron and its designation were revived later in 1944, and the Black Sheep squadron has continued to function ever since, seeing action in Korea, Vietnam, and Iraq.

(continued on page 46)

(continued from page 45)

Major Pappy Boyington, commander of the Black Sheep Squadron, briefs his pilots. NATIONAL ARCHIVES

After World War II, Boyington wrote a book titled *Baa, Baa, Black Sheep* and later served as an advisor on a television program of that name, in which he was played by actor Robert Conrad. His personal life was a troubled one, marked by drinking, womanizing, and multiple divorces. His record and memory were honored in 2007, when the airport in his hometown of Coeur d'Alene, Idaho, was named in his honor. ★

range, and all of a sudden I saw tracers going by me, and I thought, "Oh, man, I got a Jap on my tail." I looked around and, heavens, it was another Corsair. The guy was so anxious to make a kill that he was shooting at a plane that was far out of his range. I just thought, "Buddy, before you put one through me, I'm getting out of here." So I dove out, and that was my only chance to shoot at an enemy plane.

We did a lot of bomber escorts. If you're escorting bombers your job is to keep the Zeroes away from the bombers, so you don't go out there and chase them, because while you're doing that you let other ones come in and get to your bombers. You just stayed with the bombers on the bombing missions. I was over there thirteen months, through three tours of duty. The first tour was with the Black Sheep, for twenty-eight missions. I was in two other squadrons after that, and flew fifty-eight missions with those two squadrons, for a total of eighty-six missions in the South Pacific. After a while I had some jungle problems, some of the things that you get from the jungle like fungus and so forth. They finally released me to come back in October of 1944.

I had to stay in the service because the war was still going on. They sent me to instrument flight-instructor school, which I wasn't really happy about. That made me an instrument flight instructor. I was in that category until I was discharged in December of 1945.

The Black Sheep had the best camaraderie and was the best corps of any outfit I was ever affiliated with. I think a lot of the sacrifices people made back then haven't been duly recognized by a lot of today's people. There were a lot of sacrifices made then, and we certainly wouldn't be enjoying the freedoms we have now if things had gone the wrong way back then.

AFTER THE WAR . . .

The war interrupted Glenn Bowers's studies at Penn State. Following his time in the service, he returned to Penn State and eventually received his undergraduate and graduate degrees. In 1948, he went to work as a wildlife biologist for the Pennsylvania Game Commission and moved through the ranks to the position of executive director, which he held until his retirement in 1982. Mr. Bowers's wife of nearly fifty-seven years, Betty Lehr, passed away in 2000. Together they had two children.

☆ Wesley Mullen ☆

Ridley Park, Pennsylvania

∙∙∙

Wesley Mullen landed on Normandy Beach on D-Day. He was also involved in the fighting at Saint-Lô. In one encounter, his platoon lost twenty of twenty-eight men.

∙∙∙

I was pretty young when I quit school and joined the Army. I just thought that was the thing to do. I was seventeen at the time, but they didn't call me into active duty until I was eighteen, which was about a month later. I actually had chosen the Navy, because my father was in the Navy. I went down and had a physical and they turned me down for flat feet. I tried the Coast Guard and they turned me down for flat feet. Then the Army took me with flat feet. It didn't bother them.

I was immediately sent out to Fort Riley, Kansas, with the 1st Cavalry. I enjoyed the training. It was a lot of walking and a lot of exercise, and we trained with rifles. We were originally going into the cavalry but the government did away with the horse cavalry because the horses were too big of targets, so we all ended up as replacements in the infantry. After a few months of training we were sent overseas by way of Nova Scotia and England, where I joined the 1st Division in Swanage, England, which was a little town on the English Channel.

I've heard a lot of people say they had extensive training for D-Day and for the invasion, but we had no training. Occasionally we would take a hike out of Swanage, run a half-mile, and go in the woods and sleep for four or five hours, and then run back into town and look like we were running all day. That's about all the training we ever did. We stayed there from October to June of 1944, and then we went to Plymouth, England, and boarded LCLs for the invasion of Europe. It was extremely rough with the rain and bad weather. We started over to France in the early morning of June 4 and had to turn back because it was so rough. Then they changed it and we went over on June 6.

That day there was a tremendous number of Navy ships on the Channel, lined up and firing at the beach. When you're that young I guess you don't think about how serious it could be, because I never concerned myself. It was just something we were going to do. The LCL was very uncomfortable. You were in bunks five high, in cots. It was very close quarters, but you didn't expect to be on there too long. And the water was very, very rough. Fortunately for me I don't get seasick so it was okay for me, and fortunately I knew right away when I got on this ship to get on the top bunk, because everybody else was sick. So I was on a top bunk where it was fairly safe. When we were approaching the beach, we were sitting in back of the cruiser *Augusta*. We came out from behind it and headed for the beach and we hit a sandbar and couldn't get off of it. An LCVP—which is the kind of craft you always see in the movies with the big door in the front that always drops down—pulled alongside of us and we went over the side and into that and then went into shore.

The thing I vividly remember is when that door dropped on the beach we had to push bodies aside to get ashore. There were bodies floating in the water all over. That was the 16th and 18th regiments which had gone before us. When the 1st Division went in, the 16th Regiment went first, then the 18th, and then the 26th, so we were not the first wave that hit the beach. It was fortunate for us because the 16th Regiment lost 90 percent of their men. The 18th lost about 70 percent. They did all the work, and then we walked right over them. When we landed on the beach, in my platoon of about sixty men, we lost one man, and he got hurt getting off the ship.

As we crossed the beach, there were marked areas where there was a narrow pass across the mine field, which was maybe forty yards across the beach, and then a big embankment which went up forty to fifty feet. We got across to that without any problems, then we went up that path and had an assembly point on top of the bluff. The 18th had already made it to the top, which made it very good for us.

LSTs put personnel and cargo ashore during the Normandy invasion in June 1944. U.S. COAST GUARD COLLECTION, NATIONAL ARCHIVES

There was an occasional sniper, but not heavy fire. The two regiments before us made it easy for us because they had taken a lot of the heavy fire. I no sooner got to the top when officers ran over—and there were four of us there, and one sergeant—and they wanted us to take a patrol out immediately. They wanted the patrol to contact the 29th Division, which was on our right. There was a big gap between the two, and the message we had for them was to close this gap. They were to move over toward us because there was too much of an opening. So the four of us took off running. I don't know if we ran a quarter of a mile or three miles, I have no idea, but we finally found them. They were in a heavy fight with the Germans in a cemetery. We were able to get behind them and give them the message and then went back to our outfit. We never got fired on or anything. We got back to our outfit and they had already moved out and we had to run to catch up. For the next seven days we never stopped.

We were at the farthest penetration of the beachhead; that was to Caumont, France. During that time you slept ten minutes and were on your feet again, then you'd fall and sleep for five minutes and get back on your feet again. We had no food. They were unable to get food ships ashore for some reason. We carried a couple of K rations and that was about it. I think it took us about seven days to get to Caumont, and then we set up a line of defense. We dug in really good because we were there a long time. We'd get parts of houses and anything we could get to put on top of our holes.

By that time our kitchen unit caught up with us and we started getting food. We would eat once a day, around midnight. Of course you didn't want to make any noise because the Germans would hear you, so you went back to the kitchen and you would eat a little further back of the lines. You never knew what you were eating because it was dark. It was mashed potatoes and gravy and oatmeal and whatever you got, but it was food. We were in Caumont for about twenty-eight days. The Germans were constantly probing trying to find out where our lines were. Every night they were coming in their patrols shooting at us or trying to find out where our lines were. You always had two men awake to make sure they didn't get there before you. It was a long twenty-eight days. We slept on the ground all the time. I've often thought back and wondered, when did I get washed or when did I go to the bathroom, but I can't remember when we ever did these things. I mean it's a normal thing, and yet washing was not normal. It was probably weeks before we got washed or shaved.

After twenty-eight days the 5th Division relieved us and we went back behind Saint-Lô. We were going to be the spearhead to go out through Saint-Lô. We set up pup tents and had a nice rest there. During that time our planes were coming over, and I mean thousands and thousands. The sky was just full of airplanes and they were bombing about a one-square-mile area in front of us. After three days of that we took off and eventually broke through Saint-Lô and reached our object, which was La Ferté Macé, where we surrounded one of the German armies. We were sitting on top of a big hill, and down below we could see the Germans trying to get out of this pocket they were in. Every time they tried, the artillery would just slaughter them. It was so bad they eventually surrendered the entire army. From there we took off again across France.

During that time I had one of the worst days I've ever had. We started the morning with only twenty-eight men in our platoon. We kept losing a man here and there. You see in the movies where the guys knew where all the guys were, but you didn't. Two or three days later you'd say, "Where's Joe?" and nobody knew. "I think he got wounded, I think he got killed" . . . nobody knew. You never really knew what happened to the fellows who were with you all the time. So we had twenty-eight men, and the Germans hit us in the front. We were walking down a highway—we were on the left, the other platoon on our right—and the order was to go over the fence. We had two tanks sitting in the field and we were to get in between them. Three men and I were put behind one tank, the corporal and three other men were

LCI(L)s

Originally designed as a vessel for rapidly transporting British commando raiders from England to Normandy, the LCI(L), or Landing Craft Infantry (Large), played an important role in many amphibious assaults of World War II. These included action in North Africa; the invasions of Italy, Sicily, and southern France; the invasions of Guam, Leyte, Okinawa, Iwo Jima, and other Pacific sites; and the invasion of Normandy on D-Day.

Unlike the LST (Landing Ship, Tank; see page 60), the LCI(L) was built primarily to carry troops, not weaponry or vehicles. Its flat hull and shallow draft was designed to facilitate beach landings, with rapid delivery of troops to shore. Ordinarily, with the ships' spartan accommodations and limited food and water supplies, they were intended to be occupied for only about forty-eight hours. They were not intended to be oceangoing vessels, although some did function in that capacity, carrying troops across large stretches of the Atlantic and Pacific.

LCI(L) ships were built in two versions, both measuring 189 feet long and 23 feet wide. The first, introduced in 1942, carried 188 troops and 75 tons of cargo, with a crew of 24; 1,031 of these were built. The second, introduced in 1943, carried 209 troops and 75 tons of cargo with a crew of 29; 605 of these were built.

The Army, Navy, Marines, and Coast Guard all used LCI(L)s. In addition, the United States leased at least two hundred of them to the United Kingdom, which assigned them to the British Royal Navy or the Canadian Navy.

Early models were built with ramps on both sides of the ship to deliver troops to the beach, while later versions employed a bow ramp like those of the LSTs. LCI(L)s were powered by eight General Motors diesel engines, generating 1,600 horsepower.

The first LCI(L) was built at the New York Shipbuilding Corp. in Camden, New Jersey, launched on September 27, 1942, and commis-

LIBRARY OF CONGRESS

sioned on October 7 of that year. It was sunk by German aircraft bombardment at Bizerte, Tunisia, less than a year later, on August 17, 1943.
Shipyards in Massachusetts, Oregon, and Texas also built LCI(L)s.

With their relatively small size compared to aircraft carriers, destroyers, and battleships, they gained a nickname: "the Waterbug Navy," supposedly uttered by an admiral looking down on them from a larger ship
and thinking that they resembled insects skimming the surface of a
pond. Although they operated out of the limelight, at least one LCI(L),
LCI-220, got a big splash of publicity when it appeared in a photo
titled "Landing in Italy" by George Rodgers on the cover of the March
21, 1944, issue of *Life* magazine.

Besides troop-carrying LCIs, other types were built or modified
for special purposes—some carried rockets, guns, or mortar launch-
ers, while others were used as command posts known as flotilla flag-
ships. Some delivered demolition specialists (frogmen), and still others
carried depth charges to be used against Axis submarines.

After the war, some LCI(L)s participated in occupation duty in
Japan. There being little civilian use for them, most were transferred
to the U.S. Maritime Commission or the State Department, from
which they were sold between 1946 and 1948 and scrapped. ★

put behind the other tank. Everybody else went to the front skirmish line in front of us. Within seconds a German tank that was well-hidden knocked the two tanks out, and all the men between them surged forward and jumped into a ditch in a little road coming off the main road. I jumped up on a tank and I could see the guy on the other tank doing the same thing. We were trying to see if we could help the guys in the tank, but flames started coming up and the tank started shuttering, so we jumped off and ran to the ditch. When we jumped into the ditch everybody was dead. I have no idea whether it was gun fire, artillery, or what hit these guys. It had to be very quick. The lieutenant was one man I saw, and the top of his head was off.

There were eight of us then. We ran up the bank, and the Germans were down below. We could see them coming out of the hedge row. This corporal said to me, "Go up there and see what's going on, and what we are supposed to do here." The first man I walked over to was named Owens. He said something, but then he was hit all over and he died just like that. I was running up the ditch now and I found five men who were badly wounded. Some had holes in their chests, and as I made it back to that road, medics were coming over the top into the ditch. I told them we had five men back there. A lieutenant came over and said, "Get the men out of here, we're withdrawing." That was the first time I was in the Army that we ever pulled back. I immediately ran down and got the other eight men and we went up and helped the medic get the five men on stretchers.

We got them out and we pulled back, but we lost our whole platoon that day except for the eight of us. It was apparently a trap set up by the Germans, knowing we would all jump into this ditch. They must have zeroed in on it. I don't know what actually got these men, but we lost everybody: the lieutenant, all the sergeants, everybody. It was just a bad day, probably the worst day that I had ever seen in combat. Then we had to pull back a little bit and regroup. We got some replacements and then I didn't know anybody in the platoon anymore. I was a stranger there.

After that we ran across Europe until we hit the Rhine River. We were about twenty miles away, preparing to cross the Rhine River at Remagen, Germany. They were bringing in big boats that looked like lifeboats from ocean liners, and we were supposed to start practicing. We were in a comparatively safe area, looking down on the Rhine. Our object was we were going to go across that river in those boats. It never happened; we got word one day that the Remagen Bridge had been taken by a few guys. We were to drop everything, grab our rifles and ammunition, jump in the trucks and jeeps and run over twenty miles upriver to the Remagen Bridge. So we didn't have to cross in a boat. We didn't cross the bridge either, because the bridge was pretty weakened by the Germans. Right next to the bridge they built a footbridge about a foot wide on pontoons, and we went across on that. And as we went across, two German planes came in and dropped one bomb that went between us and the bridge, but we did go across and set up a defense line on the other side around Remagen.

After that we went on to the first big town in Germany, Aachen. We were on the edge of town, and on the night of October 17, 1944, the lieutenant came to me and said, "You are now squad leader, and tomorrow I'll put you in for first sergeant." That sounded pretty good, more pay. The next morning at six o'clock I got the word, "Take your men and take off." Every morning we would get our orders to move out, and everybody would take off and start moving across the streets. You didn't do it in crowds because you made too many targets; you would do it a couple here and a couple there and try to get across to take the houses out.

So Robbie Robinson, from Philadelphia, and I were the first two. I said, "We'll get across the street and the rest of the guys can come over in twos." I got as far as the curb and this guy with a machine gun was sitting in a doorway, and he lowered the boom on me. He hit me in the stomach, the head, the hand, and the chest, and of course I went down. Robbie went down too, but he wasn't hit. He gave me a shot of morphine and tried to do what he could for me. It was now starting to rain, and the rain was going into my ear and driving me crazy, so I asked for my helmet and I had a big hole in the side of my helmet. I didn't know if a bullet had gone through my helmet or around and hit me in the back of the head. The medics wouldn't come out, but they threw a first aid kit over to Robbie and he got up to get it and they shot him. He got hit in the shoulder and the ear so he just took off and went over the wall and now I'm lying there by myself. I laid there from six o'clock in the morning until noon. I couldn't get my legs moving or I would have crawled back. I tried to walk, but I couldn't move. I never felt that I was going to die. I probably should have, but I didn't. I just think I was too young to realize, and that's why they use all these young kids, I guess, because they don't have enough sense to know how dangerous it is.

About noon the lieutenant yelled, "Wes, how are you, are you alright?" I said, "Yeah," and he said, "Can you walk?" and I said, "No I can't move my legs." The next thing I knew, he was beside me with a stretcher. He rolled me over on it and grabbed it and ran back to the wall and got me over the wall. They got me on a jeep and rushed me back to a field hospital. I don't remember a whole lot since I was getting morphine; Robbie had given me a shot of morphine, when I went over the wall at noon they gave me a shot of morphine, when I got to the aid station they gave me another shot of morphine, and by this time I'm feeling no pain.

The next thing I knew—and I don't know how long it was, a day later or three days later—I was in a hospital in Paris. I couldn't walk, I couldn't move my legs, and my thumb was broken in about six different places. So who walks in the door but the lieutenant who saved me, and he had patches all down his chest. He said, "It's nothing serious, it's just a lot of scratches. As soon as I can find my clothes I'm going to get out of here and go back to the outfit." The next morning MPs and officers were all around my bed wanting to know everything he said. Apparently he found his clothes and took off and went back out and they were out looking for him, so I assume he got back to the outfit.

They sent me by airplane to a hospital in Birmingham, England. There were so many patients that you rarely saw a doctor, and I just laid in bed. The nurses were unbelievable. They worked sixteen hours a day and were always there helping you. One nurse took an interest in me and kept making me sit on the edge of the bed; then she would have her arms around my shoulder and make me get up and walk a few feet. I was getting ribbed a lot from the guys saying, "You're lucky, you got a private nurse." But this nurse was just helping; she would have helped anybody else.

Right after Christmas I had been walking for about two weeks, and I was sent back to my outfit. I was supposed to be going home; I had changed my clothes, my money, but I didn't go home. I think they were desperate for men. We had been reading in the papers that the German Army was in full retreat and the war was over in Europe. Well, it wasn't. So to get replacements, they went to the hospitals. And all the truck drivers and all kind of support personnel behind the lines were sent up to the front lines. I rejoined the 1st Division at Malmedy and from that time on it was all the way through a lot of small battles. I got wounded again in the Harz Mountains. We were going up to the top of the mountain and mortar shells came in behind us and I got hit in the legs, but it wasn't serious, and the medic was right there and he cleaned it up a little bit. I went down to the aid station and they put a few stitches in my legs and I was okay.

We went about twelve miles into Czechoslovakia and we were then told to withdraw because we weren't supposed to be in Czechoslovakia because that was Russian territory. So we pulled back to the German border and I was put on an outpost with four guys. Our orders were that the Germans were going to come in to surrender, the war was over, and that we were to keep them where we were, and not to let them into town. They told us there would be a few people coming, but there were thousands. German soldiers, tanks, trucks, and families kept coming in and surrounding us. We were sitting in the middle of all of this, and thousands of them kept coming. They all seemed very happy that the war was over and it was done.

We eventually pulled back to Nuremberg where we were guarding prisoners for the war trials, and because I was in the regular Army I didn't get sent home. I was supposed to serve three years in the Army. Every time the chance to go home came up they would say, "Wes, you're not married, you're regular Army, so forget it." I stayed there for the Army of Occupation and didn't come home until October 1945. It got me other medals; the Army of Occupation Medal, the Cold War Medal, and things like that.

Finally in October I was shipped home. There was no big fanfare or anything, you just came home. I came home with a fellow by the name of Murray from Chester, Pennsylvania. I was living on Pine Street and Darby. I got out of the cab and went up to the house and he took off and went on to Chester. There was no fanfare or anything. We just got home. Within a week I went back to work and it was no big change. It was just done, that's all.

I've never had nightmares about it, but I feel very fortunate that I came home and so many of my friends didn't come home. They talk about all of these heroes and the only heroes to me are the ones that didn't come home. They gave up everything so you and I can sit here. But you're not doing things over there to be a hero. You're doing things to save your life.

AFTER THE WAR . . .

After leaving the service, Wesley Mullen married Marie Smith in 1947. He went to work as a meat inspector in the Philadelphia area and attended the University of Chicago, Ohio State University, and Penn State University. In 1980, Mr. Mullen retired from his job as a compliance officer with the federal government. He went on to work in a law office, in real estate, and as a crossing guard. The Mullens have a son and daughter, five grandchildren, and two great-grandchildren.

☆ Grant Lee ☆

Enola, Pennsylvania

••

Grant Lee was a gunner on an LST, transporting men and supplies across the English Channel for the D-Day invasion. He was later sent to the South Pacific, where he served in the invasion of Okinawa.

••

I was in high school, living a normal life, until we heard about the Pearl Harbor attack. I was only about fifteen years old. Then one day in April, 1943, I got a letter from the government: "Greetings. Report to Carlisle Courthouse." So my mother took a whole group of us boys up to Carlisle, and that's where I left her. They put us on a bus and took us to Harrisburg, Pennsylvania, and inducted us on June 2, 1943. They put us on a bus and ran us up to Scranton, put us on a train, and took us to the Naval Training Station in Sampson, New York. Then they sent us out to Great Lakes, Illinois, for gunnery training for two weeks, and there I had a pointer and a trainer that couldn't be beat. We were on a 40-millimeter, and we had to shoot at sleeves pulled by Piper Cubs. We knocked five sleeves down. Then all they had left was drones, like a small toy plane that they could fly around. They put them up, and we knocked down four of them out of five, so they said, "Secure your gun. You don't need any more practice."

Then they sent us down to Evansville, Indiana, to pick up our ship, the 491. We went out into the Gulf of Mexico and around the Keys to go up to Quonset Point, Rhode Island. We went into Norfolk, got some supplies, and went on up through New York and the Long Island Sound. We got to Quonset Point and they shored our tank deck with timber and brought fresh hams in. We had a space there about twenty-six feet wide and 150 feet long, and had twelve feet deep of fresh hams. We were supposed to take them over to England for the troops.

After we got situated in England we started making mock invasions of southern England. We had 24 LST's. LST means "Landing Ships, Tanks," but later on, it was changed to "large, slow target." I was a gunner's mate in charge of the number-one gun on the bow. When I went into the service I wanted to be a gunner's mate, because I had gunned before I was in the service and I liked guns.

One group of eight LST's was in the English Channel on what they called "Exercise Tiger" to make a mock invasion at Slapton Sands, at the little town called Norcroft, when a German E-boat came down the channel. They thought we were oil tankers, and they charged us with torpedoes, sunk two of the LST's, and the other one made it to the shore. They patched up their damages so they wouldn't sink, and got towed to dry dock to be repaired for the Normandy invasion. There were 749 casualties from that German E-boat.

The Americans wanted to get tanks to shore, so they thought they would try a flotation device. They put a tank in a flotation off of the LST's ramp and had to start up the tank's tracks to move it—that's the only propellers they had. As they started them up, the tank ran right out of the flotation and sank. I don't know if the fellows got out or not, but that tank sat in the English Channel for thirty years.

[General Dwight D.] Eisenhower had said, "If anybody gets caught talking about the Tiger operation you'll get general court-martial and maybe get shot." So nobody would talk about the Tiger operation for twenty or thirty years.

After practicing and running back and forth in different harbors, and anchoring and going into the docks and that kind of stuff, we then were set up for the invasion of June 3, 1944. On June 2 they loaded us to take off for the evening of the 3rd, and we went up the English Channel. When we were ready to turn in toward Normandy we turned around and went back. Then on the evening of the 4th, the same thing happened. We went up so far, and they turned us around and sent us back. We found out later that the tides weren't right, the wind wasn't right, nothing was right.

LSTs

The workaday naval vessel known as the LST (for Landing Ship, Tank) was one of the most useful ships of World War II.

Modified from a British design known as the Tank Landing Craft, the LST was built in several variants at shipyards in the United States, England, Ireland, and Canada. Many of those built in America were constructed in Pennsylvania, at the Philadelphia Navy Yard, by the Dravo Corporation on Neville Island (in the Ohio River northwest of Pittsburgh), or by American Bridge Company (a division of U.S. Steel) at Ambridge, Pennsylvania, a few miles downriver from Pittsburgh.

Other LSTs were built farther down the Ohio at Jeffersonville or Evansville, Indiana, or on the Mississippi in Illinois. Still others were built along both coasts in Bath, Maine; Boston; Baltimore; Wilmington, Delaware; Norfolk and Newport News, Virginia.; Charleston, South Carolina; and in California and Washington. In all, 1,052 American LSTs

(continued on page 62)

NATIONAL ARCHIVES

World War II LSTs that were later named for Pennsylvania counties

LST Number	Name given on 1 July 1955	Builder	Date Launched	Service Notes	Combat Honors	Struck from Naval Register	Disposition
LST-57	Armstrong County[1]	Dravo Corp, Pittsburgh	4 December 1943	Took part in Normandy invasion	1 battle star WWII	11 August 1955	Sunk as a target, 1956
LST-845	Jefferson County[2]	American Bridge Co., Ambridge, PA	7 December 1944	Supported Asiatic-Pacific ops. Also served in Korea	5 battle stars, Korea	1 February 1961	Sold for scrap
LST-850	Juniata County	Chicago Bridge & Iron Co., Seneca, IL	3 November 1944	Took part in invasion of Okinawa	1 battle star WWII	1 November 1958	Sunk as a target
LST-887	Lawrence County[3]	Dravo Corp, Pittsburgh	7 October 1944	Took part in invasion of Okinawa. Also served in Korea	1 battle star WWII; 3 battle stars, Korea	1 November 1960	Sold to Indonesian Navy; renamed Tandjung Nusanive (LST-1)
LST-902	Luzerne County	Dravo Corp, Pittsburgh	16 December 1944	Served in Korea, Vietnam; 10 campaign stars, Vietnam	2 battle stars, Korea	12 August 1970	Unknown
LST-1038	Monroe County[4]	Dravo Corp, Pittsburgh	6 January 1945	Supported Asiatic-Pacific ops	1 battle star WWII	1 November 1958	Unknown
LST-1041	Montgomery County[5]	Dravo Corp, Pittsburgh	20 January 1945	Supported Asiatic-Pacific ops	Did not see combat	1 June 1960	Sold to West Germany, but did not serve in German Navy; scrapped in 1968
LST-1086	Potter County	American Bridge Co., Ambridge, PA	28 January 1945	Supported Pacific operations	Did not see combat	9 August 1960	Sold to Greek government, served Hellenic Navy as HS Ikaria (L-154)

Note: The Navy also acquired postwar LSTs that were named for Tioga County (built 1953) and York County (built 1956).

[1] Also named for a county in Texas.
[2] Named for counties in 26 U.S. states.
[3] Named for counties in 11 U.S. states.
[4] Named for counties in 17 U.S. states.
[5] Named for counties in 18 U.S. states

(continued from page 60)
were built during World War II. Of these, 117 were transferred to the Royal Navy or the Greek navy under the Lend-Lease Program.

LSTs were essentially transports, designed as seagoing, flat-bottomed, low-draft vessels that could land armaments, troops, and cargo directly on a beach. Upon landing, two bow doors opened, and a ramp was lowered, allowing tanks, artillery, and other vehicles to be driven ashore immediately. They were configured with a main deck above and a hold or tank deck, which carried tanks and heavy equipment. Lighter vehicles and cargo stored on the upper deck could be lowered by elevator to the hold deck to go ashore. Where conditions did not allow an LST to get close enough to shore, the crew could assemble portable pontoon sections to form a causeway reaching from the ramp to the beach.

Measuring 328 feet long and 50 feet wide, LSTs could carry 1,600 to 1,900 tons of payload, plus as many as 16 officers and 147 enlisted personnel. LSTs were utilitarian, but not fast. Their speed of 14 knots was half that of a powerful battleship.

The first LST to be built in America, LST-1, was constructed by Dravo at Neville Island, beginning on July 20, 1942. It was launched on September 7, 1942, and commissioned on December 14. Its first mission was in the Mediterranean, where it supported Allied invasions or assaults on the island of Sicily and at Salerno and Anzio, Italy. Later it took part in the D-Day invasion of western Europe at Normandy. For its service during World War II, it earned four battle stars. It was decommissioned in 1946 and sold for scrap the following year. ★

So then, the evening of June 5, they sent us up the channel again. Our ship was just rocking something terrible and, of course, it was at night so we couldn't see. Nobody had any lights on. We found out later on that battleships and cruisers were passing us like we were standing still. The battleships and cruisers that were sitting out in the harbor were lobbing shells over our heads onto the beach. If anybody saw *Saving Private Ryan*, that's about as true a story as you could possibly get, except you didn't see the first three waves that went in.

As an LST would go in to the beach they'd drop a stern anchor, and that would aid them in getting off of the beach when the tidewaters would come back in. You would have to leave that anchor one hundred or two hundred yards out from the ship before you hit the beach. When we went in, we hit another LST's anchor and punched a hole in the bottom of our ship. So we had the welders go down and seal the compartment—weld that anchor to the bottom of our ship inside—then go outside and cut the cable off.

With the Americans shooting or softening the beach up with shells, every time a shell would hit it would cause a crater. That meant it would blow the sand out, and you'd have a hole. When the LCVPs [Landing Craft Vehicle, Personnel] would go in they'd hit these sand mounds and couldn't go any further, and they'd drop the guys out right down in the crater in the water. With seventy-five-pound packs on their back they could not get out. They couldn't walk up the side because the sand was going out from underneath them. So after two or three boats had gone in, when the fellows would go off the end of the ramp they'd be walking over the bodies of the other men to get to the shore. There were about three-thousand that didn't get shot, they drowned. On Normandy Beach there were twenty-three-foot tides. So from high tide to low tide you might have had anywhere from a mile to a mile and a half of beach. And when the tide went out you could see the fellows—the Americans—still in the craters made by the shells.

By the time we got in there they had captured a lot of Germans. The Germans weren't really captured, they gave up, held their guns up over their heads, said, "Don't shoot," and they gave themselves up. So they used the Germans to go down in the craters and pick the Americans' bodies out and put them on a front-end loader. Then when the front-end loader got full they took it up on the dry ground and just dumped the bodies like cordwood.

The next morning the tidewaters were coming in, and there was an LCT [Landing Craft, Tanks] that came in down the beach behind us, and just as he got directly behind us, he hit a magnetic mine. There were eleven crewmen on board, and in about two minutes they were completely gone. There was one fellow that our small boats picked up, and they brought him into shore on a litter. He was still alive, but his arms and legs were shredded. We had the doctor come out and look at him, and he asked the doctor to help him, so the doctor got some morphine. He couldn't find any place to inject it but in his chest. Then the doctor told the pharmacist's mate to get a blanket, but by the time he got the blanket there, he was gone. That LCT that hit that magnetic mine saved us from getting hit on that mine, because once we'd have gotten tidewaters under us enough to move back, we'd have hit it.

We got off the beach and went back to England, into Falmouth dry dock, and had the anchor removed from the bottom of our ship and a

Exercise Tiger

In preparation for the D-Day invasion of Nazi-held Europe, Allied troops conducted a massive, yet top-secret, rehearsal at Slapton Sands, on the southwest coast of England. The site was chosen for its similarity to Utah Beach, one of the prongs of attack in the Normandy invasion of June 6, 1944.

One element of this planning was Exercise Tiger. Lasting eight days, from April 22 to 30, 1944, it turned into a costly and embarrassing failure when a mix-up in radio frequencies, among other circumstances, resulted in an Allied convoy being attacked by German Schnellboot (E-boat) vessels—small, fast torpedo boats. The casualties included 749 American servicemen—198 sailors and 551 soldiers.

Late in 1943, about 3,500 residents had been evacuated from eight English villages to make way for the exercise, and they were kept from their homes for nearly a year. As the exercise took shape, it involved 30,000 soldiers and three hundred ships, including thirty LSTs (Landing Ship, Tank).

In the simulation, Allied troops "bombarded" Slapton and began landings on April 27. Early the next day, a flotilla of eight American LSTs with a single British escort, the corvette HMS *Azalea*, was preparing to simulate a follow-up landing. They carried engineers, physicians, and members of the signal and chemical corps, as well as a smaller number of infantry. A second British escort was supposed to accompany the group, but it was laid in port with a hole in its bow.

Shortly after 2 A.M., the convoy was attacked by a group of nine German E-boats that had slipped across the English Channel from their base at Cherbourg, France. Three LSTs were hit; two of them sank immediately, one within six minutes. The other one limped back

plate put over to seal it up again. We made about another half a dozen trips from England to Normandy and either Utah Beach or Omaha Beach, depending where they wanted the supplies. We made shuttles back and forth until one day we got notice to pick up anchor and head for the to port. Four LSTs returned fire, but the E-boats escaped by using a combination of smoke and speed.

It later surfaced that the LSTs had been given an incorrect radio frequency, and while the British escort had been warned about the approaching enemy, its commander believed that the LSTs had gotten the same radio alert. They did not.

Those servicemen who were not killed in the initial attack either drowned or died of hypothermia in the 42-degree water. Many drowned because they had not been trained on the correct way to apply their lifebelts. This made them top-heavy, resulting in the pathetic sight of their feet being out of the water while their torsos and heads were submerged.

Allied commanders were keen to recover the bodies of as many casualties as possible, but especially those of ten officers who had been briefed on exact details of the D-Day invasion. Had they been taken prisoner and forced to divulge their knowledge, the curtain of secrecy surrounding the greatest naval invasion in history would have been compromised. All ten officers' bodies were recovered; all had drowned.

Exercise Tiger continued, and another rehearsal, code-named Fabius, completed the training for the Allied assault on the Nazis' Atlantic Wall. To avoid revealing anything about the coming invasion, U.S. commanders hushed up the incident, although it was listed in subsequent military press releases after D-Day. Years later, various parties tried to claim that it was a cover-up, but it had been mentioned or described in the military newspaper *Stars and Stripes*, as well as numerous books and official government reports. To many of the war-weary involved, it was just one more cost, among many, of fighting evil.

The sad fact of the story is that more men died in Exercise Tiger than died in the actual invasion of Utah Beach.

Many years later, and mostly through the efforts of British retired policeman Ken Small, a memorial to those who died in Exercise Tiger was placed overlooking the coast at Slapton Sands. ★

Mediterranean area. We were going down to make the invasion of southern France.

Our ship was the flotilla flagship, so we had to lead the other LST's in the invasion. We had small boats hit the beach before daylight and after daylight, but they didn't soften the beach up because there wasn't anybody there. So the beachmaster directed the ships to come in. There were five or six LST's on the beach, and right ahead of the beach was nothing but a mountain.

The beachmaster notified another ship, the LST-282, to come into beach, but he reported that he couldn't go in right away because his engines were down. So we went into beach. We were in there about twenty minutes when the 282 came in. He got within fifty or one hundred yards of us when general quarters sounded, and here over the mountain came a German bomber with a buzz bomb underneath it. It made a big circle, went back behind the mountain and came back over it a second time and released the buzz bomb. It hit LST-282 right in the engine room and caused a big fire. On their tank deck they had two tractor-trailer loads of high-octane gas for the airplanes; one was in the back end of the tank deck and the other was in the front. When the fire got to the first truck, that explosion went off, and it just looked like somebody took a can opener and opened up the main deck of that ship. It just blew a hole right up out through the ship.

There was an ensign on the bow, and the Army and Navy personnel were jumping overboard because there was no way they could fight the fire. It was too intense. The officer on the bow said, "Don't you guys jump overboard. You'll be put on report for abandoning ship without permission." Well, by the time the other tank truck of gasoline went off they didn't have to jump, it just blew them overboard. The reason the ensign didn't want anybody to jump overboard was because he couldn't swim. So when he did get overboard, the others saved him.

After that invasion we went down to Florence, Italy. We hadn't had any mail for thirty days and we had about thirty bags of mail waiting for us. We went into Florence, but we had to go through a minefield to get in to get some fuel, so we left one of the ensigns off to go get the mail and bring it back to the ship. Well, the ship got fueled up and we got out of there. We left word with the ensign that he's to try to get a seaplane and take the mail to Naples, Italy, and we'd pick him up there. We got back out of Florence, and on the way down to Naples we got word that the airplane didn't make it over the mountain. So we lost thirty bags of mail and an ensign.

We then shoved off and went back to the United States and went up to Quonset Point again where we got our ship modified. We had a single 40-millimeter gun on the bow and a single three-inch 50-millimeter on the stern of our ship. When we went back to Boston they took off the three-inch 50 and put on a quad 40, and they took my single 40 off the bow and put a twin 40 on.

After we got fixed up there, they put an LCT, the 554, onto the main deck of the 491 and they sent us over to the South Pacific. We got into the Okinawa invasion, but before that we were in Guam, where they loaded our tank deck with five-inch projectiles—ammunition. We were so heavy in the water that they had pontoons on the side of our ship. We sat in the harbor for eighteen days and nights until a typhoon came along, and we had to go out and head right into the typhoon for three days. Our main deck cracked from the main cargo hatch over to one of the small cargo hatches and we thought we would lose the ship. We had four welders there trying to weld that crack shut, but every time the ship would go up in the air and come back down, the crack would open up again. I was one of the welders who helped to do the welding for three days.

We survived it, and after the storm was over we went into Okinawa and sat there until they could get us a spot to go in. They took us up the northern part of the island where there was a lagoon, and they had the underwater demolition team blast the coral reefs out wide enough and deep enough that we could get in.

There were many LST's that the Japanese suicide planes would dive right into. If they dove into us there would not have been anything left of any of us because of that ammunition we were carrying. If it went off it would have been the end of us, period.

After the Okinawa invasion we ran from Guam, Saipan, Tinian, and also down into the Philippines. Then we'd come back to Guam and get loaded up with personnel. We took off to make the invasion of Japan, and about one hundred miles from Tokyo Bay they turned around and sent us back. The third time they sent us back we were about a day out of Saipan and we heard that the war was over.

AFTER THE WAR . . .

After returning from the service, Grant Lee received his high school diploma and then held various positions with the Mechanicsburg Navy Depot. After retiring from the Navy, he worked for companies that received government contracts, where he enjoyed working on jobs from start to finish. Mr. Lee married his current wife, Marian, in 1980. He has two sons from a previous marriage.

★ John Scott ★
Mechanicsburg, Pennsylvania

• •

**John Scott was a bombardier in a B-24 in bombing
raids over Europe. He flew fifty-one missions
and earned the Distinguished Flying Cross.**

• •

I was a clerk in the Reading Railroad working out of the Reading Terminal in Philadelphia. I enlisted in the Army from there. I knew that the draft was close to me so I thought I'd go enlist to see if I could get into what I wanted. I always wanted to be a flyer. When I was a kid I used to make model airplanes and fly them, and I thought I was going to be another [Eddie] Rickenbacker. When I went home from signing my enlistment there was a letter there from the draft board, but I beat them to the punch.

They put me on a train to Fort Meade, Maryland, where they assigned us our clothing and gave us our first shots. We took some examinations down there to find out what we might do in the Army. After that we got back on the train and went up to Philadelphia again through a station called Frankford Junction, which was near where I used to live. Then we crossed the river and went into Atlantic City where there was a big crowd at the station, a band playing; you might think we won the war. The Army had just taken over all the hotels in Atlantic City and this was to be the basic training camp for the new recruits for the Air Corps. So we started basic training on the Boardwalk and the beaches of Atlantic City.

Atlantic City at that time was a place where new fellows coming in for basic training had their choice of what school they wanted to go to; there was mechanic school, sheet metal worker school, radio school, and cooks and bakers school. That was the one they all hated. They didn't want to be cooks and bakers, but some of them got pushed in there. I was transferred from training to headquarters to do typing, so I only got five weeks of basic training. After I was there a while I went to the lieutenant in charge and asked him if I would be eligible to take the test for aviation cadet training, and he said he would get back to me. Two or three days later he came in and said I was all set to go, it was just a matter of having an opening to go up to Fort Dix to take the examination. So I took the examination and another physical and I was qualified to go to aviation cadet training. That was around October 1942, and in December I got a notice that I was on call to go to San Antonio, Texas. When we got to San Antonio I took more tests to find out if I was qualified to fly.

They gave us three selections; pilot, bombardier, and navigator. I picked pilot first, bombardier second, and navigator third. When the orders came out I was assigned to bombardier school. I didn't like that, but I went anyway. I was sent to Ellington Field in Houston, Texas, for ground school, where we learned higher mathematics like calculus and trigonometry and also English, just like the college courses. We also learned about engines and the make-up of aircraft and what made them fly. Then you learned to be a gentleman, because you were going to be a commissioned officer so you had to be a gentleman.

After that I went to Big Springs, Texas, where we were introduced to what they called the Norton Bomb Site. It was highly secret at that time; so secret that when I went to Big Springs, they had a safe where they kept these bomb sites. You and another fellow would go to the safe and pick out the bomb site and the two of you would carry it to the airplane you were flying that day. One guy would install it and the other guy would stand outside with a .45 automatic attached to his side. Then when the pilot came we would take off.

We used practice bombs. We used to call them Blue Buddies. They were one hundred pounds and had sand in them and a charge that made them flash and explode when we dropped them. There would be about ten of those bombs in an AT-11; that was the kind of aircraft we flew in bombardier training. The target was about three hundred feet around, and a shack sat in the middle. The idea was that you were supposed to hit that shack. We hit all around it, but we hit the shack very few times. That was my first experience with doing any type of bombing.

I had never been in an airplane in my life. The first airplane I flew was when I got to bombardier school. The only people on the plane were the pilot, another bombardier student and me. The pilot would line you up on the target and say that it was all yours, because he had set the plane on automatic pilot. Then it was up to you to do the job. He'd get you to the target, and once you dropped the bombs he would shut the automatic pilot off and take over and fly to the next target. The highest we went at the time was about 10,000 feet. Later on in training they brought in B-18s and they got us up to 15,000 to 17,000 feet. We learned to work with an oxygen mask on at that altitude and bomb from that altitude.

After I graduated from Big Springs I was sent to Clovis, New Mexico where I was assigned to a crew. There were ten members on a crew: a pilot, a co-pilot, a bombardier, a navigator and six gunners. From Clovis we were sent to Alamogordo, New Mexico, out in the middle of the desert. The barracks we stayed in had a door with slats in it, and when the wind would blow it would blow sand right through the middle of the barracks. Then we got a notice to pack up because we were going to Charleston, South Carolina, because they were going to explode the atom bomb at White Sands, right there at Alamogordo. We never knew why we were chased out until years later when we found out they had set off the atom bomb in White Sands.

When we left Charleston, South Carolina, they sent us up to Mitchell Field in New York by troop train. When we got up there they told us to go outside to pick up an airplane. There were B-24s lined up like you had never seen; it looked like a new car lot. These things were all brand new and had just come from Willow Run in Detroit with about five hours total time on them. So, our job was to go out and pick up one. We were supposed to leave in two days, so we did have a night in New York City. The next day we came back and took off. We were the first ones to take off, then it started to snow and they closed the field down. We went from there to West Palm Beach, Florida, where we got orders in an envelope right before we took off. We were instructed to go to 15,000 feet then open the orders up and that would tell us where to go. When we opened the orders it told us we were going to Italy.

That sounded better than going to England, because England was right in the heart of the war at the time. So we flew to Trinidad, then to Maracaja, on the coast of Brazil, and from there all the way over to French West Africa, and from there we went to Tunisia. In Tunisia they gave us orders to go to Manduria, Italy, right above Taranto—where the boot is—twenty-five or thirty miles inland.

When you were scheduled to fly on a raid you went into a hall where they had a big screen with a curtain on it, and when the curtain raised up you saw where you were going that day. I remember my first combat mission very vividly. I was scared to death. I just hoped that I remembered everything they had taught me. The first mission was to Toulon, France, where the Germans would take submarines to repair them. The target was made out of concrete, and most of the bombs hit that thing and bounced when they hit. The only way to hit it was to come in at a lower level. We couldn't do that with a heavy aircraft because they were in a side of a mountain, and we would probably have ended up on the top of the mountain.

I was based in Italy the whole time. The main targets were places like Wiener Neustadt, Austria, where they were building a Messerschmidt factory—I made a number of raids there—and Ploesti, Romania. I made seven raids there. Ploesti was the main supply of oil for the Axis. They had antiaircraft around the whole city and when they put it up you knew you had to go through it. If you were lucky, you were in first group that went through, but when you were in the back, boy, your group got hit hard.

The crew flew fifty missions, and I flew fifty-one. The reason I flew fifty-one was because I had a friend who was a pilot and his bombardier was sick and he asked me one night if I would go the next day with him. We went to Wiener Neustadt. It was one of the roughest days I can remember. When I came back I was supposed to go to the movies with the other three officers of my crew, and I remember sitting there that night, and I just stared. I was in shock, I guess, because the flak was tremendous, and the fighters; I saw guys going down and planes going down, and I just kept thinking that I hope we make it. We did, thank God. So that's how I got fifty-one, because I flew that one extra mission.

On my last mission we went to Ploesti, which had flak and fighters, and we got hit pretty hard. We had our hydraulic system knocked out and the radio system knocked out, and we had a malfunction in the landing gear. It kept dropping down and that caused drag, and that drag was using up our fuel. Our tail gunner, named Lemke, was hit in the back with flak, and it came out in the front someplace and down through his leg. The pilot said to me, "Go back there and get Lemke out of the turret." I asked Joe Clark to help me, because Lemke was a pretty good-sized man. So we got him down on the deck in the back of the ship and I unzipped his flying suit and, boy, all I could see was blood. We used to carry packets in our 'chute harnesses that had sulfur drugs and morphine, so I got the sulfur out and poured it in his wound. Then I got a bandage and put it on his wound and zippered him back up. The guy was in pain, so I took the morphine and—I never gave anyone a shot in my life—I gave him a shot in the leg, and that quieted him down. We didn't know if we were going to make it back. There was some talk about bailing out, but we all agreed we would stay with the airplane because we felt that if we threw Lemke out the harness would catch him in his wound and probably kill him. As it ended up we made landfall in Italy at an airfield someplace north of where we were stationed. We were at about 8,000 feet and everything stopped; our fuel was all used up, so we made one sweeping turn and just as we were coming down on the final approach there was an airplane sitting right on the end of the runway. Our engineer was shooting off warning flares, but the plane never moved, so we finally went over top of him. When we hit the ground we slid down the runway, sparks flying. I figured that was it, but it didn't catch fire or explode. We finally came to a stop and nine of us got out and the ambulance took Lemke out. That was the worst experience I had. I thought after all these missions that they were finally going to get me on this one, and that was my final mission. That's what I got the Distinguished Flying Cross for.

I was back in the States in August of 1944. I got notice that I was to go to Charleston, South Carolina, as an instructor bombardier. So I was instructing new guys on crews how to bomb in combat and what to look for. One time they brought in this new crew that was in the place they called "Tail-end Charlie," down in the back. They had superchargers in the engines because when you got up so high there wasn't enough air there to ignite the fuel, so they needed these superchargers. Sometimes they would act up and run wild, and on this particular day the pilot was having trouble with the supercharger. He was down under another plane and he made a swing and up went into the other plane, and the propellers cut right through the back of the cockpit. Out my window I could see the propellers go right through that ship. They just rolled over and straight down they went, and the other plane did the same thing. We lost twenty men just like that, in an accident. We lost a lot of men that way.

I saw a lot of young fellows who died, they were in the prime of their life, and they died. I hope young people today appreciate what they were trying to do for them. Because if we hadn't defeated the Nazis and the Japanese, God knows how we would have lived in this country.

AFTER THE WAR . . .

John Scott retired from the U.S. Air Force as a lieutenant colonel in 1972, after serving twenty-eight years. He took up a career in real estate as a salesman and a broker, and he also worked as an appraiser for the Pennsylvania Department of Transportation. He retired from that position in 1982. John married Mary Richard in 1943. They have two children, six grandchildren, and four great-grandchildren.

☆ Lewis Eppihimer ☆
North Wales, Pennsylvania

....

**Lewis Eppihimer enlisted in the Marine Corps when
he was fifteen years old. He served in the South Pacific,
including five months on Guadalcanal, where he
contracted malaria and yellow jaundice.**

....

I was fifteen years old, working at Sears and Roebuck in Philadelphia in
the mail department, sorting packages. Pearl Harbor was bombed on
December 7 and I went down to the courthouse on December 8 and signed
up. I originally wanted to go into the Navy for submarine service, but the
line was so big you couldn't even get close to it. I went upstairs there and
saw this marine all decked out in his blues and medals and he had me right
away. They gave me three tests and supposedly I passed all three.

Previous to that I had been in the CCCs, that was the Civilian Conservation Corps, and to get into the CCCs you had to be seventeen. I went to our
family doctor and said, "How about signing a note for me saying that I was
born on March 14, 1924, instead of 1926?" Which he did. But even at age
seventeen you couldn't go in without your parents' permission, so I had my
cousin sign the papers for me. My dad gave no resistance because when he was

sixteen the First World War broke out and he signed up. But my grandmother got wind of it and she hitched up the buckboard and went up to West Chester and grabbed him before they could take him away. So he didn't want to stand in my way. He had wanted to go. And I had my one uncle who won the Distinguished Service Cross, the Croix de Guerre, and Legion d'Honneur. We've had Eppihimers who fought in every war, including the Revolutionary War. That was my kick. I wanted excitement, I was bored, and it was during the Depression. And I was lucky, I had a job. When I went to grade school I was a straight-A student, and I read everything I could get my hands on. I probably appeared a lot older than fifteen years of age.

So the recruiter said, "When do you want to leave?" I said, "Right now is as good as any." I left from the old B&O Railroad over at 34th and Market in Philadelphia and we went down to Beaufort, South Carolina, Parris Island. My first reality check was the drill instructor. His name was Earl Pike, and the first thing he said was, "Okay, all you little girls, off the train." He said, "For the next six weeks, I am going to be your father, I'm going to be your mother, and your father confessor. Your soul may belong to God, but your ass belongs to me, and I will make a marine out of you, you can bet on that." And he did. We got six weeks' training; it was close-order drill, and then we went out and fired rifles. I qualified on rifle and missed by one point for sharpshooter, but I made sharpshooter on pistol, which was the .45.

We left Parris Island and went up to New River, North Carolina; it was an old tent city. The 7th Marines had come up from Guantánamo, the 5th came down from Iceland, and out of that nucleus, they formed the 1st Marine Division. We did some training, and on April 4 or 5 they told us we were shoving off. We had a case of beer under our bunk, so we had to get rid of the beer real fast. We had beer in our pockets, beer in our packs; we had beer all over, because we weren't going to leave any beer behind. We got up to Norfolk and got aboard the USS *Heywood*; it was a bucket of bolts that they had converted into a troop carrier. We came down off of Cape Hatteras in April, and Cape Hatteras, as any sailor will tell you, is just about the roughest body of water in the world. I thought sure as hell that thing was going to sink; I thought that was the end. But we finally got through it and we went down through the Panama Canal. Going through the locks really impressed me; I thought that was great. Then we got out onto the Pacific side, going through all the little islands. I thought that was fantastic, it was really pretty. After we got out of there, the following morning, we woke up and I'll tell you, I had never seen so many ships in all my life. We had picked up a convoy coming down from San Francisco and San Diego. We didn't know where we were going from there. You could look out at the ocean and see the flying fish and the dolphins; they would always follow the transports.

About the second day out they had general quarters. They herded us all below decks and battened the hatches. I got to thinking to myself, "If this ship ever gets hit, and that guy who battened the hatches, if he gets hit, how am I going to get out of this coffin?" So from then on, I never slept below decks, I only slept above decks. In the mornings, you'd hear the loudspeaker, "There will be a clean sweep down fore and aft, empty all trash cans and ashtrays." And then a little voice would say, "And hose those Marines off the deck." So I guess that's how the sailors got their jollies. We were on the ship thirty-one days.

We went down to British Samoa to set up a perimeter of defense while the Seabees hacked a one-mile airfield out of a solid coconut grove. That was no mean feat, because if you ever saw those coconut trees, they're tough, but they hacked it out. We had no combat yet, just training. We'd do twenty-five-mile night hikes, and we'd go up over the mountain, Mount Vaea. Incidentally, on the top of that mountain is where Robert Louis Stevenson is buried. He's got a nice little tomb, and they take care of it. But you would go up and look down and see the Seabees, Navy construction guys, with their floodlights and welders and arc flashes; it was like a little city. They worked around the clock.

Every now and then they used to mix up a batch of what they called "White Lightning." They said they were getting it from torpedo juice. We'd go down there and they'd give us a little bucket of it. Another interesting thing, our company had a little compound, and it was all fenced in. At night you'd get a helmet full of water; you heard the old expression "Marine bath?" Well, that was a Marine bath; out of a helmet of water. Everybody's out there naked, and I guess whichever part was the dirtiest got washed, then the following day, the other part got washed. The Samoan girls would come up, and that was a field day for them; they'd all be pointing. I always said I lost my modesty a long time ago.

We finally left British Samoa and we went to American Samoa, Pago Pago, and they gave us liberty there. We got off the ship and the slop chute was open, that's a taproom in civilian parlance. The big thing there was you could get in line and get two cans of beer, then you could get back in line and get two more and two more and two more, until either you got filled up with beer, or you got ossified, and they carried you back.

From there, we went into Espiritu Santo, but we were only in there for about fifteen minutes, and they told us we had to get out. There was a Jap sub pack on our tail, so we got out of there. We finally hit Guadalcanal on September 17 or 18. The plan to go into Guadalcanal was on the spur of the moment, because they found out that the Japs were building an airfield there. We couldn't tolerate that, because if they had an airfield there that would leave Australia and New Zealand exposed.

They had an admiral who was in charge down there; Admiral Gormley, and he was afraid of his shadow. At that time we only had two aircraft carriers left because of the Battle of Midway, where they had absolutely decimated the Jap fleet, but lost a carrier. We only had three, now we were down to two. So he was afraid that he was going to lose his other two carriers and he took off, and we never saw him. So we unloaded and went into the Canal. The first night on the beach the Japanese sent a battlewagon (warship) down, and that had fourteen-inch guns. And along with the five-inch guns and the fourteen-inch guns, they just started blowing the hell out of everything. That was our baptism. That went on every day; the constant bombings and strafing and the shelling. But the prize was the airfield. They put up a perimeter defense around the airfield, and they were holding on. After we got off of the beach we moved inland and set up a little bivouac camp. To get the feel of the terrain we'd go out on patrols and look around and see what was happening. That went on for a few weeks.

Around October 7 there was a concentration of Japs coming in on the west side of the Matanikau River, and that was our first baptism. We were going down a valley and shot a couple snipers. We had a kid by the name of Eberle from Asbury Park; I think he was our first guy that got killed, then Master Gunnery Sergeant Ballou got killed. We advanced, and by that time they were dropping mortars on us. I think we sustained a few casualties, but we got up to where we wanted to get, up on the ridge. That night we had a second lieutenant by the name of P. M. Hatch, a real nice guy, and a buddy of mine, Ray Mullen, he was First Scout and I was always in back of him. Ray always tells the story that when we went into the Canal all the officers were told to take off their insignia, all the NCOs to get rid of your stripes, because that's who the Japs would kill first.

That night we went down to reconnoiter to find out exactly where the Japs were. Coming back up the slope, the password was "Honolulu." They used l's because the Japs couldn't pronounce an "l." They would say "Honoruru." We came up and were giving the password, and we had a kid by the

Guadalcanal

The battle for Guadalcanal, a two thousand–square-mile island in the southern Solomons of the western Pacific, was the first United States offensive action of World War II. After the invasion began on August 7, 1942, the follow-up campaign to secure the island lasted six months. Although the Japanese troops occupying the island were initially surprised by the attack, they and their reinforcements fought back and forth against the Allies, each side taking and retaking ground over the ensuing months.

Guadalcanal's value to the Japanese was as another fortification for disrupting supply lines between the United States and one of its key allies in the region, Australia, and to extend its presence and control in the region. For the Allies, it was a strategic toehold in their objective of neutralizing Japan's air base at Rabaul, in the northern Solomons, and in the eventual drive to recapture the Philippines and ultimately conquer the home islands of Japan.

In May 1942, the Japanese had taken nearby Tulagi Island (see page 26) without resistance and established a seaplane base in the harbor there. Two months later, the Allies discovered that the enemy was building an airfield at Lunga Point on Guadalcanal. The Japanese intended to base forty-five bombers and sixty fighters there, but the Allies took a preemptive strike when 11,000 U.S. Marines invaded the island. The Japanese troops and construction workers fled into the interior.

By the end of the following day, Allied forces captured the unfinished airfield and set about using the construction supplies left behind to complete the job. They named the facility Henderson Field, in honor of Marine major Lofton R. Henderson, a pilot who had died two months earlier in the Battle of Midway.

Unwilling to let the Allies enjoy such an easy occupation, the Japanese launched several air and naval attacks over the following months. Meanwhile, they landed additional troops on the island with orders to "rout and annhiliate" the Allies, employing a nightly destroyer run from Rabaul that the Allies dubbed the "Tokyo Express." For their part, the

An aerial view of Guadalcanal and Henderson Field. NATIONAL ARCHIVES

Americans built up a fleet of fighters and other aircraft at Henderson Field, numbering sixty-four planes by the end of the first month.

A series of battles took place by air, on the ground, and at sea. Ground fighting was made more difficult by the island's terrain—old volcanoes and mountains projecting up to eight thousand feet high, with ravines and rivers to inhibit troop and vehicle movement. Jungle conditions forced troops to fight at close quarters, and the hot, humid atmosphere fostered the spread of malaria, dengue, and various tropical fungi.

Skirmishes on the ground included the Battle of the Tenaru and Battle of Edson's Ridge; at sea, actions included the Battle of the Eastern Solomons, the Battle of Cape Esperance, and the Battle of Santa Cruz Islands. As the months passed, the struggle became a war of

(continued on page 80)

(continued from page 79)

Wreckage of a SBD scout-bomber, still burning after it was destroyed by a Japanese air attack on Henderson Field on Guadalcanal, 1942. NAVAL HISTORY AND HERITAGE COMMAND

attrition, with each side suffering not only casualties but also from tropical disease and, for the Japanese, a lack of adequate food and supplies. Japanese troop strength peaked at 30,000 in November 1942. That same month, on November 12–15, naval forces fought the climactic Battle of Guadalcanal, which the Americans won, ultimately determining the outcome of the entire Pacific campaign. Organized resistance to the Allies ended on February 9, 1943, when the Japanese evacuated 13,000 men.

In the six months of the campaign, American forces lost 24 ships and counted 1,490 dead, 4,804 wounded, and 55 missing in the sea battles. The Japanese also lost 24 ships, but also lost 600 planes and counted 25,000 deaths.

The significance of Guadalcanal was that it represented a reversal of the previous American role of reacting to Japanese initiatives and instead going on the offensive. It also secured a valuable base from which to counter further enemy aggression in the region. The ultimate outcome of the war in the Pacific was decided by the Allied victory on Guadalcanal. ★

name of R. E. Smith; he was a Cherokee Indian from North Carolina, he opened fire and wounded a couple of the guys. He shot Hatch through the lung. So we told them, "Call up, get an LST in there, and we'll take him down to the beach." But they said, "No, we can't afford to lose six more guys." So Hatch laid up there on the ridge all that night, and the following morning when we really went into battle, they took him down to the beach and put him on an LST, but he died on the way in. We felt real bad about that, because as I said before, he was a terrific guy. R. E. Smith, after he had inadvertently shot Hatch, went into depression, and I really felt sorry for him. He wandered off, and we found him two or three days later down in the valley. The Japs had gotten hold of him, and they cut him all up. He was dead, so I guess he was happy.

The engagement out there lasted about three days. They tell us we knocked off about one thousand Japs. Our kill ratio was pretty good. I think out of the entire campaign, which lasted about six months, we lost 1,750 killed and we were credited with killing between 38,000 and 40,000.

The night of October 23 was the Japs' big push. They had about 34,000 soldiers coming down to the island, and they had aircraft. We took up a position down by the Matanikau River, and me and a few other guys were supposed to go out on what they called "Listening Post." We went up a ridge that was solid coral; you couldn't dig a hole in there to save your butt. Our company, the F Company, had taken a few casualties and we were spread pretty thin. The ridge was overlooking the beach and it was wooded below us. That's where Mitchell Paige's machine guns were setting up. G Company was in the back, and E Company was in back of that. I had a position out on one finger of the ridge, all the way out on the end. While we were up there they dropped a mortar on us and killed a buddy of mine, a guy by the name of Bill Long. He'd come from Gadsden, Alabama, and had an accent so thick I could never understand him, but he really was a nice guy. They asked me if I wanted to bury him and I said, "No, I don't want to bury him. You bury him."

That night we heard a commotion down in the position we had just left. The Japs had come through there, and the 1st Battalion, Chesty Puller's outfit, moved in. Those guys did themselves proud down there. They supposedly knocked off about 1,300 or 1,400 people. So we were sitting there, I guess it was two-thirty in the morning, and we heard all this rustling, and we thought, "Uh-oh." Down below it was all tall Kunai grass, and you could see it waving, and there was no breeze, so you figured they were coming up. I looked over on the other side and a captain, I'm not going to mention his name, he pulled about thirty Marines out of the line. Why? I guess he got plain scared; that was probably what it was. I noticed those guys were leaving, and I was looking around and I got to thinking, "I'm the only one out here." Anybody in their right mind would say, "This is just not the place for me." In the meantime our platoon sergeant Jenkins came up and was crawling along the ridge. He said, "Don't move. They're all around us." He went back and we later found out that he got wounded because, unbeknownst to us, the Japs had set up a 31-inch long machine gun, what they called a Hotchkiss gun. A little while later a guy by the name of Schaffner, he was the sergeant, came up and the same thing happened. By that time I figured out that I had no business being out there. I couldn't go up on the ridge because the machine gun would have a clear line of fire. The only thing I could do was skirt around the edge of the ridge there and get back up to company headquarters.

I had two hand grenades with me, so I got up on my knees, dropped them on those guys, and I took off, back to company headquarters. By the time I got up there the Japs were starting to come up the ridge. They looked like ants. You ever see a bunch of ants running? Well, that's what it looked like. The Marines were breaking out the hand grenades, and lobbing them down, and they were still coming up. I went back to pull some more boxes of hand grenades up there and as I was bent down, I had my rifle leaning against the boxes, and I noticed a guy running at me with a bayonet. I don't know what I thought, but when he just about got to me, I dropped and pulled my rifle over, and it caught him in the throat and he went down.

We were still throwing hand grenades and they were still coming up. I don't know how many of them got up on the ridge. Everybody was firing like crazy, and there was Mitch Paige with his machine gun and the belts draped around him and he started firing and got a load of them. He was shooting over our heads at whatever was standing, and he got them. Finally, that was over.

After that battle I went back to where I had dropped the two hand grenades and there were six dead Japs. In one guy's pack he had a brand-new pair of blue shorts and a blue shirt. I took my clothes off; they stunk and were dirty and shredded, and I put this blue shirt and shorts on. I thought I looked pretty good. Somebody came up to me and handed me a handful of dog tags and said, "Take them down to the beach to Colonel Henneken." So I took the hand grenades and on the way down, I guess it was about twenty yards from the beach, there were three Japs on the trail; two guys holding up the one guy in the middle, he must have been wounded. They turned around and looked at me, and I was dressed in Jap clothes. I guess they thought I was a Jap, so they turned around and went about their business. I couldn't go back and shoot those three guys because I didn't know who else was around there, so I just went running past those guys and busted out of the brush onto the beach. Well, I'm telling you, there were about forty Marines right there. They all dropped, and I hollered, "Don't shoot! Don't shoot! It's me, Eppi! Eppi!" They knew me from being a platoon runner.

After that we started dragging all the dead Japs together to where my position had been. The engineers came up and planted charges that blew it up and buried all of them. Supposedly, we had knocked off about nine hundred that night. After that we went back to our old routine, patrols and what have you; then around November 2 they decided that we were going to go out and cover a landing. We thought, "That's great. Some more Army's coming in. Maybe they'll bring some food with them." We went out to Koli Point to meet the landing. It was foggy and I was standing out there and I heard all clanking and clunking, and heard guys talking in Japanese. I thought, "What the hell is this now?" I thought our army was coming in, but the Japs unloaded at Koli Point about five hundred yards up the beach from us. They sent a patrol of five or six men down toward us and our guys killed them all. Out of their packs we got Chesterfields, Lucky Strikes, and Camel cigarettes. They had been part of an outfit that had gone down through Singapore, Bataan, and Corregidor, and they had gotten a load of American cigarettes.

Then the Japs knew where we were, and they fired a .47 fieldpiece that landed right in the middle of our first squad, knocking six guys right out. My buddy Ray Mullen was one. It didn't kill him, but it wounded him a little. There was another marine, I never saw a guy with so many holes in him in all my life. By the time the corpsman got done with him he looked like a mummy. They evacuate them.

We left the island on February 5 after five months on "the Canal." I had malaria, I had yellow jaundice, which later they'd call hepatitis C, and I had elephantiasis, which is caused by a worm; it causes certain parts of your body to swell up. When we left the island we had six guys left in our platoon. We had about 369 guys left out of the battalion, and a battalion was about eight hundred men. As a fighting unit, we were done. They took us out on a Higgins boat, back to the *President Hayes*, and they pulled us up alongside of the bow. I got about halfway up and I just couldn't go. I was so weak and didn't realize it, but a couple of sailors came down, grabbed a hold of me and took me up. From there, we went into Melbourne, Australia. We were starting to reorganize when I came down with yellow jaundice and they sent me to the hospital. When I finally got out of there it was September 1943.

They started training in earnest then because we were going to go into New Britain, but I was in bad shape by that time, so then they sent me back to the States. I went to the hospital at Oakland, California, and was quarantined there. Then I went to the Philadelphia Navy Yard and while I was there I'd have liberties. That's when I met my wife. Then they sent me up to Klamath Falls, Oregon. I think the theory behind that was the cold weather might knock the worm out for the elephantiasis I had. When I came out of Klamath Falls I went back to the depot of supply at Broad and Washington in Philadelphia.

In June 1945 they sent me back down to Camp Lejeune for re-evaluation. I went to one doctor and told him that I had malaria and yellow jaundice and that I was having headaches. He sent me to the eye doctor who gave me the eye chart, and I was starting to see O's instead of C's, and C's instead of O's, and B's instead of E's. And he said, "You're not doing too well. Do you have trouble with your eyes?" I said, "Nah, I just get these headaches." And then I told him about the malaria I had. He said, "I don't think you're ready for re-evaluation. I'll give you a permanent no-duty slip until either tour date of discharge or until you get a medical discharge." My enlistment was up December 8, so from then on all I did, they had these sixteen-foot sailboats with a centerboard, and I'd go out on them every day, sailing on the Back Bay. On October 25 they called me in and they said, "Okay, you're medically discharged." And I went back home.

I learned two things from the war. I learned that every generation has to fight for their freedom, I don't care who they are. And if they don't, then we're going to be in bad shape. Fortunately, we have the volunteer army, and we have these young guys and young ladies who want to go and want to fight for their country. And when they get to the point that they don't want to do that . . . I doubt that day will come. I hope it never comes.

AFTER THE WAR . . .

Lewis Eppihimer finished high school when he returned from the service and married his wife Ruth in 1944. Together they raised two daughters. Lewis also became a Freemason in 1947. He worked as a driver with Tasty Baking Company for twenty-seven years. Now that he has retired, Mr. Eppihimer enjoys shooting pool and playing pinochle.

☆ Frank Galicic ☆

Cecil, Pennsylvania

••

Frank Galicic arrived in Europe with the 11th Armored
Division just in time to experience the Battle of the Bulge.
He was also involved in the liberation of a concentration
camp and served post-war occupation duty.

••

Before the war I was working in the coal mine in Sygan, Pennsylvania, for the National Mining Company. My dad got me the job in February, and in June when I turned eighteen, I was drafted into the service. Back then they didn't wait. As soon as you were eighteen they were ready to draft you. If I would have joined, I think my dad would have shot me. He was so against me going in the service, and I couldn't convince him that I did not join, that I was drafted. It took a few years after I was out to convince him that I was drafted. He finally accepted it.

My first dealing with the military was in the Submarine Corps. I said, "Submarines! It's bad enough being on top of the water and you want me underneath? No way!" They said, "What about the Navy?" And I said, "The pond is too big." So they said, "Okay, you're in the Army now." I didn't mind going through the enlistments. Outside all of the shots, it wasn't bad. Every time I turned around they were giving me a shot of this or a shot of something else. After we were done with that they had us on a train with two sleepers, and we didn't know where we were going. We got to Pittsburgh and thought maybe we'd be stationed in Ohio. Well pretty soon we found out that Ohio was out, Indiana was out, Chicago was out, and we thought, "Where are we going?"

We hit Texas and ended up with the 816th Anti-Aircraft, 40 millimeter. I spent a year training with them, and it ended up that they deactivated us; they didn't need the 40s anymore. The German planes were pretty well shot up, and the 90s were sufficient to take care of what they were doing. So they sent me down to Camp Carson, Colorado, to the 90th Infantry Regiment where I had eight weeks of infantry training. I had a T5 rating and they made me a squad leader. Well, a lot of times you tell the guys in your squad to dig a foxhole and they look at you and laugh, they aren't going to dig it. Then the sergeant jumps all over you, giving you heck.

After our training I was transferred to Camp Cook, California, and joined the 11th, and we were there ten or twelve days. Then we got on a troop train and came back to the East Coast and headed overseas to England. On the way over we were being threatened with German submarines, but we had ships that had depth chargers. They were all around us, dropping them off, and they finally scared the submarines off. We were about fifteen days on the water getting there. We got into England and the sun was shining and it was a beautiful October morning and I said, "Oh man this is a nice country!" About two days later it started to rain and never quit.

In December 1944, we were slated to go to somewhere in France, but a German breakthrough came on the 16th, and on the 17th we were crossing the channel getting ready to go over to the Bulge. Our orders changed overnight. So we convoyed from Cherbourg to Belgium. When we were going through Paris we had women hanging on our trucks and tanks and giving us big loaves of French bread; they were just so glad to see us. We had our Christmas dinner right behind the lines, fifteen or twenty miles back. Each day they would take us up a little closer and around the 29th we went into combat, and boy that Bulge was bad. The snow was deep and cold, and in the foxhole at night me and my buddy—we dug a long enough foxhole for two of us to get into—and I'd say to him, "Who wants to stand guard duty first?" and he would say, "I'll stand guard duty first and I'll call you in two hours." So I would sit in that foxhole and in about an hour you were numb, your feet and toes and everything. You would wake up and you'd stand up and start moving your feet and your arms to try to get the blood circulating and you'd say to him, "You might as well go ahead and go to sleep because I sure can't sleep anymore." Then in about an hour he would be awake and he would say, "I can't take this anymore, I'm froze." And that's the way it went on in the Bulge. It was just cold.

One time there was a fire in a haystack out in the field and it was just blazing away. I said to this lieutenant, "As cold as it is why can't we go down to that haystack and get warm?" He said, "If you want to go, go. But I don't think you'll live more than five minutes because some sniper will have you." Well, I wasn't cold anymore, I forgot about it. That night we emptied a barn out—it had thirty or thirty-five cattle in it—and we put down a bed of hay about four feet deep on top of all that manure, and that's where we bedded down for the night. The next morning when we woke up we looked out and the cattle were lying out there with their feet up in the air. They got killed by artillery shells. The Germans were shelling half the night, just dropping shells down because they knew we were in that area. We got relieved the next day by the 17th Airborne. After about two days on break we had to go back and help them out, because they were losing ground. That was their first time in combat too.

After we got everything straightened out, we were staying at a farmhouse in Belgium. The sergeant had the mess hall set up there in a big tent, and we would eat outside. He'd make pancakes and believe me, I never ate pancakes so good in all my life. We started out getting four pancakes, and when we were done we'd go back for seconds, and they would ask how many you had the first time and how many you wanted the second time. And if you would say four, they would say, "no take eight" and they would put all that syrup and butter on them and they would just melt in your mouth.

We drove into the Battle of the Bulge in half-tracks. The half-track was a vehicle with treads on the back—it didn't have wheels on the back—and it carried ammunition or rations. It had seats on both sides for the squad to sit on and up front there was a ring mount with a .50-caliber machine gun. I had never seen a half-track until I joined the 11th Armored, but because I had truck driver information they put me on as assistant driver. A lot of times you would be going up to the front and they'd be throwing artillery shells back at you, and sometimes they would throw air bursts that would explode in the air. A lot of times we would stop and jump out to try to get under the thing to protect us from getting hit with shrapnel. It was scary.

The Bulge was one of the worst battles, because you had the cold weather and you had a lot of artillery. You would come out of the foxhole in the

Half-Tracks

Tanks were developed as a weapon during World War I, but they were limited in their strategic capabilities. They could take a position, but not hold it, because they outpaced the armored infantry that followed. Conventional motor vehicles such as scout cars were neither rugged enough nor flexible enough to keep up with tanks under combat conditions. In particular, they encountered difficulty in operating over rough or soft terrain. Thus, during World War I, tanks were relegated to a support role, moving with, rather than ahead of, advancing troops.

The solution was to develop a vehicle to carry sufficient manpower along with the advancing tanks to occupy positions once they were won. A hybrid design, known as a half-track car, often simply shortened to half-track, filled this need. It consisted of a conventional truck cab, engine, hood, front wheels and suspension, and armored body, but a tracked propulsion unit in the rear, resembling those used for traction on tanks.

The U.S. government began to develop designs for its own half-track after experimenting with French and American prototypes at the Aberdeen Proving Grounds in Maryland during the 1930s. Two similar types evolved, the M2 and M3, from which many variants were built or created as field modifications. These variations resulted from their configuration as either primarily personnel carriers (carrying ten to thirteen passengers) or as armored assault vehicles with machine guns, mortars, or cannons mounted atop their bodies. The M3A1 version, a personnel carrier powered by a 127-horsepower gasoline engine, weighed 10 tons fully loaded and could reach 45 mph.

Production was contracted to four companies that had previous experience building motor trucks: Autocar Motor Co., Diamond T Motor Company, White Motor Company, and International Harvester. From 1941 to 1943, White and Autocar produced 11,415 M2s. White, Autocar, and Diamond T built 12,499 M3s. To speed production, the

A U.S. Army half-track. NATIONAL ARCHIVES

government added International Harvester, which built 11,019 variants known as M5s and M9s.

The U.S. military was not alone in developing half-tracks. Italy, France, the Soviet Union, and Japan also mass-produced them. Germany built more of them than any other nation—nearly 100,000 between 1934 and 1945—and used them in invading Poland, France, and the Netherlands.

American half-tracks eventually found their way into most of the theaters of World War II, beginning with the Philippines in 1942 and spreading, in succession, to Africa, Italy, and Europe. They were used primarily by the Marines in the Pacific and by the Army elsewhere. The greatest deployment of American half-tracks came in the D-Day invasion of Normandy in June 1944, and the subsequent drive across Western Europe to capture and defeat Germany. Half-tracks equipped with antiaircraft weaponry were notably effective in downing planes of the Luftwaffe.

After the end of the World War II, half-tracks found limited use in the Korean War, and their role eventually was taken over by the armored personnel carrier, and more recently, the humvee. ★

morning and it seemed like there was eight or ten inches of snow, and you would look down at the half-tracks and there would be big black spots all around them from artillery. It's a wonder anybody survived.

One day they told us we were going to be on the lead tank. That's when we heard a shot go off and our lieutenant had put a bullet through his foot. He said that it went off accidentally, but if we were not going to lead the point I don't think he would have shot his foot. Anyhow, we drove two or three miles down a lowland with woods on both sides, and boy, these three Tiger tanks just played heck with us. I was behind the tank, looking over to my left and I could see the 75-millimeter artillery shells from our tanks. We were hitting their tanks on the front end. The Germans had about twelve inches of armor on their front, so their nose was well protected. I watched one tank throw four shells into them and every one ricocheted off.

The 11th Armored was under [General George] Patton's command for the Battle of the Bulge, but the only time I got to see him was when he was coming up to the front past us when we were on a break. I never met him personally, but he kept the Armored moving. Once we crossed the Rhine it was just a matter of time. We were taking town after town; I don't know how many towns we liberated in that short three or four months. Our division took 76,229 prisoners. We turned more that 30,000 prisoners over to the Russians and to other infantry units because we just couldn't handle that many.

We heard rumors that there were concentration camps. When we liberated one camp we knew there was something going on because we saw prisoners along the road lying in the ditch with their faces down in the water. We were told later that the Germans were fleeing the concentration camp and were taking prisoners with them and they were trying to hurry up. These prisoners were so thirsty and so hungry that some of them would get down to drink water out of the ditch and the Germans would shoot them behind the head with their pistols. We saw about a half dozen laying there like that, dead. When we got to the concentration camp a lot of the guys stayed in their vehicle, but I got out because I wanted to see what was really going on. I opened up some of the doors and sometimes I found a body or a part of a hand or a leg that hadn't burned. Then I went inside and they were making lampshades; if you had a nice tattoo, they would take the hide off of you and make little lamp shades out of that stuff. They took their teeth, their glasses, just everything. And talk about smell. God, you couldn't believe how bad it smelled; there were probably a couple thousand bodies outside the building piled up five or six feet high that weren't burnt yet. It was sickening. You couldn't believe that people would do stuff like that. I mean, you hear of people shooting each other and think that it's cruel, well this was really cruel; not just one but thousands of them. It really just makes you sick in the stomach. But the prisoners were so happy to see the Americans.

About three weeks before the war was over they transferred me to Reconnaissance. I got in an armored car and we were going out to try to locate the Russians that were in the area. We had a trap door in the bottom floor of the half-track, and when I was leaving my sergeant said to me, "Frank, why don't you take some of those cigarettes? Half of them have to be yours, why don't you take some when you leave?" I opened up the trap door and there must have been fifty or sixty cartons of cigarettes in there. I took one carton of Old Gold. I probably could have had thirty cartons. After the war ended they were taking our money and transferring it over from one type of money to another, and they said our money would double, whatever we turned in. If we turned in one hundred we would get two hundred back. So I went down the street trying to sell this carton of Old Gold. Everybody was offering twenty dollars and I said, "Nope, thirty." I wouldn't give up. Finally about eleven-thirty at night I sold them for thirty dollars. I turned the money in a couple days later and got sixty for it. I sure wish I would have taken all those cartons because I could have made a killing even at twenty dollars.

I was in Austria when the war ended, in a town called Ufer. Linz was close by, and it was right on the Danube River. Tanks were driving into Linz and the people threw so many flowers at them, they were so happy to see them. That was the time to look for something to drink, so we saw a guy with a big crate of something and he said it was wine. He said he got it at the train station, so me and my buddy ran down to the train station and, sure enough, they were stacked up, big crates full of wine wrapped in straw. I found a dolly and we started pushing the dolly down the street. We went up to the room and started passing wine out and drinking, and when we were about half bottled up they came and told us that the war wasn't over, and that we better straighten up. By then we all just laid down and took a nap. When we woke up in the morning we felt like we had big heads. Then they told us the war was over that day, so we went back to drinking for another day.

We were transferred to a town in Austria called Gummern, a little town up high in the mountains. We had a nice lake there, a resort, and the guys rigged up a boat with a jeep motor in it so we could ride in the lake. We were really living it up there. I was ready to sign up for six more months of duty, that's how good we were having it there. Finally they said they were breaking up the division, and they sent some of the guys to the 90th Infantry Division, including me.

They said I was going to pull Occupation Duty until my time came to go home, so I was sent to Achberg, Germany, and spent five months in that area with Occupations. I was living like a king there; no KP, no kind of duties. You had two civilians cooking for you. All I did was drive the lieutenant, who was acting captain.

I came home on March 9, 1946. It was no picnic, and I hope no one would ever have to go through another war, but what I saw and where I've been I wouldn't trade for anything in the world, because I made it.

AFTER THE WAR . . .

Frank Galicic was discharged from the Army in 1946 and soon went to work in construction. In 1951, he married his wife, Eileen, and then started working at the Shenango Neville Island Foundry in Pittsburgh, where he worked for the next thirty-one years. Mr. and Mrs. Galicic parented four children. Following his retirement, Mr. Galicic took up camping as a hobby and enjoyed it for many years.

☆ Ed Halluska ☆

Monroeville, Pennsylvania

••

**Ed Halluska worked on the highly classified
Manhattan Project in Los Alamos, New Mexico, where
he machined uranium for the first atomic bombs.**

••

I was a tool-and-die maker at Westinghouse when the war started. They had
a draft lottery and my number was about in the middle, so I wasn't drafted
until six or eight months after they started calling boys in. At that point I got
a deferment because the work I was doing was essential to the war industry,
so I wasn't drafted until February of 1945.

I was sent to Fort Leonard Wood, Missouri, for about two weeks for
indoctrination and security checks before I was sent on to the Manhattan
Project; that was the code name for Los Alamos. At the time I didn't know
that. All I had was orders to take a train ride into Lamy, New Mexico, which
was eighteen miles from Santa Fe. When I got to Santa Fe I was taken up to
Los Alamos, forty-five miles out; actually, the Manhattan District. The
thought came to my mind that I was going to New York, but it was just a
code name. In fact, everything about Los Alamos was very secretive.

When I was drafted I didn't know what I would be doing. I had actually signed up to go to the Navy. I thought I could go to school there for a while, but when I reached the Induction Center in Pittsburgh I was sent to Army General Service. That's when they explained to me that there was a project. I didn't know what it meant, but we went to basic training and security clearance at Fort Leonard Wood.

I sat up there for a couple of weeks before I was given any assignment, but they did a lot of background checking on my family. When I went into the tech area in Los Alamos there were about five hundred people that had the badge to go into the tech area where they assembled all the top scientists. Dr. Robert Oppenheimer was in charge. Leo Szilard, Ed Teller, and Niels Bohr were all there under different code names, and all up there to design, develop, and test the bomb.

I was given very little information except to be very careful. The uranium was very expensive— "Save every little chip!" They showed me little bits and pieces of what to do, and we weren't allowed to talk to anybody about it, just do your work. I didn't know what I was doing until much later.

Uranium was mined and sent down to Oak Ridge, Tennessee, where they had a big plant to take the uranium that was mined—which is uranium 238—and separate U-235, which is explosive, critical material, less than 1 percent of uranium 238. They had a big gaseous diffusion plant there to do all the work to get the precious U-235, which they would send up to Los Alamos in lead-lined tanks. I did machining on that metal, which was very, very expensive. Somebody said it was $1,000 a gram. There's twenty-eight grams in an ounce, so I had material in a lathe and milling machine that was worth millions. Every little chip was precious, so we had to recover it. I just machined it to specifications that they gave me.

They cautioned me to keep a water supply on it. The minute the water would go down or lose velocity there would be sparks flying out. This was a very unstable metal, and I worked with very primitive tools. I just had rubber gloves and a mask and overalls. Today nobody touches it; it's all done by remote control. In those days, it was "Hurry up and do the work."

A metallurgist I worked with was living in the barracks with me, and we'd walk home at times and he'd start talking about what he was doing. He said, "You know, Ed, this is a massive bomb." That was when I first discovered we were doing something really important.

I worked alone in a hot room in Building CM20, Chemistry/Metallurgical Lab. The machines and everything were there; a milling machine, a grinder, the tools, and a lathe. They would bring the material in with lead-lined tanks, and I would machine it, and collect all the scrap. It was the only place in the U.S. where the mail was censored, so in any letters you sent home you couldn't mention anything about what you were doing.

I would often pass Dr. Robert Oppenheimer in the tech area. He wore a porkpie hat, and of course, we all knew who he was. He was in charge, and everybody was there to work. We worked around the clock actually, in some cases.

My wife, Helen, moved out to Albuquerque, about ninety miles away, and got a little apartment there. I was able to visit her on the weekends. That's when I told her that I might get exterminated because of the work I was doing. But it turned out great.

They made the first test on July 16, 1945, in Alamogordo, New Mexico. Everything up to that point had been theoretical. They tested a miniature bomb—which I had machined parts to—on a tower about one hundred feet up. They did it right at daybreak; this was in a remote part of New Mexico. They said people saw the flash in Albuquerque, two hundred miles away. Of

Mushroom cloud from the atomic bomb dropped on Nagasaki on August 9, 1945. The picture was taken from one of the B-29 Superfortresses used in the attack. WIKIMEDIA COMMONS

course they had a cover story: that an ammunition dump blew up, and that was what was in the papers. But that was the first test on July 16. Once they knew it was successful, they dropped bombs on Hiroshima on August 6, and on Nagasaki on August 9. They killed more than 100,000 in both cities, but it scared the Japanese and they surrendered on August 15, within six days. Saved a lot of lives.

After the war my wife was able to move to Los Alamos. First we lived in the barracks, and then we got a little Hanford house to live in. Our son was born there, and on his birth certificate, instead of having Pittsburgh, Pennsylvania, or Monroeville, Pennsylvania, his birth certificate address is Box 1663, Santa Fe, New Mexico, because Los Alamos was not acknowledged as being a place at all. He was born in 1947, and it wasn't until a few years later that they opened the city up; and now it's the city of Los Alamos. You can go in and out now, but prior to that you couldn't get in without a pass.

As I said, I was drafted in February 1945, and when the war ended they said they wanted us to stay on as civilians. So I was discharged in March 1946 with the agreement to come back and work at least six months on the project. I ended up staying seventeen months. A number of my friends got the discharge and went home, but I felt it was important. I continued doing the same work as a civilian as I was doing as a GI, but I got 25 percent more in hazard pay because of the nature of the work. We didn't come back home until August 1947. I spent about two and a half years there.

I think history is important. It's something I participated in, and I'm glad I had the opportunity. Again, going back to being blessed, I think that was a blessing because they could have picked any number of people to do the machining that I did. It wasn't difficult; it was something that I did and I just had to be careful and not spoil anything.

AFTER THE WAR . . .

. . . .

Ed Halluska received his Army discharge in 1946 and returned to Pennsylvania in 1947. He was rehired at the Westinghouse plant in Pittsburgh and worked there as an engineering supervisor for thirty-eight years before retiring in 1977. Mr. Halluska married his wife in 1942, and they currently travel six months a year on cruise ships teaching the game of bridge.

. . . .

☆ James Sipple ☆
Woodlyn, Pennsylvania

James Sipple was an Army Air Corps gunner on a B-24
bomber. On a mission over Linz, Austria, his plane was
shot down and he was taken prisoner. He describes life
as a POW at the hands of his German captors.

I was twenty-one and was employed at Reading Coal and Mining Company in Lucas Gap, Pennsylvania, just outside of Mt. Carmel, in August of
1942. Two friends and I decided to enlist, so we joined the Army Air Corps.
When I joined up they asked where we wanted to go, so we picked Sacra-
mento, California. We took basic training out there at March Field. We actually tried to get into the Coast Guard first, and the Coast Guard said the one
fellow was too short, the other fellow was color-blind, and to me they said,
"We'll take you." I said, "Not without the other two." So we left and joined
the Air Corps. I thought that would be a better place to be, I don't know
why. I just thought that was the best deal.

After going through basic training they sent me to Ontario, California, to
become an aircraft electrician. I finished that course and went to a ground
service unit. While I was there they asked if we would like to go to radio

school, then come back to the unit. At the same time we would pick up a couple of extra stripes because we would be qualified to cover more of the electrical system on the airplane. So I went out to Sioux Falls, South Dakota, for radio school. I spent three or four months there and was just about to graduate and somebody in Washington decided that everybody who was in the Air Corps on detached service from their outfit was now Air Corps unassigned. So I no longer belonged to the ground service group. Then they said to me, "How would you like to go to gunnery school?" I thought, "That's great because gunnery pays flight pay and you get extra money." So I said, "Sure." I ended up in Laredo, Texas, and finished that course down there.

At gunnery school they start you out shooting a shotgun at skeet. You go from different positions and you learn how to lead the skeet, which are the targets they throw out; and you fire with a shotgun. After we completed that training we were given machine guns. We had to learn how to handle the machine gun, tear it down and put it back together again blindfolded, so that you would be aware how to handle it in case you had a gun jam anytime you were in flight. You were also given a course in aircraft recognition so you could recognize what the silhouettes and front view and tail view of enemy aircraft where. We went out with a pilot who flew the front seat of an AT-6—the gunner was in the back seat—and they had a .30-caliber machine gun on a swivel on the rear cockpit. The pilot would make a run on another AT-6 which was towing a sleeve, and the bullets we had were marked with coloring so any of your shots were recorded as you hit the target. That's how they kept your score.

From there I had to report back to March Field in California, where I was assigned to a crew that was captained by Jim Robinson from Pennsylvania. He was a Penn State graduate, a very nice fellow. I got to be the waist gunner, which was the position that was open on their crew. All the fellows on the crew were real good fellows, easy to get along with, very cordial. Just a jolly bunch of fellows; we all got along fine.

Our aircraft was a B-24. We had four officers: our pilot and co-pilot were both officers, our navigator and the bombardier were also officers. The other six of us were enlisted men; one was our engineer, one was a radio man, and one was an armor man, and three were assistants to the engineer, radio man, and armor man. I was the assistant radio man. The gunners manned the nose turret, the top turret, the belly turret and the rear turret, and then you had the two waist guns, one on each side with .50-calibers. The turrets all had two .50-caliber guns in them, so they had a little more manpower.

We were assigned to pick up an aircraft at Hamilton Field in San Francisco and fly over to Florida. We left from there with an envelope with sealed orders. We opened them after we were out about an hour and found out where we were going. We were going over as a replacement crew to an organization that was already over there, the 461st Bomb Group. We took the southern route and went down through Central America, down to South America, into Brazil, from there to Natal, over to South Africa, and got over to Tunis. We left from there and went over to Italy. When we got there we were assigned to the 461st Bombardiers Bomb Group, in Cerignola, Italy, which wasn't too far from Foggia. The crews that were over there already had trained as a group, so they were more familiar with each other than we were. We were more or less strangers.

We were a heavy bomber. We carried as much as two thousand to four thousand pounds of bombs, and the missions we flew were in northern Italy, France, Romania, Yugoslavia, Germany, and Austria. On one particular trip we were flying the number four position as they say; you start with six airplanes in a box, you have a lead airplane, one on each wing, another one just below each wing again. We were making a bomb run and they called for the bomb bay doors to come open. No sooner had that happened then the nose gunner called on the intercom that he had a flashlight come through his turret. Apparently it was lying in the bomb bay doors on the ship ahead of us and fell out and came through his turret. He was complaining about how cold it was getting in that turret up at 22,000 feet. That was one little incident we never forgot.

During another raid I was in the waist gun. On this mission they gave us boxes of tinfoil they used to decorate Christmas trees with. They thought if we would throw the tinfoil out it would distract the radar so they couldn't track us and get a good reading for their antiaircraft firing. I was busy throwing out tinfoil and the flak started to come up. Just as I reached in the tinfoil box a piece of flak went through the airplane and it cut out a piece in about a three-inch rectangle. The skin of the airplane came down and fell in my hand on the box, but the flak went on through, thank goodness. So I started dumping the tinfoil boxes at a time instead of buy the handful. I thought they needed a little more distraction.

The antiaircraft fire came from 88-millimeter guns. It got to look pretty heavy some days, you could almost go out and walk on it; it was pretty thick stuff. We had lost a number of airplanes by it and a lot of fellows were injured, because when it burst it used to break up as shrapnel and go through the airplane in different areas. A number of times we'd get back and count the number of holes we could find in the airplane from that particular mission. A lot of times you would see a ship going down beside you; one that they have to bail out of after they were hit. You would count chutes and try to keep a record of the number of chutes you could see coming out of an airplane. When we got back from the mission we were always interviewed by the Intelligence Department. They wanted to know any target areas or any activities we saw en route or coming back. And every time we saw troop movements or boats or trains or river movement we would give it to the navigator. He would make a record of it and pass it on to Intelligence when we got home, and they would keep it for future missions.

We would have about twenty-four planes go out from our group on each mission and we would meet up with other groups along the line to the target area. You would have one hundred or more airplanes going on these missions that would go in pretty much at one time, so there were quite a number of planes they could shoot at. It didn't take much to pinpoint us and they usually got something. We weren't running into much activity with German fighters at the time, but on July 24, 1944, we were on a mission to Linz, Austria, and we ran into 125 fighters. They came in at us and shot down eleven of our planes, including my own.

Our job was to shoot down these fighters before they would get to us, and I was in the waist on the right side of the airplane. We got hit on the left side, the one and two engines on the opposite side of me. We were on fire and I saw the smoke coming up over the bomb bay area, which is where the oxygen tanks and radio equipment were. So I disconnected my oxygen and my communications and went to look over the bomb bay and saw that the smoke was coming from down on the wings; the engines. When I started back to my position the captain signaled for us to bail out. After I put on my chute I saw a German fighter come up alongside of us, so I fired at him before I left. I thought that I couldn't pass this up. He did start smoking and he tailed on down, nose down ahead of us. After that we all bailed out, and all ten of us got out of the plane alive. The nose gunner was the last one out, and he was only out ten seconds when the airplane blew up and came down to the ground in pieces. We were all fortunate to get out alive, but we were all picked up and captured.

We had what they call an escape kit, which gave you a small map and a compass so you might be able to orientate yourself. When we were in the chutes coming down, I flew over the Danube River; and being it was in July

I thought, "Well if I'm lucky, I'll try to stay out of sight during the day and make it to the Danube River, find myself a nice healthy log and float the river at night and try to get down to Switzerland." But that never happened. I no sooner got out of the chute when a German soldier came up and said, "For you the war is over." And I said, "Yeah, it looks like it." He spoke English. He was from Canada. He was originally a German and had moved to Canada with some of his family, then he decided to come back to Germany for a visit and when he did Hitler threw him in the Army.

We walked down to a little area where there were split-log benches. He had me sit down there and we smoked my cigarettes. He was telling me about Canada and that he had no use for Hitler, but there wasn't much he could do about it. He was forty-five or fifty years old. They used to send older soldiers out to round up those who had bailed out, and at the end of the day they would come around with a bus and pick us up. The first night was more of a concentration camp than anything. We stayed there a day or two and then went to another camp for interrogation. When we got there everybody was kept in solitary.

When they interviewed you the German officer had you sit down and offered you cigarettes and made you feel at home. He wanted to know our names, our ranks, and serial numbers and all that stuff, which was what we were supposed to pass on, and that was the limit. Of course that never satisfied them. They wanted to know where we were flying from, what kind of airplane, what the targets were, and all this stuff. I never gave them anything of that nature, so finally he gave me a sheet of paper that asked questions about where you flew out of, your bomb load, targets, and anything that might have pertained to that particular flight. I just left it blank, and he said, "There is a question there that says who captured you." I said, "That was a German soldier who picked me up and that is the only thing I know." He said, "If we don't get the necessary information from you people we may turn you over to the SS and they may treat you a little differently."

We stayed there a day or two and then we all left as a group on a train, and were sent into a regular prison camp near the Polish border in Germany. We stayed there in a barracks that had sixteen men to a room. We had four double bunks with wooden slats, burlap bags filled with straw for mattresses, and a heavy, horse-hair blanket. Occasionally we would get some boxes from the Red Cross that had quite a variety of stuff in it. It had chicken pâté and graham crackers and powdered milk, raisins, cigarettes, a toothbrush and toothpaste, chocolate bars, a pack of chewing gum, and it was a treat to get those. After we were there a while, that stopped. The Germans had a hard time getting food for themselves. A lot of the food we got was just soup or maybe a potato, or once in a while you would get some bread. You didn't get an awful lot to eat.

To pass the time we would discuss sports and we'd go outside and play ball, we'd play leap-frog, football, whatever we could do to pass the time. At night they would put us in the barracks and let the police dogs run loose in the camp. So we would play cards or read a book, or you would do some sewing and mending. There were American prisoners who had put together a radio, and they would tune in to the British broadcasts on how the war was going and they would give us reports they had heard from the radio. That's how we kept up a little bit on what was going on with the war movement.

I was in the camp from July 1944 until February 6, 1945, when they said they were going to put us on a march to stay away from the Allied troops. They told us to take what we wanted with us, and I took an overcoat and a blanket. As we were marching I used to try to get the names of the towns we were going through. I kept a record of it on the inside of a cigarette pack; the towns and the mileage.

We marched with five hundred to six hundred in a group and we never knew how far we were going. One day we would go north, another day we'd go south; it would depend on how the Allied troops were closing in. I remember in particular February 14, Valentine's Day, it rained all day. We marched about twenty miles and at the end of the day they said, "Here's an open field, you can sleep here." It was still raining so two of us went together and put the blanket and one overcoat on the ground, and we put the other overcoat over the two of us, then another blanket on top of that. It was a wet and cold night, and the next day when we woke up the blanket and over-coat were pretty wet and pretty heavy. We didn't know if we wanted to lug them with us the next day, but it was a long war so we figured we better take it along.

We marched for the best part of the winter. In fact, it wasn't until May 2 when we found out we were going to get liberated. When the officers rounded us up for the march like they normally did, they just told us that we weren't going anywhere; the British were coming in and the Germans were surrendering. A British troop came in and picked us up and told us to go down the road about five miles and take over the town, go in and help ourselves. He said we would find British people there who would guide us around. So we found the place and got into one of the houses and found something to eat.

We had been marching from February 6 until May 2. A lot of us lost a lot of weight, and a couple of our fellows died on the march. I guess the morale was pretty strong when you stop and think of it, because most of us made it. We were finally sent to La Havre, France, at Camp Lucky Strike, they called it. When we got there they deloused us and gave us some clothes and put us aboard ship. I went into the service at about 150 pounds, and with all the eating and outdoor exercise I was about 175 after a month. When I got out I was 140, so I lost about 35 pounds.

We got on the ship and went to Boston. I got there on May 11. The next day they put us on trains and sent us to Fort Dix, New Jersey, where they gave us fresh clothes and a sixty-day leave. I went home and my girlfriend was still waiting, so we decided to get married. I was going to be reassigned and then probably sent to Japan, so I got on a train and started back, pulled into Washington, DC, and while we were in Union Station in Washington the announcement came out that the Japs had surrendered. That was a lot of reason to cheer. I continued on to Miami and they put me up in a hotel right on the boardwalk, on the beach. The only thing we did after that was report for meals and roll call. I stayed in Florida until the end of August, when I was sent back up to Indiantown Gap. I got discharged from there on September 5, 1945, and that was the end of my war activities.

I was very fortunate. I think that those who didn't make it paid a tough price, and if it weren't for them paying the price, we wouldn't be doing what we're doing today. It might be a different story.

AFTER THE WAR . . .

James Sipple married Jane Williams while on leave, after his release from prison camp. Upon discharge from the service, Mr. Sipple returned to his job in electrical maintenance. In 1948, he began his career with American Airlines, where he worked in a variety of positions until his retirement in 1980. The parents of two sons, the Sipples traveled to many of the 461st Bomb Group reunions until 2001. Mrs. Sipple passed away in 2003.

☆ Marion Yurkis Lurz ☆

Doylestown, Pennsylvania

••

Nurse Marion Yurkis Lurz worked at a tent hospital at Bizerte, Tunisia, and in Italy, where she tended to servicemen wounded in the assault on Monte Cassino.

••

I graduated from training at Abington Hospital in 1940. I worked in a hospital, I worked outside the hospital, I worked private duty, I did a lot of things because I wanted experience in everything. In the meantime, my friend and I both got letters from both the Army and the Navy, saying, "If more of you nurses don't join the service, you're going to be drafted." So we decided we would join. And that's how we got in.

We both went to Fort Story, Virginia, on January 3, 1943. There we had our, what was called, "basic training." We were shown how to wear the gas mask and go through a gas chamber—which we never did use—and all the rules and regulations of the Army. And by March, we got orders to go overseas. There were four of us, all friends. We were placed on a train and told not to speak to a soul. They didn't want anybody to know what we were doing. We were just going on a vacation. We were going to Camp Shanks, New York, but we were not to tell anybody that, so we just chatted among ourselves. We weren't there too long. We met our unit there, not all of them, but the commanding officer and a few of the officers. Then came the time to board our ship, the *Edmund B. Alexander*. We boarded the ship carrying all of our luggage. The only thing we didn't carry with us was our big luggage, our suitcases. Everything else was on our shoulders. We stood in line until a couple of the nurses fainted, and finally we boarded the ship.

We were in a huge group of ships. As far as you could see there were ships. And it was okay on the ship, we had our quarters downstairs and we were fine. At three o'clock one morning, about the third day out, there was a boom, and the ship shook. And another one. Boom, the ship shook. We thought we were hit, of course. I'm not one who panics quickly. I thought, "I'll wait a little bit." I had an upper berth and so did the gal across from me.

NATIONAL ARCHIVES

We watched all the rest of them down there screaming and hollering, going up the hall, trying to get up on top to get off the ship. Finally, on the PA system, they said, "Go back to your rooms. Everything is fine, everything's under control. A boiler blew up." I don't know whether that's what really happened, but that's what we were told. When we got up the next morning and came on top, we were the only ship in the Atlantic. The rest of the convoy was gone.

We had two little ships that circled us constantly. "Tin Cans," they called them. They just kept going around our bigger ship. We limped, if you can say a ship limps, into Oran, Algeria, rather than Casablanca, where the rest of them went. We got off the ship, loaded down with everything we could possibly carry, and stood in line. Nothing moves fast in the Army, you know. The rumor was, "Don't worry girls, you're going to be placed in a very nice hotel in Oran." We were finally piled into vehicles, and we ended up on Goat Hill. Goat Hill was just a plain old hill where we set up tents and slept on the ground. That was our hotel. We were there for about three weeks. We were issued a helmet full of water every day, and that was to take care of bathing yourself or your clothes or whatever. One helmet full of water. That was for the three weeks we were there. There was a shower nearby, which was open to the sky. I think it got buzzed a little bit by the Air Corps. We could take a shower once a week.

Finally we all were piled onto a train, called a forty-and-eight train. It was supposed to carry forty men or eight horses, so it wasn't exactly luxurious. We were on our way to Bizerte, North Africa. And going in the other direction from us was a train full of German prisoners on their way to the United States. We had no water on the train. We got so hot and so thirsty. There were natives along the tracks as we would come into a little station. They were selling water. That was not for me. I'm very fussy. But my friend bought some and drank it, and she ended up with an infection. And they said since I was her good friend, I could take care of her.

We set up our tent hospital at Bizerte, like *M.A.S.H.* Everything went along pretty well for three days. We had patients, of course, right from [Erwin] Rommel's war there in North Africa. On the third day, at three in the morning—there was always bombing at three o'clock or so in the morning to wake you up—a German plane tried to bomb our hospital. He was probably aiming at the motor pool, but he missed the motor pool and almost hit the nurse's quarters. The next morning one of our units that was protecting us there said, "For heaven's sake, get the crosses on top of your tents so they know that you're a hospital." Those crosses went up fast, and we were never bombed again. They'd come back and buzz us, but we weren't bombed.

On one occasion, as our big bombers were flying over the German planes, they managed to shoot one down, and it landed only about a mile away from our hospital. And believe me, such a bang when that came down. That was the only thing we had any danger from. Otherwise, we were pretty safe.

We were serving as a German prison hospital over Christmas of 1943. And believe me, we never had any problems with those prisoners, because we were guarded by the Senegalese. The Senegalese are a French-African tribe of very tall, big, husky black people, wonderful people. And I'm so glad they were on our side, because they were very stealthy, and that's what the Germans were so afraid of. The Senegalese were so stealthy, nobody would know they were there. But those were the soldiers that guarded our hospital, so we had no trouble.

Most of the Germans were young kids, and they wanted that war over as much as we did. But there were some who were pretty arrogant. They were superior to everybody, you know, but most of them were not that way at all. Most of them wanted to go home, just like ours wanted to go home. One night, it was Christmas Eve and a friend of mine and I were walking through the area and we heard some singing far off somewhere. I said, "Let's go see where that is." We found the tent. It almost makes me want to cry. Here was this group of German soldiers, they had made themselves a Christmas tree and decorated it with cotton and so forth, and they were all singing "Silent Night" in German. And we joined them in English. I was in tears. They wanted to go home. We did, too.

We had very little to entertain us when we were in North Africa, but they did bring in movies to show us on occasion. Bob Hope came when he was in North Africa, and he was wonderful. For exercise we would play Ping-Pong, and I got pretty good at it. We Army nurses played the Navy nurses, and we beat them.

In the middle of April 1944, we were ordered to Italy. We arrived on a hospital ship, near Naples. We arrived after one of the worst battles they had in Italy. There was one small American hospital hit, completely annihilated. But when we got there the Germans had moved on. They were up in Rome. And Monte Cassino, that's where we had an awful lot of patients. We were so upset that they kept sending soldiers up that hill and they were mowed down. And we would get them, the ones that were still alive. Finally they had

Nurses

World War II, a highly mechanized and global war, brought more injury and death than had any previous conflict. In the midst of this, U.S. military nurses helped relieve the suffering of countless hundreds of thousands of soldiers, sailors, Marines, and airmen. They served not only in military hospitals, but also near battlefield front lines, and on hospital ships, hospital trains, and medical airlifts.

Congress had established the Army Nurse Corps in 1901 and the Navy Nurse Corps in 1908. More than 21,000 Army nurses and more than 1,300 Navy nurses served during World War I. In the interwar years, those numbers shrank to 1,000 Army nurses and 500 Navy nurses. During World War II, their ranks grew exponentially to encompass some 57,000 Army nurses and 11,000 Navy nurses.

Among the first nurses to treat casualties in World War II were those in the Navy who were serving aboard the USS *Solace*, a hospital ship that was docked at Pearl Harbor in Hawaii when the Japanese attacked that installation on December 7, 1941. Eighty-two Army nurses were also stationed at Honolulu when the attack took place.

Thereafter, nurses served in every theater of the war, from North Africa and Italy to Normandy and the Battle of the Bulge; in the Philippines and Okinawa and dozens of other islands in the Pacific; and in the China-Burma-India Theater. By serving in field and evacuation hospitals near the front lines, they proved the ability of women to function under enemy fire.

The presence of women as military nurses preceded and presaged the passage of legislation in 1942 to establish the WACs and WAVEs, in which women served the military in transport, secretarial, and other noncombat roles, thus freeing men for actual warfare. This act, which established the right of women to serve their country in the military, took place over the objections of the traditional male-dominated military establishment.

Both Army and Navy nurses were taken prisoner by the Japanese in the Pacific and held as POWs, during which time they continued to function as a medical unit, treating fellow Allied POWs. Among these were the celebrated "Angels of Bataan and Corregidor." In Europe, an Army nurse aboard a plane that was shot down was taken prisoner and likewise held as a POW by the Germans. She continued to provide medical care to other POWs until liberation.

A sudden increase in the ranks of military nurses brought two results. One was that the influx of nurses was so great and so rapid that the Army and Navy did not have a formal training program in place until July 1943, when a four-week training course was established for newly commissioned Army nurses. From then until the end of the war in September 1945, fifteen training centers graduated more than 27,000 inductees. The second result was that the military was accused of depleting the ranks of civilian nurses, to the detriment of health care for American citizens. As a result, Congress passed the Bolton Act, which established a Cadet Nurse Corps program, in which the federal government subsidized the cost of a woman's nursing education in exchange for a promise to work in essential military or civilian nursing until the end of World War II. This program resulted in about 150,000 graduates by 1948, when it was discontinued.

On the home front, the American Red Cross served as a first-level recruiting arm for nurses, maintaining a roster of First Reserve nurses from which women would be called to active duty. According to Mary Beard, director of the Red Cross Nursing Service, the rate of recruitment reached as high as 250 women per day after Pearl Harbor. Within two months of that attack, the Red Cross had more than 25,000 women on its list. Military officials wanted twice that many; then the Army changed its mind in December 1943 and thought the nursing corps had enough women. The result was an order to the Red Cross to quit recruiting. The military then changed its mind again and tried to jump-start the Red Cross recruiting network, which had fallen into disorganization and disarray from the previous order. The result was a perceived 10,000-nurse shortage. President Roosevelt even proposed a bill to draft nurses, which came within one vote of passing in Congress, but an Allied victory in Europe rendered the proposal moot. ★

to bomb the Monte Cassino monastery and then we took it and everything was fine after that. Then we became another German prison hospital.

They moved us on to southern France, at the Riviera. There was a hotel that had been abandoned, so we set up our hospital in the hotel. I had just been promoted to first lieutenant, so I had charge of the soldiers who were wounded the worst. I was set up in the front of the hotel. Above us there was a balcony where they had medical patients. We used to wave to those guys up there, they were all Americans. There was one lieutenant who probably had pneumonia. He had been shipped to us for treatment. We got to know him fairly well, but of course, as soon as they were well enough, back to the front they would go. Sadly, about three weeks later he was back on my ward, minus his legs. He had apparently stepped on something. I was so sad I just wanted to sit down and cry, but I didn't, of course. They told us that when we went into training that we would have to immunize ourselves from becoming emotionally involved with our patients. You can't do that. You do the best you can to help every patient. It wasn't easy of course, and there were times when it was hard. We had some bad burn cases from patients who were caught in tanks that were burning. But we were commended for the good job we did of sending them back, recovered as much as possible. That was a nice compliment. We worked hard.

From that hotel we were transferred to an abandoned TB [tuberculosis] hospital, which was arranged in layers so patients could be in the sunshine. We were there until the end of the war. One morning I came on duty, and my whole ward was Japanese. I turned to the right and said, "My God, is Japan attacking Europe now?" And they said, "No, these are American Japanese, and wait till you see them." They were the nicest guys, the bravest guys, they were the most highly decorated men in Europe for what they did, and they were proving that they were good Americans. Believe me, I was very fond of my Japanese patients. They were wonderful. They kept making things for me, weaving me a belt, and that sort of thing. It was just so nice.

When we went home after the war was over I was listening to some soldiers being interviewed, and one Japanese soldier said when he got back, he was still in uniform, and he boarded a bus down in Virginia. Some woman in the back of the bus said, "Oh, another dirty Japanese." The bus driver pulled the bus over, he turned around, and he said, "You apologize to that American soldier, or get off my bus." And I thought, "God, that's marvelous." Nobody knew how hard those guys fought over there. They were wonderful. After the war was over I got to know a couple of them in Willow Grove, and they are great guys. That's one thing you learn when you travel all over the world, that, basically, human beings are alike. They may get bad leadership somewhere and be taught bad things from the time they're little, as they are here in our own country, but basically, the people are all good, I think. I didn't see any really bad people.

I was very proud to have been a part of my county's health service, very proud to be able to do my part against someone who attacked us. We were attacked, so we had every right to go to war then. And I was very happy to be there and to do the best I could.

AFTER THE WAR . . .

When her service with the Army Nurse Corps was completed, Marion Yurkis Lurz went back to school and earned a degree in education. She taught nursing for nine years. After that she traveled around the world as a nurse. She worked for a patient in Europe, as a first-aid nurse at the rim of the Grand Canyon, and in a nursing home. Throughout it all she raised three children and "did her best to raise them as she was raised."

☆ Will Ketner ☆

Harrisburg, Pennsylvania

••

Will Ketner was a pilot in a B-17 bomber, flying missions against railroad yards, bridges, and oil refineries in Europe. Out of five students from his high school who enlisted at the same time, he was the only one to survive the war.

••

I was working at a weekly newspaper and also working at a radio station in my hometown of Roaring Springs, Pennsylvania. At the newspaper they called me "Editor," but I wrote, sold ads, wrote sports, and took the paper to the post office. At the radio station I was an announcer and did one of the first local news broadcasts for station WFBG in Altoona. I was eighteen, try-ing to save money to go to college.

Then after Pearl Harbor everything changed. I'll never forget it. It was a very pleasant Sunday afternoon, and my dad and I were deer hunters, so we took a walk to the mountain and my sister went along. We told her to be quiet and not unwrap any candy wrappers, and then we sat there; it was such a pleasant afternoon. When we went back to the car my dad turned the radio on and we heard all this business about Pearl Harbor. It sounded like a play or something, but when we got home, my mother was crying. Then we heard President Roosevelt's speech, and everybody was going to go into the service. I knew I'd probably be drafted, but I wanted to fly. I always liked to run outside and look at the airplanes when they went over.

Quite a few of us went in and enlisted. There was a patriotic spirit in the country, and I was caught up in it. Five of us from my high school enlisted at the same time. I'm the only one of the five that came back, and all four of the others were only sons. That has given me a guilty feeling for many, many years because I'd see their families. It was Frank Kemp, Gerald Miller, Max Green, and Jack Keeting, and they all died in the war. My mother had five children, and three of her children were in the service. My brother, who's still living, was in the Army, on the ground in Europe. I was in the Air Force, and I had a sister who was in the Navy, so my mother had three stars on her flag in the window, and that was typical at that time.

When I enlisted they brought us to Harrisburg, Pennsylvania, to an armory where we were processed, put on a train, and sent to Miami Beach, Florida. We were living in hotels there, but we were not permitted to use the elevators. We learned to dislike Florida immensely, because we'd have to run down the stairs for reveille in the morning, run back up the stairs to get in our fatigues, and go out in the golf course to drill. I'll never forget, we had a drill sergeant from Scranton, Pennsylvania, and he was a big, tough fellow. He called us the AEF, the American Exiles in Florida, and he would make us march in the hot sun and carry rifles, and he'd laugh. He said, "You thought you were going to be flying." Well, we did, too.

We were there for about a month or six weeks, and then there was a succession of assignments. First we went to Nashville, Tennessee. At Nashville we had what was called "Classification." They gave us a lot of tests there to determine whether we qualified to be a pilot, a bombardier, a navigator, or a gunner. You never knew how you were going to make out till you got your orders for the next station, which was Maxwell Field in Montgomery, Alabama. That was sort of an exposure to flying. There were planes there, but we had some ground school and we had tests in the high-altitude chamber to see what our oxygen tolerance was. We were there about six weeks, and then we were sent to North Carolina State University at Raleigh where we studied meteorology and navigation. They called us "CTD," College Training Detachment. In fact, my first flying was at Raleigh-Durham Airport. I had ten hours in a Piper Cub. Ten hours isn't very much, but that was my first flying. I was nineteen and very nervous, but a little cocky too.

I had all my ensuing flight training at Douglas, Georgia. That was called "Primary Flight Training." I flew the Stearman PT-17. That was open cockpit with a bi-wing. That's the first one you did aerobatics in. You had to do a slow roll, and you had to be sure you were strapped in because you had an open cockpit. You felt like Snoopy. You had your goggles and your white scarf, of course, but while you soloed there, and had every phase of training, you had this idea hanging over you that you might wash out, meaning you flunked the test. You'd be in a barracks with some guys tonight, and tomorrow they were gone, washed out. Some of them were not coordinated, some were afraid to fly, and some couldn't handle the faster, more powerful planes.

We went from Douglas, Georgia, to basic training at Cochran Field at Macon, where we flew a BT-13. That was a low-wing plane with variable speed propellers. It had more power and was a faster, heavier aircraft. Then we went to the next phase of flying, at Moody Field, Georgia, where they had a more powerful plane with two engines; it was more like a light bomber. I graduated there. That was where you got your coveted wings, if you made it. There were 326 in my graduating class, and I had the honor of being the outstanding cadet in my class. So my mother and my father were invited down, and my mother was up on the stage to pin my wings on me. It was a proud moment for her.

I was kept there at Moody as instructor for three or four months. I wasn't asked if I wanted to be an instructor. I suppose they had a need for them, but my class went on. Some went on to fly P-38s; some went to P-51s. The P-38 was graceful, it was fast, and it looked like it was action. They called it the Lightning. The P-51 was a favorite, too. It was a good, reliable plane. We all wanted to be assigned to fighters, but we had no choice in that.

When I was getting ready to go overseas I went to Sebring, Florida, for another stage of my training. They put me in a B-17 and I was what they call "Checked Out," getting so many hours flying it and landing it, and then they sent me to Gulfport, Mississippi, where I picked up my crew. You were assigned nine other fellows. You'd come in, say, "Hello, I'm so-and-so," and you'd start to fly. We flew fake bombing missions and fake gunnery missions out over the Gulf of Mexico, flying in and out of Gulfport, Mississippi, night flying, daytime flying. Anybody who's been in the military knows you build a camaraderie that is almost like a brotherhood, and we did. We knew that we might live together and die together. I told my crew that I wanted to fly in everybody's position for a half hour so I could appreciate what they had to do, and they put me down in the ball-turret. I was there five minutes and that was it, I wanted out; I couldn't have made it being a ball-turret gunner.

You learned a lot about England in a hurry. It was usually rainy or misty in the morning. We were wakened at four or five o'clock for a briefing. We'd line up and take off maybe one every minute, and we'd get above the rain, and all of a sudden, there was a glorious blue sky and vapor trails everywhere you looked; hundreds and hundreds of vapor trails. Then coming back from the mission you'd always look for the white cliffs. That song, "The White Cliffs of Dover" is for real, because you could see those white cliffs. There was a little church off the end of the runway at our base at Molesworth, England, and it had a steeple on it, and when we'd come in, we'd lay our left wing on that steeple and turn on the steeple as sort of a pivot, and we'd be lined up with the runway. So we'd always look for that little church.

I got there toward the end of the war, and we worried about being shot down on the next-to-the-last mission. Everybody was superstitious. We had one mission to Pilsen, Czechoslovakia, and the Skoda works there; it was an armament plant. General Eisenhower had notified the Czech people that we were coming. It was three days in advance, so the civilian population could evacuate. That's okay, but it also gave the Germans three days to get every flatcar and truck with antiaircraft guns that they could around the target area, and we knew that was going to happen. As we approached the target, the antiaircraft fire was like a black cloud.

We were supposed to make a visual run, but there was an under cast, and we couldn't see. Visual run means you have to see the target, you don't use radar. We were about 25,000 feet, but the weather forecast said it was going to be clear and it wasn't. So we had to make three passes before the cloud cover cleared and we could see the target. And of course, we were being shot at on all three of those passes. And you start figuring the odds. With the anti-aircraft fire you'd hear a popping. It hit our plane in the aluminum fuselage and it would pop little holes. But the good Lord was with me. We had major battle damage, they called it, on a large majority of our planes that day, but we got back all right.

I remember one mission to Royen, France, which was a seaport. It was the coordinated effort of the Air Force and the Navy. It was a perfectly clear day, and as we approached the target we could see forever. We were at 25,000 feet, and there was to be a couple of groups of B-24s come in at 18,000. They were coming from the east and we were coming from the north. And the Navy had some ships that they lined up out in the water. We could see the ships firing, we could see the flames from their guns, and then we could see the bombs hitting from the B-24s. Then ours were the last on the target. It was almost like it was a lesson at West Point, where they show you the way it should be done. But it didn't always happen that way. We had one mission where we must have plowed some farmer's field because we sure missed the bridge we were supposed to hit, but we had a nice bomb pattern back about a mile before the bridge.

Some missions were "milk runs." A milk run meant it would be easy, but you never knew who was waiting for you. On the day of a milk run you had a briefing in the morning before you left, and they'd show the map where you were going and give you an IP—that was the initial point—which was a decoy. You never went straight to the target. When they gave you the briefing, they would say, "This should be a routine mission. We don't know of any fighters in the area." We called that a milk run; you could fly there and back and not get shot at. Sometimes you felt embarrassed that you called it a mission, but then there were other times when they would say, "Oh, this one looks easy," and boy, they'd be after you all over the place. I didn't have that many of them, that's why I say I'm a lucky survivor. My friends Russ Jensen and George Klaus and the ones who were shot down and were prisoners; they're the heroes. I survived because I was lucky.

Our major targets were railroad yards, bridges in advance of armies, oil refineries, submarine pens, and things like that. You tried your best to avoid civilian targets, cities. Now, Cologne had marshaling yards all around it, but Cologne has a cathedral that was never touched. The spires of that cathedral were not damaged, and that was the good Lord there, that wasn't our marksmanship.

We didn't have phone calls home and we didn't have mail from home. My father, I think sent me three letters when I was overseas because he was not a letter writer. His letters were never emotional, never love letters. We were hunters, and he would draw me a little map where he went rabbit hunting. He wanted to keep my mind on things that meant something to me. My mother was ill, on the other hand. She would be a little more emotional, and she would write more often. But my dad always signed the letters "Your father, Blair F. Ketner." It wasn't "Dad." It was always "Your father, Blair Ketner." I still have some of them.

The war in Europe ended and bingo, I was supposed to go home and go into training with a B-29 and go to Japan. The B-29 was a bigger aircraft than the B-17, and it was being used in the Pacific. It had a longer range and a bigger bomb load. Most of us were told, "You're going home. You're going to spend maybe a month learning to fly a B-29, and then you're going to the Pacific." Well, they gave us some old B-17s to fly home that were going to be junked, and that was our assignment. The ground crew wrote on one engine, "Wilbur Wright was here in 1902," and another one said, "Kilroy was here and left" and "Don't count on me. I'm tired." Well, on the way home, between Iceland and Greenland, I lost both inboard engines and we thought we were going to go down. I told my radio operator to call Greenland Radio. Our plane was number 777. I said, "Every two minutes tell them our position in case we go down, in case we don't make Greenland." Five years after the war I was working at a radio station in Altoona. The engineer and I were sitting there making small talk, and I said, "Art, what did you do in the war?" He said, "I was a radio operator in Greenland." I said, "That had to be boring." He said, "It was until some idiot in Army 777 kept calling me every two minutes to tell me where he was." And I said, "Well, you're looking at the idiot."

One more thing. When I went overseas my church back home gave me a little bible, and my minister said, "Always keep in mind Psalm 91." When we got to Iceland we went to the chapel there—and we knew we were getting close to the shooting war—and we went in. The chaplain spoke to us, and said, "Always rely on Psalm 91." By this time, I was a believer, and here's Psalm 91. It's been marked and read so many times.

"I will say of the Lord, 'He is my refuge and my fortress, my God. In Him will I trust.' Thou shalt not be afraid for the terror by night, nor for the arrow that flieth by day. A thousand shall fall at thy side and ten thousand at thy right hand, but it shall not come nigh thee."

I'm a lucky survivor, I'm no war hero. I'm a lucky survivor.

AFTER THE WAR . . .

After the war, Will Ketner returned to his hometown of Roaring Springs, Pennsylvania, and worked for radio station WFBG for several years. He then went to WVAM and managed that station until 1966. Mr. Ketner then went to work for the Pennsylvania Department of Agriculture, where he directed trade shows. In addition, he served as the Deputy Secretary of Commerce, Secretary of the Public Utilities Commission, and later the Director of Personnel for the Republican Caucus in the Pennsylvania State Legislature. He retired in 1987.

☆ Jim Duratz ☆

Meadville, Pennsylvania

....

**Jim Duratz saw street-to-street combat in the Philippines,
during the recapture of Manila, and served as an MP
in Germany for the post-war Nuremberg trials.**

....

I was a student in high school, and when I got out of high school I volunteered and went directly into the service. I wanted to go to the Marine Corps, but at the time they were filled and they decided that they'd rather have me in the Army. So I ended up in the Army, in the infantry. That was 1943 and the war was still going on pretty good.

I went to Fort McClellan, Alabama, for basic training; that was a sixteen-week course. Training was tough. It was typical Army infantry training. There was a lot of walking, fighting, shooting, drilling, and discipline; a lot of discipline. When we went in as recruits, the first thing we saw was the class ahead of us leaving, and they were a trained group of soldiers. It made us look pretty bad. But at the end of the sixteen weeks when we left, we made that class coming in look pretty bad, because we were trained soldiers. There was a big difference between that first week and the end of the sixteen weeks; you were a different person.

After basic training I came home for about a week on furlough and then went to California, and then overseas. We were pretty sure we were going to the South Pacific when were sent to San Francisco, but they didn't tell us exactly where we were going. While we were on the ship everybody was betting where we were going to go, but that was mostly guesswork. We played cards and really didn't talk about the war too much, because we didn't know much about it, except what we learned through the news. But we knew we were going to be in a war, so we just accepted that.

We were on the ship about forty-five days before we reached our destination, the Philippine Islands. After landing at Luzon we joined the 37th Division. We were replacements for people who got shot or killed. The 37th Division had been there a long time; they were one of the first divisions to leave the States to go to the South Pacific. They got there in June 1942, so those guys were seasoned veterans by the time we got there.

After we joined our unit there was a one hundred–mile trek, with the goal of recapturing Manila. There were some skirmishes on the way, but nothing too serious. That took about a month, but we were walking all the way. They just kind of threw us into the battle, and from our training we knew pretty much what to do. You got to know your people and how to dig a foxhole. We knew the fighting was going to be hot in the jungle, but in

Ruins of the city of Manila in the aftermath of street-to-street fighting in the Philippine capital. NATIONAL ARCHIVES

Manila, it was more like street fighting, and there was a lot of fighting in Manila. We had to take it block by block. A lot of people died and a lot of people were wounded. We stayed there for a couple weeks before we left on Easter Sunday to go up into the hills to take Baguio, which was about 6,000 feet into the mountains, and it was cold. We had been accustomed to heat in the jungle, and we moved right into the cold. I think the first night there it rained and our clothes got a little stiff from the cold. That was quite a change, but we learned to live with it.

But by the time we got to Baguio, the Japanese had pulled out. By then they were pretty well beaten, so Baguio was kind of easy. We just kind of walked into Baguio, but it had been tough getting there. When they raised the flag after the capture of Baguio, it was just after Franklin Roosevelt died, and they raised it at half-mast, I remember that. So in a way, it was a big day, but it was also a sad day because we lost our president. That's when Harry Truman took over.

We didn't stay in Baguio very long. They put us on trucks and hauled us up further north and back down into the jungles again to Balete Pass, which is where the Japanese decided they were going to make their last stronghold. Something happened there that was really quite unusual. A regiment of the 25th Division was there when we got there, and we were to take their place. They had tried to break the hole through the pass and couldn't make it through, so they left their positions and we moved in. They had told us about how it was a very tough situation. I moved into a foxhole there with my buddy. I no sooner got in the foxhole than I found a deck of cards and I said to my friend, "I don't know how much trouble they had if they were playing cards. We never had a chance to play cards, and they were here playing cards." We just made a joke out of it, and I put the cards in my pocket. We were there for a couple days, and they decided we had to try to break through. We made a reconnaissance patrol the day before to see what was up there, and we didn't see anything so we came back and reported that everything looked quiet. It was hard to understand why they were having so much trouble. But as usual in the Army, they didn't really tell us much. But the next day, we went up and there was trouble. They just came out of nowhere and they were all around us. We had a tough time there, but we finally held our hill. It was ours, and it was ours to keep; we weren't going to give it back. That went on for a couple weeks and finally the Japanese decided it was ours. Then we were pulled off and sent to another area. By this time the Japanese had been starting to surrender and things were quieting down.

But I'd like to go back to that deck of cards now. When I came home from the service I joined the Pennsylvania State Police, and eventually was transferred to Meadville. I ended up going to college in Meadville, and I became friends with a fellow by the name of Andy Costa. I played golf with him a lot; he was a very good friend. In fact, we'd get together with a group of people and go to Florida to play golf. On one of our trips to Florida, after we finished playing golf, we sat around in his room and were talking, and the subject of the war came up. Andy started telling me about being in the Philippines, and I said, "Well, Andy, that's where I was." He was in the 25th Division, and he mentioned Balete Pass and said, "When we left there, I left a deck of cards." I said, "Andy, I think I picked up that deck of cards." I know that's hard to believe, but it's true.

After the Japanese surrender we prepared to come home. When I got home they were asking guys to go over to Germany as occupation forces. Most of my buddies had gone to Europe, so I thought, "Well, I'm going to go over." I volunteered to go to Germany—the war was over then—and I was assigned to the 1st Division as an MP. I thought it was going to be a lot easier than it was, but there were still German soldiers who hadn't given up, and they still caused some problems. There was a group called the SS that had a tattoo that looked like an "S." They tattooed another line through each one of those to make it look like an "8," and they called themselves the 88. So we were assigned the task of trying to find these guys. It got a little touchy for a while; they were kind of bad.

We found some and had a couple firefights, but we got over that. It took a little time; I was over there for about a year and a half. After that I was reassigned, and got involved in the Nuremberg trials. I hauled some prisoners to Nuremberg for the trial. One of the exciting things that happened to me there was that, on one of the trips I was in the hallway, and I looked into the room that I was walking by and saw Hermann Göring. I saw him just a couple days before he took that suicide pill, but at the time, it didn't mean much to me. I knew he was big, but I didn't realize that he was second under Hitler.

Then things changed in Germany, and I became a safety director. It was more like a vacation then; I spent time in the Alps in southern Bavaria, and as a safety director, I traveled all over Germany in the last six or eight months. I also spent time at Hitler's Eagle's Nest. In Munich, there was a little bit of war damage, but anything south of Munich in the Alps wasn't battered up like most of the cities up north. I went to Regensburg first and it was pretty bad, and I went through some cities that were completely demolished. It was sad.

As an MP I learned to speak German fairly decently by being there. And of course, most of them there could speak English, especially the younger

Balete Pass

The Battle of Balete Pass was among the conflicts necessary for Allied forces—American and Filipino—to retake the Philippines from the Japanese in World War II.

The Japanese had driven the Allies from the Philippines in 1942, resulting in the infamous Bataan Death March and Gen. Douglas MacArthur's promise, "I shall return." He made good on that oath on October 20, 1944, when the Allies landed at Leyte Island, four hundred miles southeast of Manila. The Philippine capital city was situated on Luzon, the northernmost and largest of the three main groups of islands making up the Philippines (Visayas is the center island and Mindanao is the southernmost island).

Extending about 460 miles north-south and 140 miles east-west, Luzon occupies 40,240 square miles, about the size of Kentucky. Its strategic importance in the Pacific war was that its northern tip lay just two hundred miles from Japanese-occupied Taiwan and just five hundred miles from the Ryuku Islands of Japan proper. Before the dropping of the atomic bomb caused Japan's surrender, the Allies were planning an invasion of Japan to end the war. Luzon would have been a key staging area.

Under the command of Army general Walter Krueger (1881–1967), the U.S. Sixth Army began its amphibious assault on Luzon on January 9, 1945, invading the island from the northwest at Lingayen Gulf. Allied forces recaptured Clark Air Base by the end of that month, and by early March, following a second amphibious landing, they had reoccupied the city of Manila. U.S. infantry and paratroopers and Filipino soldiers and guerrillas participated in the Battle of Manila, during which an estimated 100,000 residents were killed.

From there, the Allies—Americans, Filipinos, and some Chinese—moved north to engage Japanese forces dug in throughout the lush, tropical, mountainous country, with the aim of forcing them to give up their Philippine stronghold by driving them off the island. The enemy was represented by the Japanese Army Shobu Group, commanded by General Tomoyuki Yamashita (1885–1946), nicknamed "the Tiger of Malaya."

Northwardly, Luzon's central plains give way to rugged terrain with heavily forested mountains rising to altitudes of between 4,500 and 5,500 feet. The U.S. Army 25th Infantry Division, comprising the 27th Infantry Regiment, 35th Infantry Regiment, and 161st Infantry Regiment, began pushing north from San Jose (about one hundred miles north of Manila) toward Santa Fe, a crossroads village that lay perhaps twenty-five miles north, on the other side of Balete Pass. The pass was a low point in an eleven-mile-long mountain spine known as Balete Ridge.

This drive began in February and continued to its climax, three months later, in the Battle of Balete Pass, which lasted from May 4 to May 10. Troops encountered snipers firing down from the mountains surrounding them, and found the going to be extremely rough. The land was heavily forested and overgrown with thick jungle vegetation. Route 5 was a gravel, barely-two-lane-wide road linking San Jose with Santa Fe through the Pass. Another way north, the Villa Verde Trail, included a fifteen-mile stretch that was scarcely passable for foot soldiers, let alone jeeps or supply trucks. The Allied ground assault was aided by aerial support in the form of B-24 and B-25 bombers, P-38 and P-51 fighters, and all-purpose A-20 bomber-fighters.

When the Allies finally captured the pass, it opened the gateway to the two hundred-mile-long, forty-mile-wide Cagayan Valley that ran all the way north to Luzon's northern coastline. This victory effectively defeated the remaining Japanese forces in the Philippines. Allied casualties in the battle numbered 2,195, with 545 killed.

Balete Pass was renamed Dalton Pass to honor Col. James L. Dalton II, 161st Infantry Regiment Commander, who was killed by a sniper as he led allied Filipino and American troops northward in pursuit of the fleeing Japanese.

Since 2003, the local government of Santa Fe has held an annual observance to celebrate May 13 as Balete Pass Day. May 13, 1945, was the day on which General Krueger declared the pass to be free of Japanese. ★

people, because they studied English in school. But the older folks seemed like nice people. I got along fine with them. As a matter of fact, I had a German fellow working for me cleaning my room. I ended up being a godfather to two of his sons. But the young folks, I don't think they liked us, but they recognized the reality and knew we were going to be there, so they accepted it. By the time I left there things were fairly decent. Really, we had very few problems, but as an MP I had to investigate everything that had happened.

When I returned home, it was hard to make the transition. I had a brother and sister and a mother and father when I came back, and just to get to know them again after four years was a chore. I had never smoked cigarettes before I went, but when I came back, I was smoking cigarettes, and my sister squealed to my mother and father that I was smoking cigarettes. I'd been gone for four years, and still didn't want to admit to them that I smoked.

Since the war I haven't had any reason to talk about it much. If I'm with somebody and the subject comes up I'll talk about it, but I never made a speech about it or anything like that. I would talk about it if I was just with a group of guys, especially with another guy who was there; another GI.

Our generation's dwindling pretty fast now. There were sixteen million in uniform in World War II. There's less than four million left now. I don't think it should be forgotten; it meant a lot. In fact, I was just in Gettysburg yesterday on some hallowed ground down there and thought about what the war meant to us; and I hope we don't forget that.

AFTER THE WAR . . .

In 1948, James Duratz enlisted in the Pennsylvania State Police and was transferred to Troop E in Erie in 1949. He resigned from the State Police in 1953 and graduated from Allegheny College in Meadville that year. That same year he married Helene Barco and went to work for Westinghouse Corporation in Pittsburgh. Mr. Duratz left Westinghouse in 1959 to manage the cable television system in Meadville and became a pioneer in the developing cable television industry. He went on to build cable systems in California, Pennsylvania, and Titusville, Pennsylvania. Mr. Duratz is currently the Chairman of the Board for the Pennsylvania Cable Network.

☆ Graydon Woods ☆

Schnecksville, Pennsylvania

· ·

**Graydon Woods fought through the hedgerows around
Cherbourg and Saint-Lô in France and participated in
the victory march through Paris after that city's liberation.
He also fought in Belgium and along the Luxembourg–
Germany border, where he was wounded.**

· ·

Just before I joined the armed services I was laid off. Since I wasn't work-ing, my friend and I decided to join the National Guard at least to get a couple of dollars for Saturday night. Then in February 1941 the government passed a law that we had to have a year's training, so they federalized us, and we went to Indiantown Gap, Pennsylvania. That was our first stop.

Indiantown Gap was still just mud roads, and the barracks were only half-finished. But that's the way it was in those days. We started our training there, did our exercises in the field, and all kinds of calisthenics and rifle practice. Then we went on maneuvers down to Fort A. P. Hill, Virginia. And that's where we had our first war games, making believe that somebody was going to capture us. Then we came back to Indiantown Gap.

On the way back to the Gap from A. P. Hill a woman came out and told us that the Japs had bombed Pearl Harbor. So when we got back to Indiantown Gap we were put on the alert. In those days, they didn't know what was going to happen. We were restricted to camp, but on New Year's Eve of 1941 they gave us a four-hour pass to go to town and get our final shopping done. So me being a lone, brave soldier, I went out, and hitchhiked a ride over to Allentown from Indiantown Gap. In those days, all you had to do was put your thumb up and the first car coming by would pick you up. Route 22 was an old two-lane highway at that time. There wasn't that much traffic, but my buddy and I got a ride to 7th and Tilghman Street in Allentown. Then we took a trolley car to Walnut Street, that's where my buddy's girlfriend lived, so we went to see her.

I didn't have a girlfriend, so he said, "I'll get you one." He took me up to McCrory's Five-and-Ten on Hamilton Street and introduced me to my wife-to-be, Florence. She worked in the jewelry department of the store. That evening was New Year's Eve. We went to some club in the square. My buddy and I stayed at the Hotel Allen overnight. It cost us a dollar a night for that. The next day was New Year's Day. Florence and her sisters made a big turkey dinner for New Year's Day, and they thought we should stay there. So we decided to stay, even though we were AWOL—absent without leave.

NATIONAL ARCHIVES

We had a very good dinner and a very good visit afterwards. That evening I told them we had to get back to the Gap. We got a bus going back, and when we got there my company was all ready to move out. They were going to Fort Beauregard, Louisiana. But I didn't have any clothes packed, so I asked the guys where my clothes were. They said "Don't worry about it, we took care of everything. You're all packed."

I was assistant driver on a jeep and I was in my dress uniform and the temperature was about four below zero that night. I just about froze to death. We stopped at Camp Lee, Virginia, overnight. The farther south we got the warmer it got. We ended up in Louisiana, where we stayed for five or six months and then we came back to Camp Pickett, Virginia, where we had a lot of training. We ended up in Massachusetts, and that's where we boarded the troop ship to go overseas in a convoy.

Those waves would carry a big ship up in the air and then put it down in a big valley of water. They were almost as high as you could see. One night we got the alert to get our life jackets on, so we put our life jackets on and got on deck. The destroyers started patrolling up and down through the convoy. Pretty soon our boat shook with about three explosions. Then the word come over that our ships got the German submarine. That was the only incident we had going over.

We landed near Swansea at Cardiff, Wales. That's where we were bivouacked while we were in England. Then sometime in June we got the word to move out; that we were heading for France.

So we got down to Southampton, England, loaded on the troop ship, and we landed over at Omaha Beach, which was the bloodiest landing of any place there was, but when we got there it had been cleared pretty well, but there were still a lot of remnants there from the landing. Several thousand fellas had been killed right on that beach.

We moved inland a mile or so and stopped for the night. We bivouacked, and they told us to dig a good foxhole. We got in the foxholes at about nine or ten o'clock, and a German patrol plane we called "Bed-Check Charlie" came over, which they did every night, just to harass us. He dropped a five-hundred-pound bomb, and it exploded. It practically knocked me out of my hole from the concussion, but I wasn't scratched. He did make a hit on a big gasoline dump, and it made a very big fire. It sort of scared me, being new in combat.

The next day, we set up a command post, and I don't know who picked where it should be, but it was right in the middle of a whole German camp, because there were Germans running everywhere. It's funny, they didn't

"88" German Artillery

The best-known piece of artillery used by the German army during World War II was a group of guns collectively known as 88s, for the 88-millimeter caliber shells they used. They were designed initially for antiaircraft duty, but soon added an important role in antitank warfare. In addition, they were used against Allied infantry, other vehicles, and pillboxes, or fortified bunkers. So feared was the 88, and so widely used, that one Australian infantryman described it as "anti-everything."

In a way, 88s exerted a small impact on the English language. The word "flak," meaning either hostile projectiles or criticism, is derived from an acronym based on the German designation for 88s—*Flugabwehrkanone*, or antiaircraft cannon.

Because the German government was forbidden to develop weapons immediately after World War I, the technology was developed by the private Krupp ironworks and manufacturing firm of Germany, in tandem with a Swedish firm. Prototypes were built as early as 1928, and the first guns of this type were completed in 1934. They were deployed during Germany's support of the rebels in the 1936–1939 Spanish Civil War.

In World War II, 88s were used on countless battlefields, and in the German invasions of Poland and France. They also were used in North Africa, and on the Eastern Front against Russia. Moreover, they were deployed in Germany for homeland defense, both on the ground and against British and American airborne bombing raids. By 1944, Germany had built more than 10,700 of the 88 guns.

With a muzzle velocity of 2,755 feet per second, the 88 when used in its antiaircraft role could fire to an altitude of 35,000 feet. In ground use, its range was greater than three miles, and at a distance of 1,000 yards, it could penetrate four-inch-thick steel armor. Later versions were even more powerful, capable of penetrating seven-inch-thick armor at that range.

"88" German artillery. NATIONAL ARCHIVES

Manned by a crew of one commander and nine soldiers assigned to a variety of aiming, firing, and reloading tasks, the 88 could fire twelve to fifteen rounds per minute. Each shell weighed more than thirty pounds and measured more than a yard long.

In its various forms, the 88 weighed five to seven tons. It was built in semistationary versions with a low profile that aided concealment and made it harder to hit. In addition, it was built on mobile platforms or trailers that were towed by half-track vehicles (see page 88). It also was incorporated into self-propelled, tracked artillery vehicles such as the Königstiger, or Royal Tiger, and Jagdpanther tank destroyers.

That the 88 was deadly is proven by the fact that in July 1944 alone, 241 American bombers that flew missions over Europe from England were missing in action—134 B-17s and 107 B-24s. Most, if not all, of these were victims of antiaircraft fire from 88s. ★

shoot at us, but the colonel told us to grab our rifles, so we grabbed our rifles and the Germans skedaddled. They went right back through the hedgerows to get out of sight. The next day we were committed to combat, and the first city we had to take was Cherbourg. There was another company that had tried to take it before, and they couldn't. So they called in 1,100 bombers one day, wave after wave of bombers, and they bombed that city until there was practically nothing left. In fact, we had to get bulldozers or tanks with blades in the front to plow open the streets.

Once we got through Saint-Lô we got into the hedgerow country. Hedgerows were everywhere. The French had the fields blocked off with piles of dirt with bushes growing on top. It was almost impossible to get from one hedgerow to another, so we had to use marching fire. You would keep shooting when you got over one hedgerow until you got to the next one and you would keep your head down.

The Germans used a lot of horses to pull their artillery and supplies, and we saw a two-wheel cart with a horse galloping and a German soldier on it running up to the German troops. He was bringing them ammunition. He dumped the ammunition off, turned around and started down the road. He shouldn't have turned his back on us, because he flew clear out of that buggy on the way past us and the horse was killed. But then the Germans shot their 88s at us. When they did that we all jumped for our foxhole. Four of us jumped in it at once and I ended up on top with all the other guys underneath me. I felt something sting me in the back, and I turned around and I reached, and my one buttock felt like it was on fire. A piece of shrapnel had landed on my pants. I picked it off quick because it was hot, but it didn't break the skin, so I missed out on my Purple Heart there. That was where our company had our first casualty of the war, a fella by the name of George Ingram, from Chicago. A piece of shrapnel went right through his shoulder. That was one of the few close calls we had at that time, but going through the hedgerows, that was another story. Replacements kept coming up and they would get picked off, but I must have had a guardian angel because I could keep going.

One day a lieutenant told me to take over the BAR, which is a Browning Automatic Rifle. All you had to do was start shooting those, and the Germans would start laying the 88s in on the area. He told me, "Take over the 88, you'll get the Silver Star." He didn't even get my name, and they picked him off. He was killed right there.

On another occasion, a fella next to me fell on the ground, and he was gasping. I asked him what happened. He gurgled something, and I couldn't understand him. He had gotten shot right through the chest. He couldn't breathe because the air was going straight into his lungs instead of going through his nose. He pointed to his chest where all the blood was, so I put his hand over there and held his hand down, and then he could breathe, he could get the air back in. I called the medics up, and they came and took care of him. I often wondered if he ever made it. But the way the action was there, it was no place to hide. We kept fighting.

We went through all the hedgerows until we finally got them cleared out. The English were coming down from the north. We were supposed to bring a pincer movement in and catch the Germans in the middle, which we did. But the Frenchmen or the Englishmen were not quite the fighters we were. They fell way back because they had to stop for their tea and crumpets in the afternoon. Eventually, our general sent them word to either get down with us, or we'd have to go up and do it for them. Then they made a big push and they did close the gap.

When we got into Paris, we went to a big park outside of the city. All the trucks came up with showers and new uniforms for us. That night we all got cleaned up, and they told us that the next day we'd make a victory march through Paris. So we got all polished up, and the next day, we lined up. They let the free French go first, which I guess they did to appease the Frenchmen. But we did the job for them.

French citizens line the Champs Elysées as Free French troops parade through the Arc de Triomphe in Paris after the city's liberation in August 1944. WIKIMEDIA COMMONS

Bed-Check Charlie

"Bed-Check Charlie" was the nickname given by Allied soldiers to nightly solo reconnaissance flights the Nazis sent over Allied troop movements in Europe after the D-Day invasion of June 6, 1944. Often, the flights arrived at the same time each night, usually around bedtime, or 11 P.M., giving rise to the nickname that implied a chaperone regularly checking on his or her youthful charges.

Flying alone, these small one- or two-engine observation planes often dropped only flares to illuminate an encampment or position. But if their crews spotted targets of opportunity, they could drop bombs and direct machine-gun fire.

The flights began on the night of D-Day, continuing for many months as the Allies pressed across France and Belgium toward Germany. The Germans also employed this tactic in Allied-occupied Italy.

American troops considered their white, yellow, and orange flares to be generally harmless, but their importance to the Germans was

Going through Paris, that was the greatest feeling you ever had. The streets were lined so solid with people. I was driving a jeep, the third jeep behind the photographer, so I saw myself on TV when I came home. All the GIs looked alike so nobody could ever pick you out, but one girl came over, give me a big kiss and put a big basket of wine on my jeep. This went on for the whole parade. They loaded us up with all they could.

One of the main attractions was the women who were collaborators with the Germans; had German boyfriends, or whatever. So the free French took those girls out in the street and shaved their heads, which was quite a spectacle. Then the French would spit on them and everything. That was the parade through Paris.

The next day we started up and headed for Germany. The Germans had retreated through Paris. They were a sad-looking mess because they were all heading back to Germany. On the road from Paris up to Germany we were held up because our P-51 and P-47 fighter planes had strafed their column of vehicles, and the road was just loaded with tanks and ambulances and invaluable. They could gather and relay information about the location of guns, tanks, other vehicles, and personnel, giving Nazi officers intelligence about where bombing raids would be most effective. More of a nuisance than an actual threat, these flights still hurt morale because GIs knew that their locations would be targeted. As a result, many units took to hiding guns and howitzers in dug-out trenches, with camouflage netting spread over them. Another measure instituted was that of a general lights-out order—even including a ban on lighting cigarettes—to avoid showing activity or giving away positions.

The solitary planes emitted a low drone that American GIs mockingly compared to the sound of a Maytag washer. In fact, "washing-machine Charlie" was a variation of the bed-check nickname.

At least one Allied "Charlie" is known to have flown during World War II. A British Mosquito aircraft made nightly strafing raids on an airfield in Barth, in the far northern part of Germany, on the Baltic Sea.

Five years after the end of World War II, the North Korean air force used the identical tactic against U.S. and United Nations troops during the Korean War. ★

trucks and cars that were all demolished. On some of the ambulances the doors were blown open and ammunition was falling out the back, so they used the ambulances for more than getting their sick and wounded out.

We got up to Germany, but our lines got so stretched out that we had to stop and wait for supplies to catch up. We evacuated one town, sent the people to where it would be safe, and we moved into a house there. In this house was a thirty-gallon crock of eggs in a water glass—which preserved the eggs—and a tub of butter. We kept the baker in town so we had good, fresh bread, and that night we had a party with fresh eggs and homemade bread. We were there until the supplies caught up with us, then we headed up through Belgium. We had battles all the way through Belgium and then we got over into Luxembourg.

We went through the Siegfried Line, and the fighting got a little rough after that because the Germans were back in their home territory. We came to one town and the Germans had just pulled out, so we went in. We were in a barroom there when the word came that the Germans were counterattacking. They really came back at us and when they got the town back, it was demolished. The 109th Infantry was on our left, and the 110th was on our right. The 109th got pushed back, so when they got pushed back the Germans kept chasing them, and they got behind us so we couldn't get back to our own lines. There were about seventy-five of us in our group, and we were out of ammunition. We couldn't do anything, but we stayed there and radioed back. They were going to send us help, which they never did. There was a colonel there with us, and he had lost all of his tanks up on the hill. They were burning. He said, "Tonight, we're going to make a break for it. Line up everybody, get a hold of the cartridge belt of the man in front of you." So I got a hold of the colonel's belt. I figured he's going to be the leader, so I'd go with him. We started on over the hill back toward our lines, we thought. The Germans heard us coming, so they threw mortars in on us. They hit quite a few fellas, because I could hear the guys yelling. The colonel said we had to charge, and go out across a different route, which we did.

We had to cross the Our River, so we started wading across. It came almost up to my chin. I was so thirsty that I took my helmet off to take a drink out of the river. When I took the drink out of my helmet, my rifle slipped off my shoulder and went to the bottom of the creek, but I had no ammunition so it wouldn't have made any difference. On the other side of the river we came to a big, open field. The artillery had set a big barn on fire and it lit up the whole countryside. The colonel said to break up in little groups of three or four and go all directions, so they wouldn't get us all. Another fella and I stayed with the colonel.

We started out across the field and the tracer bullets started going over our heads. You got so used to tracer bullets going over your head that you figured one would never get you, but pretty soon I spun around and hit the ground. I thought somebody chopped my leg off. I started moaning, so the colonel told me to keep quiet, that they would know they hit us, and they would really lay it in. I told him I was hit. He said, "Where?" "My leg." He pulled my boot off and he said, "You're just scratched. It isn't even bleeding." So I thought maybe I was scared more than anything. He said, "Let's get the hell out of here." I got up, and the first step I took, the bones went by each other, because I had a compound fracture, and I went down again. I told them to go on. I said I'd get out the next day somehow. "No," he said. "We're going to take you along." So I put an arm around each one of the fellas' shoulders and hopped on one leg for maybe a mile. We went a pretty long way.

Then we came to a road and the colonel said, "We're going to flag down one of our vehicles if it comes." We heard a truck coming up the road, and he said, "Here comes one." I said, "Don't flag him down, that's a German." The lines were all mixed up and everybody was using the same road. So we let him go by. Next, we heard a jeep coming, so we flagged the jeep down. The three of us got on the back of the jeep and he took off across the fields with us.

We got back to the aid station and the guys came out with a stretcher. They gave me a shot of morphine, and as soon as I got that morphine, boy, I thought I was in heaven. The pain stopped and everything. They packed my leg with sulfa powder or something and put me on the ambulance with about ten other guys and we headed back to a railroad siding where there was a big long train with a lot of cars on it. It was loaded with wounded fellas. We ended up in Paris where they operated on my leg. I was there for four or five days and they shipped me over to England on a hospital ship. I don't know how long I was in the hospital there.

One day, during the Battle of the Bulge, they were looking for replacements. They needed a lot of men there. When the generals went down through the beds, picking out the ones to send back, they hung a tag on everyone who was available, but when they got to my bed I had a cast on my leg up to my hip, so they hung a red tag on me to come back to the states. After a month or two I was put on a hospital ship and taken back to the Halloran General Hospital in New York. Then they shipped us down to Fort Dix, New Jersey, where I stayed until I was healed up. I was in the hospital almost a year.

Then for rehabilitation they sent me to Camp Pickett, Virginia. I was there until they figured I was ready to get out of the service. They shipped me back to Fort Dix, and that's where I got discharged. That ended my Army career.

In the Army I learned discipline, and I learned that everybody had to work together to live. There's an old saying, "Love many, hate few, always paddle your own canoe." It was a great experience. If you lived through it, it was something that really taught you the lessons of life. You're here not by your own permission, but by somebody else who's looking over you.

AFTER THE WAR . . .

After his term in the service, Graydon Woods took a job with Mack Trucks, where he worked for thirty-five years before retiring. He and his wife were married for fifty-eight years before she passed away. Together they had a son and a daughter and celebrated seven granddaughters.

☆ Ezekiel Dorsey ☆
Pittsburgh, Pennsylvania

• •

Ezekiel Dorsey enlisted in the Army Air Corps
following the bombing of Pearl Harbor. He was thirty-six
years old. His overseas service was spent repairing radio
transmitters in India, Pakistan, and Ceylon.

• •

I was born in 1905. I went to school in Pittsburgh and got interested in amateur radio. Radio was more or less in its infancy. When I was a Boy Scout, twelve or thirteen years old, I was building radios. Later I got interested in automobiles and bought a 1923 Chevrolet. It was my first car. I learned how to repair it, and used to work on it out front of the house. When I grew up and graduated from Duquesne University I went to work for Westinghouse. Then I got a garage on Fifth Avenue, at the head of Oakland Avenue. I ran that garage for a while, and then the Depression came along in 1929 and I couldn't get enough business to keep going. So I went to work for an automobile company, and I stayed in the automobile business for quite a number of years.

I got to flying airplanes about 1929. I couldn't afford to take flying lessons, so I worked on an airplane as a mechanic; instead of the guys that owned the airplane paying me for it, they'd let me fly their airplane. That was the beginning of my air career

I had my own auto garage business on Bigelow Boulevard at the Bloomfield Bridge. It was quite a large business. I had three or four fellows working for me. When December 7 came, and war with the Japanese, the first thing you know, the draft board called me up and said, "You have to get a job in an essential industry. Or you can enlist, or we're going to draft you—one of the three." I was thirty-six years old then. So I went down and saw a captain at the Army recruiting station and said, "I think I want to enlist." He said, "What qualifications do you have?" I said, "Well first, I'm an airplane motor mechanic and I've got a pilot's license. I'm an amateur radio operator; I can send and receive at least thirty-five words a minute." He said, "You report here Monday morning at seven o'clock."

I went back and told the fellows working for me "I'm closing the place up and enlisting in the Army." So these fellows went and found jobs other places. I went down to the recruiting station at seven o'clock Monday morning and they put me on a train to Fort Meade, Maryland.

The first week I was in the Army I didn't do anything except take tests for different things. They gave me tests on radio equipment, on motors, and other things. They had an opening in an essential business, which was repairing carburetors, but they didn't give me a job in the automobile business. They decided that maybe they'd be better putting me into radio. This one radio operator came over early in the morning, and he said, "Are you Zeke Dorsey?" and I said, "Yes." He said, "Get up and get your breakfast. We're going to the airport and put you on an airplane." They flew me out to the West Coast to Pittsburg, California. So I went from Pittsburgh, Pennsylvania, to Pittsburg, California.

I was called one morning to the company headquarters to see the captain. At this point I had been in the Army for three or four weeks and had not taken any basic training. The captain pulled a folder out of a bunch of cabinets they had there and said, "Look at this man's qualifications. This man's got skills we need overseas! He's a celestial navigator, he's an airplane pilot, he's an amateur radio operator, he's an expert carburetor man, and we could use him in the motor pool."

So I was shipped to San Francisco and put on a boat with 750 other soldiers. It was a very small ship, and each man had about three square feet of deck surface. Forty-five days later we pulled into Melbourne on the east coast of Australia. We spent a day there, gassed the ship up, and went out to sea again, and six or eight days later we were going up the Hugli River. That's a little river going from the southern waters up to Calcutta, India. We were in Calcutta for a couple of days, gassed up, went back down the Hugli River again, and out to sea again. In another ten or twelve days we landed in Bombay, India.

The next day they put us on a train New Delhi. They had a captain there, and he was a ham-radio operator, and I got to talking to him. "I service automobile radios, and I've built my own transmitter." And he said, "We can use some transmitters if we could get somebody to build them." He had a bunch of radio gear there, and I rooted through it and found enough stuff to build a transmitter, and I built one that worked up to about one hundred miles away. They had a lieutenant there who said, "I want you to go up to Baluchistan." Now they call it "Pakistan." He sent me there in a C-46, which we used to call "Hitler's secret weapon." It burned so much oil, it was making blue smoke all the time, and it looked like skywriting. We got to Baluchistan and they had a big transmitter that was not working that I had to fix.

While I was there one day, I was loafing, just killing time, waiting for a job to come up, and a guy came over to me and said, "They want you out at the DF [Direction Finding] station. They got a plane that's running low on gas, and he doesn't know where he is, and he wants you to get out there." So I went over there and the guy in the plane called in. I said, "Give me a count of ten and I'll give you a heading." So he gave me a count of ten and I saw his little blip on the screen, but it showed me that he was going away from the airport. I called the guy back and said, "You're on the range, all right. Take up a heading of 143 and then give me another call." He said, "Will do!" I saw him turn around, and I said, "Now you're headed toward the airport. Give me another count of ten, and I'll give you an exact heading." I said. "Take up a heading of 170 and you should be able to see the airport. What are you flying?" He said, "A C-47." I said, "Okay. You ought to see the runway. It's two miles long. I'll have the airport send out the fire trucks just in case, but you should be able to make it in." He said, "I see the airport now. What a beautiful sight! I'm so low on gas, my gauge doesn't even show. It's sitting on the bottom of the tank." I said, "You ought to be at the airport in two minutes. If you got enough gas to keep that motor running for two minutes, you got it made." So he saw the airport, he came in and landed, and as he landed he dropped the tail down to flare out and the motor quit. By that time, he had the front wheels on the tarmac. So he let her coast to a stop and they towed it off the runway. He went back to the tower and said, "I want to see the guy that brought me in. He did one hell of a job. It's a goddamn good thing we got men like that in the service, because I was really lost. I was gone." So I went up to the tower and this captain walked over to me and said, "Shake the hand that helped me consummate my marriage to Betty Grable." I said, "Holy mackerel! You're Jackie Coogan!" He said, "Yep, I'm Jackie Coogan. You got me in just in the nick of time." So that was one of the highlights of all the days I spent in the Army.

After that I was shifted over to the Pacific, to Ceylon—it's now Sri Lanka. When I got there, for about a mile out to sea there were nothing but ships. That's when they dropped the bombs on Hiroshima and Nagasaki that ended the war. Two days later they put me on a little Kaiser ship and sent me back to San Francisco, and then to Fort Dix. I was supposed to be discharged right away, but they had lost all my service records, so I was in the Army another month. They discharged me from Fort Dix and I got out of the service.

AFTER THE WAR . . .

Ezekiel Dorsey returned to Pittsburgh and reopened his auto repair business. He married Hilda Rosser in 1946, and their marriage lasted fifty-three years until her death in 2000. Mr. Dorsey owned his business until 1969, when his son and grandson took it over. He continued to work there, however, until he was eighty-seven.

☆ Luther Smith ☆

Villanova, Pennsylvania

••

Luther Smith received his aviation training in Tuskegee,
Alabama, and was one of the country's earliest African
American pilots, earning his wings in May 1943. He was
assigned to the 332nd Fighter Group in the 15th Air Force
in Italy. His plane crashed on what was to be his last
scheduled mission, and he became a POW.

••

I was fascinated by aviation as a result of Charles Lindbergh's solo flight
from New York City to Paris, France, in May of 1927. I was only seven
years of age, but that incident by Charles Lindbergh fascinated me like nothing else in my young age, and I wanted to be like Lucky Lindy. Between
then and the time I was thirteen I just thought about aviation.

At age thirteen, my younger brother and I walked five miles to the municipal airport of Des Moines, Iowa, which was my home, just to be up close to
airplanes, to see what they looked like on the ground. We had never seen airplanes except in the skies. Seeing them up close, I was fascinated by these
vehicles that could roll along the ground but also could fly in the air. The
operators at the Des Moines Municipal Airport asked me if I would be inter-

ested in having a job at the airport at age thirteen and I said, "Yes." I didn't know what I could do, but they said, "You could pick up the popcorn bags and the trash thrown on the ground from the people coming out to look at the airplanes." So they hired me and I did that for two or three weeks, but then the operators of the airplanes in the hangar asked me if I would like to assist the mechanics working on the airplanes. I thought I was in heaven. So in 1934, I began to work as a mechanic's helper at the Des Moines Municipal Airport. In fact, the local newspaper, the *Des Moines Register*, did a feature story about me, and they entitled the article "America's Youngest Grease Ball."

In 1935, when I was fourteen, the airmail pilots flew into Des Moines carrying the airmail, and they would have to have their airplanes serviced. I was helping the mechanics service the airplanes and became acquainted with a number of the airmail pilots. They were young military aviators and they had to fly in rain, storms, night; no matter what the weather was, the mail had to go through. This was a very dangerous occupation, and many of these young men were killed. But they were my heroes, and I grew up as a teenager wanting to be one of them. Unfortunately, there were no black military aviators at that point in time, in the 1930s, so that was a secret on my part, my ambition to one day be qualified so that if ever the opportunity came, I could become a military aviator.

I went away to college and studied engineering, just to get a little more technical background about aviation. Then in 1942 I was accepted in military aviation training, and that was the beginning of my military career. In 1941 there were no black Americans in military aviation service. But they decided that they would have black Americans functioning in military aviation on a separate but equal basis, so a facility was established at Tuskegee, Alabama, where the weather was warm almost year-round, for the training and the development of at least one military aviation unit. That was where black Americans were going to be trained and activated into a military fighter squadron. And that's when the 99th was formed, and the 332nd Fighter Group, and eventually a second group, a medium bomber group, the 477th. I trained there in 1942 and 1943 and received my wings in May of 1943.

The training was exactly like military aviation training for white personnel, except that it was all black. We wore the same uniforms, flew the same types of aircraft. The significant thing about our training at Tuskegee was that the commanding officer of the base was a white colonel who was dedicated to making sure that these young black American military cadets were going to be given an opportunity to be trained as military aviators. And although there was racial segregation all over the South and all around the base, on the base it was almost like an oasis in the middle of a sandy desert of segregation. Everybody was treated as equal on the base. It made us feel as if we were being trained for something very important, and our motivation was high to take advantage of that opportunity.

During training you've got to do everything right or you're going to be washed out; just staying on the ball, accomplishing each task the way it had to be done. And the way it had to be done was so exacting that the pressure was enormous. And the washout rate was tremendous. When I entered Tuskegee in September 1942, there were one hundred in my class. In May of 1943, when we graduated, there were only twenty in the class.

Then the first all-black squadron, the 99th Fighter Squadron, stayed at the training base in Tuskegee and just flew training operations for a full year before they were assigned to an operation overseas in North Africa. I was in the group that was separated from the 99th. We were still in training at a base in Selfridge Field just outside Detroit, Michigan. Benjamin O. Davis, who was the squadron leader of the 99th, returned from North Africa to take command of the 332nd Fighter Group, and we went overseas in January of 1944.

We were assigned to Italy, flying harbor patrol over Naples and the sea lanes between Naples and the Anzio beachhead, just southwest of Rome, which was being heavily protected by German forces at that point in time in the spring of 1944. Our job was not very significant as far as warfare was concerned. We were flying inferior airplanes and really weren't doing that much, but Davis was a very competent military aviator. He was a West Point graduate, and another West Point graduate by the name of Nathan Twining was the commanding general of the 15th Strategic Air Force stationed in Italy. He was aware of Davis and his experience, and he decided that he was going to interview Davis about having us become an escort fighter group in the 15th Air Force. That was the highest function of a fighter operation in military service, escorting strategic bombers with targets all over Europe and carrying out strategic bombing. Twining asked Davis if he felt that his boys, these young black airmen, could carry on that kind of a function. Davis said, "Absolutely." So the 332nd Fighter Group was reassigned to the 15th Strategic Air Force to escort heavy strategic bombers, with targets all over Europe, to reduce Germany's ability to wage war. Davis told us this was perhaps the most responsible function we'd ever seen in our lives. Our job was not to shoot down as many airplanes as we could, but to make sure that the bombing missions were successful and the bombers were protected. And when the war was over, the 332nd Fighter Group had escorted the heavy strategic bombers of the 15th Air Force two hundred times, all over Europe, without the loss of a single bomber to enemy aircraft, and that was a record that was unprecedented in the history of military aviation up to that point.

On my first mission I was assigned the responsibility of being what they call the "Tail-end Charlie." I was the last plane in the formation. I felt I was the most vulnerable aircraft in the formations because enemy aircraft can fly up on the last plane and shoot it out of the sky and the rest of the fellows in the formation wouldn't even know I was gone. But I was a pretty good pilot, so they gave me that responsibility, and I was very nervous about it. I didn't see any enemy aircraft, but that was my first mission, and I thought it was the longest mission I flew throughout my combat experience.

The first time I encountered an enemy aircraft in combat was in the summer of 1944. I'd been in combat for several months, so I was a somewhat experienced fighter pilot, but on this particular mission, going into southern France, enemy aircraft were approaching the group of bombers we were escorting and I was assigned to intercept the oncoming German aircraft. I thought if I just showed them the configuration of my airplane, they would see that I was flying a P-51 Mustang, which the Germans particularly feared because we were flying superior aircraft. But that didn't deter the Germans; they still were bent on shooting down some of our bombers. So I was able to get behind the German fighters, and my airplane was faster than theirs, so I was able to fly up on one, get behind him, and I was able to shoot him down.

Because of my inexperience in actually attacking an enemy aircraft with an airplane, I was really intent on shooting this airplane out of the sky. My biggest fear was that this enemy aircraft was going to call on the radio that he was being chased, and then pull me over his airfield where they had gun emplacements that were going to take me out. So I was trying to shoot him down before that could happen. Because of the superior speed of my aircraft, as I was pulling in behind him to get close enough to shoot him out of the sky, I began to overfly him, and I was afraid that I would be in front of him and he'd be on my tail. So I pulled the airplane over to the side, just to make sure I slowed it down, keeping him from getting behind me, and I looked into the cockpit of the airplane. I was right at the same level and very close to him, and the pilot in the German aircraft did not have an oxygen mask. I could see his face, and I was shocked to see it was just a youth in that airplane, because I could see his full face in the cockpit. My reaction was, "You can't shoot down a kid. This is not an enemy, this is just a kid." But my

Tuskegee Airmen

The American military of 1940 was no more integrated than the rest of the U.S. population. President Franklin D. Roosevelt was well aware of the agitation for equal rights, a movement with its origins in the formation of the black sleeping-car porters' union by organizer and national civil-rights leader A. Philip Randolph (1889–1979). Yet Roosevelt resisted calls to desegregate the military or to endorse fair employment policies that would open jobs in the burgeoning defense industry, which almost universally barred blacks.

A half-million blacks were unemployed, and yet they displayed patriotism by enlisting in numbers far above their proportion of the population. Blacks could not enlist in the Army Air Corps or the Marine Corps. Moreover, Gen. George C. Marshall, the Army chief of staff, opposed desegregation of the Army on the grounds that it would destroy morale. Secretary of War Henry Stimson believed that blacks "lacked the brains and bravery for flying." In the ranks, black soldiers and sailors were limited to labor and support units, and segregated ones at that.

Randolph conceived the idea of a march on Washington to demonstrate for fair treatment of blacks in the military and defense industries. In March 1941, he called for 10,000 blacks to peacefully gather at the Lincoln Memorial on July 1. He soon raised that number to 100,000 marchers, grabbing Roosevelt's attention. After a week of negotiation with Randolph, FDR signed Executive Order 8802, banishing discrimination in defense work and government employment, though not in the military. Randolph canceled the march just six days before it was to occur.

It was against this backdrop that the Army Air Force in March 1941 started an experimental program to train black military aviators. The training took place at Tuskegee Institute in Tuskegee, Alabama, a black college that was founded in 1881 by Booker T. Washington. Graduates would join the USAAF's 99th Pursuit (later Fighter) Squadron, formed as an all-black unit. Cadets entered preliminary training in the

Tuskegee Airmen. NATIONAL ARCHIVES

school's Division of Aeronautics. Further training and a transition to military aircraft took place at Tuskegee Army Air Field. Capt. Benjamin O. Davis, a West Point graduate and one of only two black line officers in the Army, was chosen to be the unit's leader. The first group of five fighter pilots graduated on March 7, 1942. A year later, with more personnel, the squadron transferred to North Africa and, flying P-40 Warhawks, saw combat for the first time over Italy on June 2.

Overseen by Davis, now promoted to colonel, a reorganization brought the 99th into the 332nd Fighter Group, an all-black group of four squadrons. Piloting P-47 Thunderbolts and P-51 Mustangs (whose tails they painted bright red), the group flew 179 bomber escort missions from June 1944 to the end of World War II. By that time, the airmen had carried out 15,000 combat sorties, shot down

(continued on page 146)

(continued from page 145)

111 German airplanes, destroyed nearly 1,000 ground targets, and sank a destroyer. White pilots were prohibited from flying more than fifty-two combat missions, but Tuskegee pilots, due to a lack of replacements, often flew as many as one hundred missions. In all, they earned 150 Distinguished Flying Crosses, 744 Air Medals, 8 Purple Hearts, and 14 Bronze Stars. Combat losses were sixty-six pilots killed and thirty-two downed or captured as POWs. Perhaps most remarkable of all, no bomber they escorted was lost to enemy attack, a fact that led to a nickname tagged onto them by white American pilots: Red–Tail Angels. German pilots called them *Schwartze Vogelmenschen* (black bird men).

From 1941 through 1946, Tuskegee graduated 994 pilots and sent 450 of them overseas. Other skills taught at military bases elsewhere produced black navigators, bombardiers, gunnery crews, and initially, maintenance crews until the latter was transferred to Tuskegee in 1942. The experiment was deemed a success—blacks had proven themselves equal to whites in the most demanding of combat conditions, yet the U.S. military remained segregated. After the war, some undermanned white units were unable to rise to full strength because of the policy, although many qualified and experienced blacks were available. Seeing such inefficiency, as well as the moral issue, President Harry S. Truman issued Executive Order 9981 on July 26, 1948, banning discrimination in the armed services. The USAAF was split off as a new, separate service, the U.S. Air Force, which, with the Navy, became a leader among the services in erasing the color bar. An all-black Air Force base at Lockbourne, Ohio, was closed and its troops dispersed to bases around the world. ★

duty was to shoot that airplane out of the sky, and I was anxious to get the airplane and get out of there because I was afraid I'd be shot out of the sky myself. That was my first experience shooting an airplane out of the sky.

One time I was on a very long mission. Our job was to escort the bombers from Blechhammer, which was in southeast Germany, back from the target to what we call the bomb line, where it was safe for them to fly back to the base in Italy on their own. It was late in the war and we didn't see any enemy aircraft, so we were given opportunities to take on German targets. When we got the bombers back to the bomb line we could then pick up targets—airfields—and strafe them, which we did. The airfield we were assigned to strafe was in Budapest, Hungary, and it was filled with airplanes and gliders. At that point of the war, in October 1944, Germany was being defeated, and because we had bombed many of their refinery fields they were low on fuel. So the airplanes were sitting on the ground, and unless they were going to fly, they didn't put fuel in them. So the airplanes had empty fuel tanks, and when we strafed them, we couldn't tell if they were going to blow up or burn because they didn't have fuel on board. I happened to see two German bombers sitting side by side, but they were under high-voltage electric power lines. I thought the guys in my flight were avoiding them because of the proximity to these high-voltage lines, but I was pretty sure that these two bombers had fuel in them, and they did. The first bomber blew up when I strafed it, and I was trying to get the second one on the same pass. I got strikes in it, but it didn't blow up. I was afraid it would be a mistake to come back to the same target, because somebody would know an airplane was going to come back and they'd try to shoot it down. When I did come back, I was able to destroy the second aircraft. But as I was pulling away from the aircraft I decided I'd better fly as close to the ground as I possibly could, because if there was a gun emplacement there I'd be a perfect target right beside these two burning aircraft. Sure enough, there was a gun emplacement somewhere on the field. I was so close to the ground, I was watching the turbulence in the grass from my wing. Because I was so low I couldn't use my instruments. I was only a few feet off the ground and the tracer bullets from the gun emplacement on the ground were just under my wing. I was turning inside, trying to turn into the field, which was full of smoke and burning debris, so the gunman couldn't see me. And that was how I was able to escape that particular incident.

When I joined up with the rest of my flight, the flight leader decided to go down and strafe a railyard not very far from Budapest. But I was so visibly shaken by my narrow escape I decided to stay up and circle and patrol over them and let the flight leader and his wingmen go down to strafe, and they strafed for several passes on the freight yard. When they finished their strafing, I wanted to go home because I knew I was running low on fuel. But then my wingman decided to go down and strafe the same railyard. When he went down to strafe I had to go to protect him, because he was my responsibility. So I followed him down. Well, I decided that I was also going to make a pass on those freight cars. This was to be my last scheduled mission. I was ready to go home. So I said, "This is the way to end up," and I strafed the same freight yard. Unfortunately, I got halfway down the line of cars, shooting at them, and a huge explosion took place, and I had to fly through it. The explosion buckled the wings of my aircraft, tore off part of the tail, blew out the windows in my cockpit, blackened the windshield, and pretty badly damaged my engine. It punctured the coolant system, and I lost the engine coolant. When the coolant ran out and was gone the airplane caught on fire, and I had to parachute out.

In those days, they did not have ejection seats in the cockpits. The procedure was simply to turn the airplane on its back, jettison the canopy, fall free, and open the parachute after you're away from the airplane. I had never done anything like that before. I was afraid if I left my seat belt fastened and turned the airplane upside down, my seat belt would hold me in the airplane. So I decided I would unbuckle my safety belt before I turned the airplane upside down. Then when I turn the airplane upside down, I'd fall free of the airplane. Unfortunately, the airplane was badly damaged in the explosion, so as I began to turn the airplane upside down, because my seat belt was unfastened, I fell partway out of the seat of the airplane. Because the airplane was flying so slowly as a result of being damaged, the airplane fell into a tailspin. I knew I couldn't get out of the airplane, so I tried to climb back into the cockpit. But I was halfway out of the cockpit because I'd unbuckled my safety belt. I tried to right the airplane to get it out of the spin, but I couldn't get back in the cockpit. I was hanging partway out of it, couldn't get back in, and then couldn't get out because of the centrifugal force of the tailspin. And I thought, "You're not going to make it." The airplane was on fire in a tailspin, coming down, heading towards the ground, and I said to myself, "So, this is how guys go."

Then my oxygen mask blew off my face, and I went unconscious. While I was unconscious, not known to me, I pulled the rip cord of my parachute, which was in a seat pack, still in the airplane. By the grace of God, the canopy of my parachute got out from underneath me and out of the airplane, and when the canopy blossomed, it pulled me out of the airplane. It fractured my right hip because I was jammed in the airplane, but it pulled me out of the airplane. The airplane kept going right to the ground and crashed, but I was in the parachute and my life was saved. I landed in a tree. The Germans rescued me out of the tree and I became a prisoner of war. That was on Friday the 13th of October, 1944.

I was afraid the Germans were not going to treat me very well. I was badly injured, so their thought was simply to give me medical attention and put me in a hospital. As a prisoner of war I was a very valuable commodity to them, because they wanted to make sure all the prisoners were something they could negotiate with on peace-term conditions when the war was over. So I was actually treated like a VIP while I was a prisoner of war. Being a prisoner, I was treated with civility, but they couldn't give me very good medical attention. I went down to seventy pounds. I had dysentery and bone osteomyelitis, which is bone disease, and I was very close to death. The treatment I received was the best they could provide, which wasn't very good because we were at war, but I'm still alive today.

I came home on a hospital ship. I was in great pain and couldn't hold food down. My stomach had shrunk, so it couldn't hold food. It wasn't a very pleasant experience at all. I was just glad to be back in the States. When the war was over and I was liberated, I was hospitalized for an additional two years. After I was rehabilitated in military hospitals I had to go before a review board. They said I was no longer fit for duty because of the injuries I sustained in parachuting out and breaking my hip. So I was retired from the military.

AFTER THE WAR . . .

After retirement from the military in 1947, Luther Smith returned to the University of Iowa and earned a degree in engineering. He married Lois Gordon and together they raised two children. Mr. Smith went on to work for General Electric Company for thirty-seven years and was granted two patents before retiring in 1988. He has been frequently honored as a Tuskegee Airman and most recently received the Congressional Gold Medal from the United States Congress.

☆ Hugh Foster ☆

Furlong, Pennsylvania

• •

Hugh Foster graduated from West Point in 1941
and was commissioned a second lieutenant in the Signal
Corps. He was involved in five North African and Italian
campaigns, including Monte Cassino and Anzio.

• •

I was a first lieutenant, a twenty-five-year-old West Point graduate stationed in Florida, and one day I was ordered to report to a Captain Jay in the overseas staging area. He said, "Lieutenant Foster, you are now commanding officer of Company E of the 560th Signal Aircraft Warning Battalion." I thought pretty well of myself at that point. I thought I had finally made the grade. And so I started asking some questions. I said, "Sir, where are the other officers?" He said, "There are no other officers assigned." "Where are the enlisted men?" "There are no enlisted men assigned." "Where's the company barracks?" "Barracks have not been allocated yet." "Where's the company equipment?" "Company equipment has not been issued yet." "Well, Captain Jay, if I understand it correctly, I'm commanding Company E, no officers, no men, no barracks, no equipment, just me and my suitcase." And he said, "You got it." I said, "Well, can you tell me anything about my new command?"

And he looked at the chart on his desk, and he said, "Yes, your company is going overseas in ten days. Be ready. Dismissed." People started to come in that day. The soldier assigned to me as my first sergeant had been in the Army for three months. From there things sort of went downhill.

I wound up in Italy in 1944, assigned to the Signal Battalion, which supported Army 2nd Corps, just below Cassino. I was told that this was the ideal level to be at. You're too far forward to have to wear neckties and too far back to get shot. Well, of course, that's not quite true, but it sounded pretty good to me. I had several instances which were close calls for me. I was up at the Anzio Beachhead for ten days and was assigned to a small room in the palace of the Prince Borghese, which had been taken over by the Army for a headquarters building. On my first night there was a German air raid, and I heard a loud thump right outside my window. Nothing else. In the morning when I got up and looked out the window, I could see the tailfins of a five-hundred-pound bomb. A dud, right outside my window. So I thanked the good Lord for that.

On another occasion I had to go out and make a reconnaissance to see where we could run our communications cables. I came up to a small village on the Arno River. I couldn't go straight ahead because straight ahead was a bridge that had been blown. I couldn't go right because the street was blocked with blown-down buildings. The street to the left was open. So I told the driver to turn left and we started down there at a fairly slow pace. I passed a high brick wall with a gate in it and an American soldier was standing guard at the gate. As we went by he called me, so we stopped and backed up. He said, "Where are you going?" I told him what I was doing, and he pointed down the road. "You see that gas station down there?" Down about one hundred yards was a gas station. He said, "Ain't nobody made it past there yet. I would suggest you try some other way."

Another time, the corps headquarters was going to set up in a park in Florence, Italy. The park was about two blocks wide by about ten blocks long along the bank of the Arno River. It was heavily forested with lots of underbrush and a few roads, bridle paths, and walking paths. That's where they were going to set up. My job required me to go in there and identify where the message tent was going to be, where the teletype equipment was going to be placed, where the telephone switchboard was going to go, and so on. I went in there in a jeep and checked out the area to see what the road network was. I got out of the jeep and began walking through the bushes, nailing up signs on the trees to identify where our various elements would go. I was doing that for about two hours, got back in the jeep and drove back out of the park. The next day, we received word that the corps was not going to go there. We had been outranked. Army headquarters was going to go in there. So I had to go back and collect all my signs. That same day that I collected the signs the Signal Troops from Army headquarters went into that park and lost six men killed and fourteen wounded in about three hours, walking through those same bushes that I had walked through without any harm.

The place I picked for my company to go then was a private estate out in the country a bit. I laid out the company area and picked a spot for the kitchen and the mess hall. Behind the mess hall was a descending gully with a footpath on it. I walked down that footpath about two hundred yards just to be sure that we hadn't parked on the edge of a German establishment or something of the sort, but it looked all right. So I turned around and came back. Later that day, one of the cooks went down that same path to relieve himself and he stepped in a bush, hit a booby trap, lost a kidney and had to be evacuated back to the States. So that was another close call for me.

As we approached Florence, I was looking for a good place to park my company to bivouac. We approached the airfield, and they had a lot of undamaged buildings in there. I thought that would be great to get my troops indoors for a change, out of the rain. So we drove up to the entrance gate; it had huge ornamental wrought-iron gates with a chain around them and a padlock on it. Well, the padlock wasn't going to stop me. I pulled out my .45, and was about ready to shoot the padlock off, and some inner sense told me, "This is just too good for your little old company, you move in here now and in three days somebody else will come along and outrank you, and you'll have to leave, and by that time, all the other good places are gone." So I put the .45 back in the holster, got back in the jeep, and looked elsewhere.

The next day, a hospital unit tried to move into that area. They wanted the buildings for hospital wards. They broke the lock off the gate and drove through. The first vehicle went about one hundred feet and hit a mine. They lost eighteen or twenty people killed and thirty or forty wounded because the area was heavily mined. They had to back off and wait for the engineers to come in and clean out the mines. So that was another close call. So this remark about being too far forward to have to wear neckties and too far back to get shot was beginning to ring a little bit hollow in my mind.

On another occasion, I was looking for a good building to put my motor section in, because the mechanics had a terrible time working, having to crawl under trucks in the mud. If I could find a good building for them to work in, they deserved it. Near the place we decided to bivouac there was an old barn that somehow had escaped any damage. The roof was still good. It had a clean, concrete floor, and I thought it was a perfect place for the motor pool. The only problem was, in the middle of the floor there was a stack of wooden crates. The stack was about fifteen feet square and about six feet high, and in each crate was a German antitank mine of a kind I'd never seen before. So I told all the others to get out of there, get away from the building, and I went over and studied the situation for a while. I picked up one of these mines and carefully carried it outside, away from the building, and set it on the ground. I moved five or six mines like that, and nothing happened. So then I sent the troops in to move the rest of them and cautioned them to be very careful. Two days later I received a War Department bulletin announcing the arrival of those new mines, which were very unstable. Sometimes they'd go off for no particular reason. The bulletin cautioned the troops, "Don't ever touch them or move them under any circumstances."

Our primary responsibility was to set up five radar sites along the coast of northwest Africa, spread over 1,100 miles from the two extremities. One was at Cape Bon in Tunisia and the other one was at Casablanca. That's about 1,100 miles by air miles, but the road miles are totally different. We had no vehicles of our own when we arrived, so we had to borrow trucks from the other companies in the battalion at night when they were not using them. Then we'd go down to the docks and read the shipping numbers on all the items that came in. Our shipping number was 184—1829–L. Anything that was marked with that was going to us. We'd load it on the truck, and take it back out to our area and then sort it out.

We had 1,320 separate pieces shipped to us, and they landed at different ports all along the coast of North Africa. They would be marked as to which radar set they belonged to so we could sort them out. To move one radar set took four Air Corps fifty-foot flatbed trailers and ten two-ton trucks. That's just the radar set and the tower and the buildings. It did not include the company impedimenta; tents and so on. We always reconnoitered the road ahead of time to be sure that we had adequate clearance under the underpasses. One of the drivers did not go through the clearance bar I had established, and on his load, a piece of radar equipment was sticking up a little too high. He hit the underpass at sixty miles an hour and swept everything off the back end of the trailer. That put a crimp in our getting that radar set operational.

We did have some humorous events. We used pigeons in World War II. The pigeon would have a little aluminum tube clamped to its leg about the size of a pencil. We had a standard message book which had some tissue paper in the back. You could write a message on the tissue paper and roll it up real small, put it in that tube, and put the cap on the tube. If you turned the pigeon loose he would fly back to his home nest. That was the theory. Late in World War II, in the fall of 1944, the Germans were still in the Po Valley, which was a major valley in northern Italy, and the Apennine Mountains formed the southern edge of it. The Army wanted to know the traffic pattern of the Germans in the Po Valley; how many trucks were going in which direction. So they sent a four-man patrol up to a lookout up on top of one of those mountains. It took them four hours to climb up there. They handed them the pigeons and told them to report every eight hours or so how many trucks moved in each direction. So the four infantrymen climbed up there, got settled, started keeping records, wrote messages, put it in the tube on the pigeon's leg, and put the pigeon back in the box. When both pigeons had messages, one of them took the box with the pigeons in it, climbed all the way down the mountain for four hours to the road, went out to the side of the road, flagged down a truck and handed the box to the driver and said, "Deliver this to corps headquarters." Not quite the way it was intended.

Well, I had several close calls, as I've indicated. I was very fortunate. It was educational. And it was a professional challenge. I learned a lot. I guess what else could I say? I came out with a whole skin.

AFTER THE WAR . . .

Hugh Foster served thirty-four years active duty in the Army, rising to the rank of major general. He married Mary Jane Schneider in July 1946, and together they had three sons. General Foster taught at both the U.S. Military and Naval academies, served on the Army general staff in the Pentagon, was the Chief Signal Officer for all U.S. forces in Korea, and commanded the Army's 1st Signal Brigade in Vietnam. Following his retirement from the service, General Foster was a frequent speaker for local groups in his area and was a consultant for the National Parks Service project to restore an Army ambulance train. He passed away in 2004.

☆ John Kepchia ☆
Greensburg, Pennsylvania

....

John Kepchia was a gunner on a Navy TBF Avenger
torpedo bomber in Bougainville in the Solomon Islands
at age nineteen. His plane was shot down over Rabaul
and he was taken prisoner. He describes his ordeal
as a POW held by the Japanese.

....

I was seventeen years old, working in a grocery store as a delivery boy, when I enlisted on September 7, 1942. I went to Norfolk, Virginia, for boot camp, and then the Navy sent me to Alabama to the Auburn Polytechnic Institute. After graduating from there I was sent to Aviation Radio School at Millington, Tennessee. After completing that I went to Hollywood, Florida, for gunnery school. By that time I was an Aviation Radioman, 2nd Class. After completing our gunnery practice we went to Fort Lauderdale. That was my first time getting into an airplane.

They would tow a target in what they called a sleeve, and we would be on the .50-caliber machine guns on the beach at Fort Lauderdale, and we would fire at them. One of the fellows firing happened to hit the tail of the airplane, and the pilot was so frustrated he released the target and flew back to the base. He said that was the end of him towing a sleeve for us. We were flying a TBF Avenger with three crewmen; a pilot, a third gunner, and the radioman. The radioman also acted as a stinger gunner, using a .30-caliber machine gun under the tail. The pilots picked their crew, and Ensign Atkiss picked Dick Lanigan and me for his crew members; Lanigan was the turret gunner and I was the radioman.

One time we were out about seven miles on our flight training when the engine in our TBF Avenger caught fire and we were in a ball of smoke and flame. We were dive-bombing on a tow target that was towed by a ship, and the pilot Ensign Atkiss—we called him Doo-Doo—he said, "Kep, you and Lanigan want to bail out?" I said, "Heck no, there are sharks down there." I said, "Come on, fly it back." So we landed. When we were coming into Fort Lauderdale, you looked down at the runway and you could see all these people down there dressed in white clothes. They were nurses and doctors and medical people and an ambulance waiting for us. But we landed all right and they put the fire out.

From Fort Lauderdale we went to Wildwood, New Jersey, and joined a squadron that was called VC52. We had torpedo planes, SBD dive bombers, and F4U fighter planes. After we practiced for some time they took the fighters and SBDs away from us, and they called us Torpedo Squadron VT305. At that time I was called to go on a night flight; I wasn't supposed to go on her, but this executive officer said that his radioman was sick. I had my white uniform on; I put coveralls on, white scarf, a jacket, and a helmet, and crawled in the plane. There were seven TBFs that took off on that night flight from Wildwood, flying along the ocean. After a long time four planes left us and the other three planes, we just kept circling around. I asked our pilot if he was lost. He was kind of furious. He said, "You mind your own business." So, here he would change the frequency on the receiver and we could never receive the tower, and every time I would change it to the tower frequency, he'd get mad and change it back. I heard one tank go dry, the engine sputtered a little bit and he switched tanks. We flew for some time and the other tank went dry. By the time he switched tanks we were down pretty low. So I finally told him, "Mr. Bigwood, if you fly up to 1,500 feet, make a flat turn, I'll pick the coast up by radar." He finally flew up to about 2,000 feet and I picked the coast up. We were at a one hundred-mile range from Wildwood and if we'd have strayed maybe another few miles, we would have been in the Bermuda Triangle. That's how that happens you know; pilot error. We landed at an Army P-47 field in Millville, New Jersey and we didn't have enough gas to taxi to the line; we were out of gas.

From Wildwood, we went to Hyannis, Massachusetts, and had a dive-bombing squadron with us. They lost a few planes up at Hyannis and at Martha's Vineyard. It was really bad weather up there, cold weather. From there we flew to San Diego and practiced dive-bombing and glide-bombing with rockets. We were one of the first planes equipped with rockets. After a bit of time at San Diego we got on the USS *Kadashan Bay*. It was a jeep carrier and they had all of our planes in mothballs. We had about 3,000 Marines on board the ship and we went to New Hebrides. We traveled alone with no escort. We could see ships burning on the horizon, and we were really frightened. We were so frightened that we slept on the flight deck; we wouldn't go down to our bunks.

From New Hebrides we went up to Bougainville in the Solomon Islands, about 250 miles from New Hebrides and about the same distance from Guadalcanal. While we were flying up there we had a lot of equipment stashed in my radio compartment on top of my stinger gun. When we were flying into Bougainville we were up about 1,500 feet, and as we approached it, that's the first time we were under fire. Man, the Japs let loose on us. We scattered. I was worried I couldn't get my gun going because of all the equipment on it. We finally landed on Bougainville. We had to bomb Bougainville itself, because the Japs had us surrounded. We had three airstrips and we could only use two of them. The Japs were up in the hills. They could see whatever we were doing and they would shell us. As soon as they would shell us we'd jump in our TBFs and run up there and bomb them. They'd pull their guns back into the caves and we'd go back down. There was nothing but marshland there, so you could never find out what they were doing. They were pretty good at that.

I was shot down on my thirty-fourth mission; it was supposed to be my last mission, up to Rabaul. There must have been a hundred planes that joined up there. We had Army, Navy, Marines, bombers, and fighters. We'd get up about 12,000 feet and go into a glide-bombing dive. When we pulled out of the dive we were down to about 1,000 feet, and when we pulled out we always tried to get as low as we could to the ground, because at that time our speed was about three hundred miles an hour, and coming out of the dive we thought that if we hugged the ground and the trees, they'd have less chance of shooting at us.

On that mission we were firing like mad and all at once we got hit in the engine. I was riding backwards under the tail, firing my .30-caliber machine gun. I had my head bent down and a shell fragment came right through the

TBF Avengers

Built to replace the U.S. Navy's obsolete Douglas Aircraft Devastator torpedo-bomber of 1935, the Grumman Aircraft-designed single-engine Avenger became the Navy's premier torpedo-fighter-bomber plane during World War II. Between 1942 and 1944, Grumman produced 2,290 Avengers (the TBF model) and General Motors Corporation's Eastern Aircraft Division built 7,546 more (the TBM model), for a total of 9,836 planes. In the nomenclature, TB stood for torpedo-bomber, and F was the military designation for Grumman and M was the designation for GM.

Crewed by a pilot, gunner, and radar operator, the Avenger was a sturdy aircraft measuring forty feet long with a wingspan of fifty-four feet. Powered by a 1,900-horsepower engine, it reached a top speed of 271 mph and had an altitude ceiling of 22,400 feet and a range of 1,200 miles. In various configurations, the plane could carry a torpedo, rockets, one to four bombs, and three or four machine guns. It was the heaviest single-engine aircraft flown in World War II.

Grumman's rollout of the plane took place on December 7, 1941, just as news of the Japanese attack on Pearl Harbor was unfolding. After the ceremony, officials placed the plant, situated at Bethpage on New York's Long Island, on high security.

Avengers could launch from either airfields or aircraft carriers, and their folding-wing design was intended to maximize the use of storage space on a carrier. After two prototypes were built in 1941, Grumman began fleet production. The first six Avengers were delivered to the Navy just as the Battle of Midway was getting underway in the Pacific. Only one of them survived that fight. Avengers went on to fight in the battles of the Eastern Solomons, Santa Cruz, and Guadalcanal. Avenger crews became adept at attacking not only surface vessels—including aircraft carriers, destroyers, and battleships—but also submarines. Among the vessels they sank were the Japanese super battleships *Musashi* and *Yamato*. In the North Atlantic, they were particularly important in protecting shipping lanes that were being attacked by German subs.

TBF Avengers flying in formation over Norfolk, Virginia, in September 1942. WIKIMEDIA COMMONS

Besides the U.S., two other Allied nations flew Avengers in World War II: the Royal Navy and the Royal New Zealand Air Force. Although Avengers continued to fight to the end of the war, their design by then had been succeeded by that of the F6F Hellcat fighter.

The most famous Avenger pilot was future U.S. president George H. W. Bush, who survived being shot down on September 2, 1944, and was awarded the Distinguished Flying Cross. A postwar squadron of five Avengers that disappeared into the Atlantic on December 5, 1945, taking fourteen crewmen with them, provided the origins for what became the Bermuda Triangle legend.

After the war, Avengers were used for research, training, electronic warfare, and search-and-rescue purposes. They were officially retired in 1960, but some Avengers found civilian work as crop dusters or firefighters. More than three dozen remain airworthy today in the hands of museums or private owners. ★

plane, skimmed my head, and went out the other side. I had blood running down my face; I thought I was just sweating from being frightened, but I don't think we were that frightened because we were too busy firing. It was after we got out of the dive when we start sweating and worrying. We were scared. The plane was smoking and on fire, and I was firing my gun, strafing, trying to keep the Japs away from us. I looked out the window and I could see coconuts, so I thought we must have been pretty low. I let the gun go, and had just gotten in my seat and put my shoulder straps on when we hit.

When we hit the ground the turret gunner, Lanigan, was upside down with his gun pointing in the air. I was sitting in my radio compartment, bleeding. I asked the pilot, Atkiss, "Are you okay?" He said, "I think I broke my back." Lanigan got out of the turret and we pulled the pilot out of the plane. We carried him fifty feet or sixty feet and laid him down in the grass. We started checking his arms and legs and it seemed like he was okay. We tried to pick him up, but he was moaning and groaning. He said, "I can't. I think I have a broken back." I went back to the plane and stuck a knife through the parachutes, and fired a couple of shots into the radio equipment and the radar so the Japs couldn't use them. Then we picked the pilot up and carried him for two or three hours. We could hear the Japs coming from all sides. We were really frightened.

We got into high brush and Lanigan saw some natives coming toward us. He pulled his .38 out and said, "I'm going to shoot them." I said, "No, wait. You can't fire a shot. The Japs are going to know exactly where we are. We'll get them to carry Atkiss." So we pointed our pistols at them and told them to carry Ensign Atkiss. We had learned a little bit of Pidgin English, and I said, "Which way are the Japanese?" One of them said, "Master Japanese that way. You go this way." I said, "Nah, baloney. He's probably working for the Japs. We're going to go the opposite way." So we made them carry the pilot, and we ran for about three hours, but finally the Japs surrounded us. We got into a clearing and there was a big log there and we laid Atkiss down. We were smoking a cigarette, and we gave the rest to the natives. Lanigan hid his .38 in his shoe. I said, "Dick, don't do that." He said, "I want to take a couple with me." I said, "What are you going to do? Fight the Japanese army with a .38? Just wait awhile and we'll see what happens." Well, the Japs came running and they set up machine guns all around us. They looked like a bunch of schoolkids at first, but it was what they called the military police, the Kampei-tai that captured us. Thank God it wasn't the army; they would've executed us on the spot.

Other Japs came running up and fixed their bayonets and started charging us. Finally a Japanese interpreter yelled, "Put your hands up, you damned fool, or these Japs will bayonet you and shoot you." I said, "You tell them to stop. We surrender." He yelled at the Japs and they stopped. They searched us and found Lanigan's gun and they beat the heck out of him; they were kicking him. I tried to interfere, I grabbed one of the Japs and he hit me in the face with a rifle butt and put me down. They were going to bayonet us right there, when this Jap that spoke English yelled at them to stop.

We were three kids. The pilot was twenty-one, my turret gunner was twenty, and I was nineteen; and you talk about being scared—oh man, we were frightened. They blindfolded us and handcuffed my left hand onto Lanigan's left hand. They marched us for quite a ways and finally put us in trucks and took us to a trench in the ground. It had a coconut-log roof on it and about a foot of water in it. They put us down in there, we were still handcuffed. One Jap came down and stuck his rifle bayonet into the ground in front of us. He had a lantern there, and he would read out loud from a book he had, with his rifle leaning up against the side of this trench we were in. So Lanigan whispered, "Put your arm over here by mine." It turned out that when he was wrestling with the Japs he saw a bunch of keys on this one guy and he said, "I grabbed one of them, the smallest one." It turned out to be the handcuff key, so he loosened our hands enough where they weren't bothering us.

We were going to try to escape, so when this Jap was sitting there, I said, "Do you speak English?" He didn't say a word. I said, "Hey, stupid, you yellow SOB." I figured that would get him going, but not a word; not a peep. So I told Lanigan, "This damned fool doesn't understand English. I'm going to get that bayonet and cut his throat." I asked Atkiss, "Do you hear that plane out there warming up?" He said, "Yeah." I said, "We must be near water. It must be a floatplane." I said, "If I get rid of this guard and we get out there, can you start that plane?" He said, "Oh, yeah." I said, "You start it and I'll sit on your lap and fly it out, and Lanigan will hang on the float." At least we'd get away from there. He said, "All right." So we had all our plans made, but by this time, they changed guards. So we had to do the same thing over again. I said, "Hey, stupid." Not a thing, I said, "You yellow SOB." I said, "Hey, Dick, this guy's one of those weirdos too. He doesn't understand anything." The Jap picked his rifle up and put a bayonet on it, and he put it right against my throat and nicked me. He said, "You SOB, the next time you call me something like that, I'm going to put it right through your throat." The Jap could speak English as well as I could.

We were in that cave for about two weeks until they finally put us on a truck. One of the Japs offered us some water out of a canteen and we each took a sip. Our planes came over and started strafing the trucks and the convoys. They made the three of us get out and into this real high kunai grass, they called it. I asked Atkiss, "How are you feeling? Do you think you could run?" He said, "I think so." So I told Lanigan, "Listen, these Japs are afraid with these planes strafing. We're going to get out of here." So we were lying on our stomachs and I parted the grass, and here's a Jap face right beside me with a bayonet. He's watching me, just shaking his head. I said, "Okay." So we were handcuffed and blindfolded and put back into the truck and the planes all disappeared.

Finally we got to a hut, like a chicken hut. They took me up a ladder and had me sit at a table and they started interrogating me; they wanted to know how many men we had, how many planes we had. I just gave them a big lot of baloney. They always told you; all you do is give your name, rank, and serial number. I want to tell you something, when you're captured by people like that you give your name, rank, serial number, what hand you wipe with, and everything else. You lie a lot, but still you keep talking, you don't get smart.

Whenever I was up in that shanty being interrogated they had a jar of white fluid hanging on the wall, and they had a long needle. They said, "We're going to give you injections." I couldn't do anything because the Japs there had me bound. When they gave me the injections I could feel this hot weather coming over me as though I was pulling a blind down. I was getting so hot the whole way down my body, and when it reached down the bottom, I let loose and defecated all over everything. They grabbed hold of me and threw me out of that hut about ten feet down on the ground into all this mud and muck and water and told me to wash. I washed my trousers off in that mud and put them back on again. I was in a daze; I didn't know what I was doing, I didn't know what was going on.

They led us up to a compound where I could see people who looked like skeletons; they were nothing but skin and bone, I couldn't believe they were our people. Next to the prison compound they had a place that looked like a dog kennel. They made us go in and when we were in there we had to be hunched over on our knees and we couldn't move. They had about seven Kanakas, the natives, in there with us. They had tropical ulcers on their feet and all over. The Japs started poking sharp bamboo sticks into us, and we just cowered; there was nothing we could do. Then Lanigan, he grabbed hold of one of the sticks, and he pulled it in. One Jap, his name was Wata, he opened the door and told Lanigan to come out. Lanigan wouldn't budge, so Wata pulled his sword out and started after Lanigan. I said, "Dick, get out there." So he got out and they hit him a couple times, knocked him down, and made him kneel on the gravel. He kneeled there for about two hours and they finally let him back in again.

Atkiss, Lanigan, and I were called two or three times a day to these huts for interrogation. One of our interrogators was a professor at the University of California before the war and could speak good English. The other man was a teacher; his name was Tukahara. They gave me a map and told me to show where our antiaircraft guns were on Bougainville, where all of our artillery was, where all the men were bivouacked, and where all the runways were. I didn't know any of that. All we did was get in our planes and fly, but I made X's for antiaircraft and zeros for guns, and I marked them all over the place. That Jap came up behind me and looked at it and he made me stand up. He knocked me down, kicked me in the ribs, and said, "You lie." So he gave me another map and on the next map I changed it a little bit because I wasn't sure what to do. Again, I got knocked off the chair and hit quite a few times with rifle butts and bamboo sticks. The third time I must have marked it where they thought the stuff was, because they said, "Okay."

This happened two or three times a day for about two weeks. After that we were called about once a week for our interrogation, just constantly asking us questions about stuff that we knew nothing about. We were there for maybe a month when we were moved in with the other prisoners. When we moved there, oh God, I couldn't believe it. The men there were nothing but skin and bone. Every two or three days we'd get rice about the size of a golf ball. In between we'd get a piece of coconut about the size of your finger. So we started losing weight. And if you had diarrhea, which everybody would get often, they would cut your food off for three days.

The Japs told us that, if one man escapes, they would execute the rest, so there was no way we were going to escape. And we were on an island with 120,000 Japs. Where would we go if we escaped? There was no place to go. One time they counted twenty men off and told them they were going to send them to Japan, so everybody was fighting to get in line. Well they counted twenty men out, gave them a good meal, gave them clean shirts, and took them down into this creek and let them get a good washing. Then they took them down further, and all you could hear was shots and screams and yelling. The Japs executed them and beheaded every one of them.

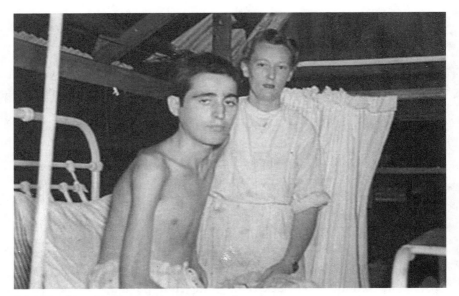

John Kepchia after his time as a prisoner of war.

One other time the Japs made about twenty men dig a trench right along the runway at Rabaul. They dug this trench and were forced to kneel with their hands tied behind their back with blindfolds on, and one Jap guard was assigned behind each prisoner. At the moment the sign was given, every one of them had their heads cut off. They fell right into the runway and were covered up. We didn't know any of this until after the war was over.

We were moved three times because of our planes bombing us. You would lie on the ground—everybody was nothing but skin and bone—and you'd be speaking to a guy at night, and in the morning, he'd be dead. That happened almost daily; one by one, the men were dying. A guy named Sanger said he was going to escape, so when he got out on work detail, he killed a guard, and was running for the jungle when the Japs up on the hill cut him down and killed him. There was no way you could escape.

Lanigan and Atkiss both died; one died the 29th, and the other died the 30th of July, just before the war was over. That's when they took a bunch of us and gave us injections. I tried to tell Atkiss and Lanigan to walk it off, "Keep walking. Don't stop. Keep walking." They just laid there, they couldn't help themselves. I cried while I held them in my arms. They just couldn't do anything.

It was near the end of the war. We didn't know it, but we thought something strange was going on because they let us all take a bath. They gave us all new g-strings and shirts, gave us a good meal and told us they were going to move us to the side of the mountain. When we got moved, they called us outside and one of the Japs said, "For you, the war is over. You are now citizens, and you are free people." We didn't know they dropped an atomic bomb. We were all crying and didn't know what to do. They said, "We cannot let you go anywhere because the other Japanese might execute you, so you must stay where you are till you are released." That was September 2. They gave us a great big bucket of rice, a can of condensed milk, and a bottle of sake. We dumped it in the rice, mixed all that slosh up and added hot peppers from the natives' garden. We all ate that until we all got really pretty sick.

One day we were loaded in a truck and taken down to the harbor; there were seven of us. An Australian corvette came into the harbor and a smaller boat came in with the New Zealanders. Man, they were about seven feet tall. They had all the Jap guards lined up. The captain came over and gave us a cigarette, and said, "I have nothing except bread and butter." So we made bread and butter and gulped it down. I weighed seventy-four pounds at that time; I weighed 164 when I was shot down.

I often told other servicemen, "If you ever had the misfortune of being captured, use common sense and do not be smart. Give your name, rank, serial number, and whatever information they want, even if you have to lie. If they ask you something, even if you have to lie, you tell them. And show respect to your captors. You would want respect from the men if you captured any, so you have to show them respect." We didn't do that at first, and we paid for it.

AFTER THE WAR . . .

After leaving the service in 1952, John Kepchia went to work for the U.S. Postal Service for twenty years. He married and raised a son and daughter. Today he enjoys two grandchildren and is a general licensed amateur radioman.

☆ Paul Matusky ☆

Lansdale, Pennsylvania

Paul Matusky joined the Army Air Corps at age eighteen.
He was a waist gunner on a B-24 Liberator late in the war
in Europe. On a mission over Germany his plane was shot
down by antiaircraft fire and he was taken prisoner.

I was born in 1925 in western Pennsylvania. I was a sophomore in high school when the war broke out. I enlisted into the Army Air Force at that time, and I had to wait until I was eighteen before they would take me. I passed rigid physical and mental tests and went into the flight-training program.

I wanted to be a fighter pilot very desperately. I guess it was the glamour of it. You'd go to the movies and they'd run movie shorts of what was happening overseas. I recall going to a movie in Dubois, Pennsylvania, and there was a scene in there of the Army Air Force cadets' physical training. They were taking physical education down on the beach in Miami, and they left the beach singing the Army Air Corps song, and that grabbed me. "Off we go into the wild, blue yonder." So I went down the street to the post office and signed papers, and in November 1943 I went into the flight-training program. Of course, I didn't last long; I washed out of flight training.

Then I wanted to be a bombardier, but at that time they weren't training bombardiers, so I trained to become a waist gunner on a B-24 Liberator. I liked gunnery school. I was apprehensive because I wanted to succeed and be on an air crew. There was some tension about being sure that you passed all the tests. You had to be able to field-strip your gun and put it together blindfolded and a number of other things, although it was a little boring at times because we had some long flying missions. On a bomb run, even in combat, very little of your time is spent going on target. It took hours over the North Sea just to get us into formation before we'd cross over into Germany. It was boring; you'd have a long time flying a mission without anything to do. But other than that, I enjoyed gunnery school.

I found out I was going overseas in the fall of 1944. It wasn't known at that time whether we were going to go to the European Theater or to the South Pacific. There was a great deal of mystery surrounding assignments. Only one person had the plans as to where we were going. We arrived in Dillingham Airfield in Britain at two-thirty in the morning, the radio was on, and Lord Ha-Ha was on the radio. Lord Ha-Ha was a propagandist for the Germans. He was a British subject who went to Germany before the war started, befriended some Germans, and he remained there after the war started and became a propagandist. And over the radio, he'd broadcast back to England saying, "Why don't you surrender? You're going to lose the war." But in spite of the fact that all our movements were cloaked in a mystery, he welcomed us to Dillingham Airfield over the radio as we went into the mess hall. He said, "We welcome the replacement crew who arrived at Dillingham Airfield early this morning." I mean, can you imagine how startling that was? Here you are, everything was kept secret, and now here's Lord Ha-Ha in Germany broadcasting over the airwaves that we'd be welcomed there.

I arrived overseas early in January 1945, and the war was over in Europe in June. So my experience overseas wasn't that long, and my combat experience wasn't that long. I wanted to fly so much that, when I got there, I volunteered to be a substitute. Sometimes an air gunner wasn't able to fly for illness, so I volunteered because I wanted to get my thirty-five missions in and go home. My first mission was February 14, 1945. The target for the day was Magdeburg, for two reasons. The Allies were in search of where the V-2 bombs were being built. The V-2s would go over England, run out of fuel, and come down. So we were in search of where these things were being manufactured, and Magdeburg was suspected of being the place. The second reason was that there was a large railroad yard there that they wanted to finally put out of commission.

When I was shot down I learned where they were making the V-2 missiles. They had carved out a mound behind Nordhausen, south of Magdeburg, and they were manufacturing these rockets underground. Had I been able to escape I could have revealed that, because I don't think they really discovered where they were until Germany surrendered. So it was a maximum effort that morning to destroy Magdeburg, at least the rail yards, because they were moving these rockets on rail.

Let me tell you a little bit about how an aircrew is briefed. Everything is done in complete mystery. When you get up, you go to the mess hall at four-thirty in the morning, you have something to eat, and then you go to your briefing room. The officers go to their own briefing—they have a special briefing—and the gunners go to their briefing. And there they reveal to you for the first time where you're going. And their intelligence was very thorough. They told us what the weather was going to be like, where the cloud coverage was going to be, they'd tell us if there was going to be any enemy-fighter opposition . . . it was just tremendous. Everything they told us at that briefing was the way it happened that day. Then you go down the flight line, you load your guns, meet your crew, go over the ship. They preflight your ship to see that everything's in shape, then for the first time, you really know where you're going. You take off through a system of flares, and the pilot finds where he's supposed to position his airplane in the formation. It takes a couple hours to get all these planes together.

You don't fly directly to your target. You use what you call evasive action, because when the Germans anticipated where the target was, that's where they would lay up their antiaircraft. And I have to tell you, they don't shoot at you from the ground; they shoot in front of you. They put up these big boxes of flak in front of you, and when you're on what was called a bomb run—they lasted about fourteen minutes—you couldn't use evasive action, you had to go straight to your target. And once that was determined by the Germans they would just fill the sky in front of you with flak. And, of course, we ran into some of it.

You did very little talking the day of a mission. I know we felt good about being assigned a mission because that was what we were supposed to do. But nobody would express any fear or intimidation. They kept it to themselves. And we minimized discussion because you might reveal where you were going to a person next to you who might have been a German spy. So as a consequence, there was very little dialogue among the crew prior to a mission, and the same thing was true when you flew. You'd communicate through throat mics, but you restrict conversation. When it was necessary, as when we were hit or if you sighted enemy aircraft, then we were all on, we were able to talk to each other.

I never shot my guns at an enemy aircraft, because they weren't in the sky at that time. They didn't have the petroleum. And we had fighter escort by this time, so we didn't have to worry that much about German fighter planes. Our big concern was antiaircraft flak.

When we were hit, the first thing we did was throw out anything that was loose, to lessen the weight. You throw out your guns and everything. That was one of the loneliest experiences of my life. We were losing altitude. I saw the formation above us, pulling away from us, and I knew we were all alone. They were going home, they were dropping their bombs, and we weren't.

When you're in trouble, there's a systematic procedure that you follow, and you have your choice, you could either bail out or you could ride it down, so we took a vote. It was unanimous to bail out. Our radioman came down off the flight deck and walked back to where I was standing, waiting to jump out. But he was reluctant to jump. It was like he was testing the water down at the beach to see if it was cold. Of course you can't waste a lot of time, so I just very courteously put my foot on his shoulder, and out he went, and then I went out. I have to put in a plug for our pilot; Hubbert was only twenty-one years old, but what a guy, he stayed right with it and was the last guy to bail out.

As I came down, I started to count the chutes. There were nine members on the crew and eight were out. Hubbert was the last to go. He was the pilot, which meant that he had to manipulate that airplane, and then step down off of the flight deck and onto the catwalk and jump. I saw the airplane off at a distance, it reared up in the air, then over on its wing, it disappeared behind a hill, and then a big plume of smoke came up. But that last guy to jump was Hubbert, so all of us got out.

When we hit the ground, the nearest town was Nordhausen. The terrain was much the same as where I was born back in western Pennsylvania, with rolling hills. It was a cold day in February, and one of the coldest winters recorded in Europe. I landed in a plowed field, and it was hard as a rock. You try to anticipate contact and bend your knees a little bit, but the ground came up on me too fast. The first thing you're told to do when you hit the ground is bury your parachute, because a huge, white thing lying out there would mean that there might be an enemy airman around. I tried to carry out my assignment burying the parachute, and I dragged it off to the side. There was a ravine and a fast-moving stream there. Most of it was frozen, but some of it wasn't. So, while I was down there trying to bury my parachute in frozen ground, I looked up on the bank and there were two German Wehrmacht soldiers with their machine guns, so that was it.

It wasn't long till we were all together, except one guy, and that was Smitty. Smitty was the crew chief; he was the guy who preflighted the airplane. He broke his leg on impact. He lay out in the field all night and nobody came to help him.

Paul Glassman was our nose gunner, and he was Jewish. When the Jewish fliers arrived in England, they were told that if they wanted to change their flight name, they could do that if it sounded Jewish, because you know what was happening in Germany to the Jewish people. But Paul wouldn't change his name; he stuck to his faith. But he made a very tragic error. He carried the Star of David in his pocket, and when he hit the ground civilians converged upon him outside of this small community where he landed, and they started to take his parachute. When they searched him and they found the Star of David, they started beating on him, the children and women first. An older farmer came, and he had a pitchfork, and he struck Paul across the face with the handle of the pitchfork. Paul ran, and he heard a shot and he thought he was hit, and he fell. He looked up to see this group of people above him, getting angry, yelling at him, and by this time two German soldiers came, took over the whole thing, cleared the civilians out, and took over. The Germans made his life miserable. They terrorized him, simply because he was Jewish.

We were taken to the interrogation center at Frankfurt. They'd take you to an interrogator and they wanted you to identify yourself as an American airman. But I had a problem with that. The night before the mission I went to the shower room and took my dog tags off, and I hung them on a nail. Guess where they were when they asked me to identify myself as an American airman? Hanging back there, still on the nail. The dog tags would have been proof that I was an American airman, so I'd be protected by the Geneva Convention. I told them my name, rank, and serial number and they said, "You have no proof of this. Where are your dog tags? You're not Paul Matusky; you're a saboteur. You're subject to being shot." But I refused to tell him any more, so up until the time I left there, I thought I was going to be shot as a saboteur.

Finally we were transferred to Mooseburg, down by Munich, in the southeastern part of Germany. We traveled by foot, mostly. The rail system was so fouled up it took us three days to go from Frankfurt to Wetzler, which was forty-eight miles by rail, because of the bombing raids. The war was over, and the Germans knew it, so they tried to befriend us. One of them came in two days before the war was over and asked us if we would sign a sheet of paper, saying that as long as we knew him, he treated us well, and every once in a while he would bring in a piece of black bread or a baked potato. We never saw him after that. We weren't mistreated. We were hungry, but when the Red Cross parcel came in we were eating better than the Germans were.

On Sunday, April 29, I went to church services. That morning, at religious service, I knew the war was over when the German captain came for roll call and he didn't have a gun in his holster. That was his way of surrendering. The 14th Infantry, spearheading the Third Army, came through, and General Patton had his white pistols, his pearl handles. They took us out of there pretty rapidly. In fact, I left a lot sooner than I thought. We went to a hospital in Paris, and were all given physicals, then we went to Camp Lucky Strike, on the coast of France, right outside of La Havre. The war was over now and the stream of soldiers and prisoners coming out went to one of these tent cities, Lucky Strike in my case.

Coming up New York Harbor, June 14, 1945, it was a foggy morning and we could hear the harbor boats and all the foghorns. All of us were looking for that statue. You couldn't see it, because it was cloudy, and then suddenly there was a break in the fog, and there she was. I could look across the lower New York harbor and on the hillside, spread out in huge letters with white stones were two words, "Well done."

After the war I didn't talk much about my experience. In fact, when I retired, most of the people I worked with didn't even know I was a prisoner of war. A lot of people used that to get sympathy from people, and I detested that. It's like, everybody who fought in the war was a hero. Well, everybody who fought in the war may not have been a hero, and the prisoners of war would use it to their advantage to gain sympathy, and I didn't care for that.

I think that young people have to realize what some people did to put this country to where it is. It affected my life immensely, the fact that I had served. I appreciate this country. My father was an immigrant. I like to believe that I am the American dream, in that I came from rather humble circumstances. I have a lot to be thankful for.

AFTER THE WAR . . .

Paul Matusky taught high school history and served as a high school principal after continuing his education at Penn State University under the GI Bill. He and his wife, Adeline, raised two daughters and two sons together. In addition they had nine grandchildren. Mr. Matusky passed away in 2005 after a vigorous battle with cancer. He fervently voiced his patriotism and was proud to be a Pennsylvanian and an American.

☆ Joseph Orlando ☆
Media, Pennsylvania

••

Joseph Orlando was a Marine Corps drill instructor at
Parris Island and served in the South Pacific on Saipan in the
Northern Mariana Islands, clearing Japanese pillboxes and caves.

••

I grew up in Philadelphia and worked at the Alloy Metal Wire Company after high school. Then I went to work for the Sun Shipyard and worked there until I volunteered for the Marine Corps.

After Pearl Harbor young people all wanted to get into the service, and they wanted combat. I know people I meet, older people my age, that say, "Oh, I didn't get overseas," and they are apologetic about that. They shouldn't be because they might have contributed more than I did to the war effort. You went where you were sent.

I went down to the recruiting office and I can remember clearly, there were two young fellows in there that were bigger, barrel-chested fellows with letters on their sweaters, and they got turned down. I thought that I would never make it because I was 140 pounds. I was thin and I had eaten about four bananas before I went in there, figuring they might turn me down on account of the weight. I had two cavities that I had to get repaired, and then

I went down to Parris Island where the dentist said I had two cavities and drilled out the same two teeth and put his filling in there. That was my introduction into the Marine Corps. Things didn't change the whole time I was there. Boot camp was six weeks plus two weeks on the rifle range, and you didn't learn much except close-order drill. And the drill instructors did what they could to make you miserable. Any marine will agree with me there. My first week or so one of the Marines got a letter with a big lipstick SWAK [Sealed With A Kiss] and a lip imprint on it, and the drill instructor made a big thing out of ridiculing him, and I laughed like everybody laughed. But this guy said "What are you laughing at?" to me and I started to say something and the drill instructor picked up on it and said "When we're done drill instruction, you two in the ring, you'll have to have a fight." I didn't know how to fight, and this guy probably knew less than I did about fighting because he approached me sort of in a charge, and he would duck and bang his head on my fist. I don't think I ever hit him, but he did bang his face. The gloves were like big pillows, they wouldn't hurt anyone, but he did this so often his face got red on the side and my reputation as a fighter was sealed.

After the eight weeks we were assigned, some to cooking school, some to transportation for truck driving; and I got picked along with another man as drill instructors. We didn't want to be drill instructors because we wanted combat. So I was kind of nervy and thought I would go talk to the battalion commander, who was a second lieutenant. In boot camp you rarely saw an officer. You called the drill instructor who might be a sergeant or a corporal, or in my case a private when I got to be one, but I thought I would see the battalion commander. Now you can't say to the battalion commander, "I don't want to be one," because that won't hold water, but I was an ex-salesman so I said, "It's an honor to be a drill instructor; however my voice won't carry so I don't think I'll be a good one," thinking he might assign me to something else. He looked up and said, "Is that all?" I said, "Yes sir." And he said, "Out, get out!" The other fellow didn't want to be a drill instructor either and he was waiting to go in after me. I just shook my head and he was out in a flash. So we were two drill instructors.

You went down to the main station and got seventy-four men, brought them back to your area, and you were a drill instructor. The only thing I knew about a drill instructor was what my drill instructor did to me. There was no training at all, so I took the seventy-four men and went out to this field, showed them how to stand at attention, and told them to stand at attention. The mosquitoes were miserable and pretty soon one of them would slap at a mosquito and I would jump at them the way my DI did to me. I said, "The mosquitoes have to eat too." So nobody slapped at mosquitoes anymore. Then I taught them how to do an about-face, right-face, left-face. The one thing we learned in the Marine Corps was to respond to commands; instant obedience. That's about all we were trained to do except for the rifle range, because every marine is a rifleman. After that I showed them how to fix their bunks and how to make them as tight as they could be. My drill instructor threw a half-dollar coin on the cot, it bounced up and he caught it. I didn't do that, but I did have them fix their bunks, and then I went down and tore them apart because they weren't satisfactory. They were fine, but you had to be miserable. My drill instructor, who was a little fellow, had said, "Any of you don't like it, step out and we'll have it out!" So I did the same thing, and I was so happy that nobody stepped out. Some of those guys were brutes and I would have gotten killed. I suppose I did a fair job, but I wanted out and I made that very clear.

From there I went to Hingham, Massachusetts, a Navy ammunition depot, where I was largely on guard duty. You couldn't take a walk in Hingham without someone stopping you and asking you if they could give you a ride. It was marvelous; they treated us wonderfully. But I wanted out of that and I got sent to Camp Perry, Virginia, which is right outside of Williamsburg, to train Seabees. I was right back to being a drill instructor, although we were much nicer to the Seabees. They were great men who were highly skilled in their different crafts and not as young as the young Marines. Williamsburg was a great experience for me. William & Mary College had a lot of lovely young co-eds who were allowed out until eleven o'clock at night and twelve o'clock on weekends as long as you passed an interview with the house mother, which I did. So my stay in Williamsburg was exceptionally nice.

I finally got sent to New River, North Carolina. You go there before you go overseas and I was delighted. Then we went to San Diego and got on the *Mormac Dove*, that's a cargo ship that was redesigned; it had six bunks high, and I was bright enough to get the top bunk, because if anyone got seasick it's better to be on the top than on the bottom. You spent as little time in the bunk as possible; you slept on deck if you could. The ship broke down as we left San Diego; we were in a convoy and the convoy kept going. So we limped into Pearl Harbor for repairs and spent two weeks there. After two weeks we started off with another convoy, and shortly after, we broke down again. It took us forty days to get to Saipan, so we were not in the first or second wave, which probably saved our lives, because we lost 13,000 men on Saipan. But the first and second waves were kind enough to leave plenty of Japanese on the island for us.

We had what we called "pushes" on a regular basis; we would camp and then we would form a long line and push against the Japanese, and there were snipers and things of that kind we had to put up with. We didn't move at nighttime and we didn't dig foxholes; I never dug a foxhole in my life. But there was a little rise in the ground here and there and you would lay down flat there to protect yourself. And I could lie down very, very flat. It wasn't conducive to sleeping, but it was conducive to thinking, and I thought to myself, "Why am I here?" And I would answer myself, "You're here because the Commander in Chief, the President of the United States, said we should be here. We're doing the right thing, we were attacked at Pearl Harbor and this is the right thing." I had no quarrel with that at all. Then I thought further that, "Hey there's a young Japanese soldier sixty or seventy yards over there and if he asks himself why he's there, he's going to get pretty much the same response as I had; because his emperor or General Tojo said you should be there, and we were the enemy." And I thought, "That's hardly logical. He and I ought to be out having a beer together and not wanting to kill each other."

The Japanese had pillboxes on all the islands and the only way to get rid of them was to approach them and put a grenade in there. In those pillboxes, the Japanese had a deep hole and put a piece of sheet iron over it, so when you threw anything in there and it exploded you thought everything was safe, and then everybody approached and suddenly the pillbox came alive again with fire. That's how we lost a lot of men on islands. Also on every island there was a mountain and every mountain had its caves and that same thing was true of caves. They would dig a hole down and put a sheet over it.

A U.S. Marine discovers a Japanese family hiding in a hillside cave after the Battle of Saipan.
WIKIMEDIA COMMONS

When I got there, we lost men. We didn't lose nearly as many as the first and second waves did, but we lost enough, too many. We were occasionally assigned to bury Marines, and I won't tell you exactly how they were buried except to say that we didn't have body bags in those days, nor did we have equipment to lower them gently, but we did it with every amount of respect and dignity that we could, I can assure you of that. I never shed a tear, but I was sad because some of my friends passed away that way.

The only time I was really scared was when we got dengue fever; I never got it, but as I understand, with dengue even your eyeballs hurt. That meant a lot of our people could not serve, and I as a corporal had to go on guard duty, stationed at this water tower. It rained frequently on Saipan, and the water towers leaked so you were standing in marshy soil. And there were toads on Saipan that jumped and that would create a splash. So when you were there with your rifle you'd be turning every time you would hear a splash until you realized it was only the toads, and then you'd relax.

There was one time we went to Tinian, which was a nearby island that had a big airfield with B-29s that regularly went to Japan to bomb. They would come back and if they had any bombs they would drop them in the ocean before they landed. We were assigned to surround this airfield one night because—we didn't learn this until later—the atomic bomb was there.

On our way back from Tinian to Saipan we were going along, and we were never closer than five paces apart, because if a sniper is going to shoot somebody, if he shoots into a group it's easy for him, but walking the way we always did, at least five paces apart, it was more difficult. We were walking along and suddenly we heard this racket in Japanese and a lone soldier came down the hill charging at us, just one Japanese soldier. The poor fellow was probably out of his mind. One of our lieutenants jumped up and down and said, "Shoot him, shoot him!" And we couldn't understand why you would want to shoot one Japanese soldier, so one of our guys got the guy and brought him along with us.

There was a cliff called Suicide Cliff on Saipan. We had soldiers and Marines that could speak Japanese and they would assure the local people who were approaching Suicide Cliff that we would take good care of them and we were not brutal. I'll tell you about being brutal; the Japanese had their civilians convinced that we were brutal, so that regardless of the assurances, these people jumped off the cliff. They threw their children off first and then jumped off the cliff to their death, which was sad, very sad.

I had a gem of a squad. I don't know if it was because the captain liked me, but it seemed like I got all the oddballs, and I say this with deep affec-

The ruins of Nagasaki following the use of the atomic bomb. NATIONAL ARCHIVES

tion. I had two Marines who had been on Guadalcanal and were assured when they got back to the States that they wouldn't go back overseas again. So here they were on Saipan, and they were very bitter. Another guy in my squad was kind of an oddball. He said he was seventeen, but he was no more than fifteen or sixteen. He wrote every night to his mother, very nice letters. But one time we got weevils in our bread and he wrote home and said, "Dear Mom, we're eating better now. We're getting more meat and they're even putting it in the bread for us."

Something else about the kid, when we went on pushes and approached a mountain with a cave, one squad had to go up to the cave. When I was assigned to a cave I would lead and the second one in the squad would follow me and the BAR man—that's a Browning automatic rifle—he would have his weapon aimed at the mouth of the cave if anyone showed up. I was running up to the mountain and the kid was right behind me, and I passed a dead Japanese soldier. Well, Marines are told to kill twice because, just because you see a man lying there, he could suddenly return to life and kill you. But this man had been dead a little while, and when you are dead in that climate there is no question that you're dead. So I ran and didn't pay much attention to him and suddenly I hear eight shots, and the kid is standing over this dead Japanese soldier emptying his rifle. Of course being five paces ahead of him, I'm down on the ground, figuring my end is near. I turned around and saw this kid, and I might have said some profanity then, but we went on up to the cave, lit a couple of the TNT bricks, threw one in and waited a little bit, figuring that maybe somebody would come out. Then we threw another one in and we were satisfied that it was okay to proceed.

When the war ended we worked six hours on and six hours off to prepare to go up to Japan. Thank goodness Harry Truman dropped the bomb, otherwise our next step would have been invading Japan, and that would have been extremely costly on both sides. We all got sick on the small boat we took because we had worked constantly, and we didn't bathe at all. We had sores under our armpits and we were miserable. It was even more miserable because we got seasick. Once we got on a larger ship we took turns having showers, got 100 percent improved, and nobody got seasick.

We were sent to Nagasaki where the bomb had been dropped. That bomb was much less powerful than the bombs they have today by far, yet when you looked at Nagasaki the only thing you could see was a concrete foundation here and there, otherwise, nothing at all. In Nagasaki the Japanese were very fearful of us and yet once we were there a day or two, there would be children walking around carrying the Marine blankets and asking for the chocolate that was in the K rations. But the older Japanese didn't want any part of us.

What I would say today is that people have to conduct themselves in such a way as to eliminate or reduce the hatreds that exist between ethnic and religious groups that have existed for years. Also, they have to work so that there are no more wars. If it comes across that I'm an antiwar fanatic, it's what I'm trying to portray. Because it doesn't make sense, we've been given the gift of wisdom maybe, reason certainly, and yet we solve problems with bullets and bombs. That hardly seems civilized. Maybe there will be a day when there will be no more wars and no more veterans.

AFTER THE WAR . . .

Following his service in World War II, Joe Orlando worked for Eastman Kodak and the Atlantic Refining Company (ARCO). He and his wife have six sons and seventeen grandchildren. Since his retirement in 1984, Mr. Orlando has volunteered at St. John's Hospice in Philadelphia. He says that his work there has made him "a better person in many ways."

☆ Pete Porreca ☆

Uniontown, Pennsylvania

· ·

Pete Porreca was trained at Armored Force School
and became a tank mechanic. Landing in France shortly
after D-Day, he spent time with Gen. George Patton's
Third Army, building temporary tank bridges and
retrieving tanks abandoned in no-man's land.

· ·

I worked in the coal mine for about nine months before I went into the
service. I was deferred twice without applying for it. My father had applied
for the deferment for me, but I didn't know it. Then some girl from the Draft
Board told me that I was deferred, and my deferment was up for the third
time. I went to see the superintendent of the mines and told him I didn't
want a deferment. He said my father applied. I said, "I don't want it. I want
to be drafted like my buddies were." Two weeks later on April 3, 1943, I was
drafted into the Army and went to New Cumberland, Pennsylvania.

I had a pretty good grade on the aptitude test there, so they wanted me
to go to school. I didn't want to go to school because I graduated in 1941
and I was tired of school. I wanted to get out. I wanted to be a hero and get
in combat. They sent me to Camp Campbell, Kentucky, where I found out

that I was in the tanks. They put me in the tanks because tanks had radios in them, and I had a good test on the dots and dashes on the aptitude test.

They sent me to Armored Force School in Fort Knox, Kentucky, where they taught me everything: every nut and bolt in the tank, every part of the guns, the gyro stabilizer, and the radio. I was never a mechanic before that, but when I came out, I was trained to be a mechanic. I didn't want to be a mechanic, but I was stuck. They gave me a promotion to T-5, which was a corporal technician, and my outfit moved to Camp Phillips, Kansas. We were there a couple months and then they shipped us overseas.

We landed in Liverpool, England, on April 30, 1944. We were there for D-Day. We were supposed to jump off on D-Day, but a German sub had sunk a boat that had tanks on it, so they gave our tanks to the outfit that was ahead of us. We didn't land on Utah Beach until August 6, so we were lucky. We missed D-Day because of this submarine sinking the ship with the supplies on it.

When we landed in France we had to go so many miles to reach the front, because the foothold at the beach was already secured. Outfits were there ahead of us, around Saint-Lô and other places. The first battle we came to, we were going to the front lines. All you could hear was artillery. You couldn't hear small-arms fire; you just heard shells being lobbed in from our artillery. The Germans were firing out too, but ours were more common.

After about two weeks, we hit a battle at Argentan. That's where the Americans and the Allies closed the Falaise Gap. The Third Platoon was in its first battle. Our commander wouldn't order the tanks in because of the hedgerow openings. The reconnaissance the night before told our company commander that it was suicide to go through the hedgerows because of the German tank guns, the 88-millimeters, trained on the openings. Our commander wouldn't go through with it, so Major General [Horace] McBride of the 80th Division ordered him to send the tanks through. He still wouldn't do it, so they busted him out on the spot. They relieved him of his command, and then the tanks were ordered through.

Of the first five tanks, four tanks were hit. There were so many deaths and injuries in those first four tanks. They lost half their men in each tank, plus the injuries. The fifth tank was bogged down. It didn't go in. About six months later this captain was court-martialed, and he was not relieved of his duties any more. They reinstated him because they thought he knew more about armored force than the infantry general did. That was suicide to order his men through that opening. So they reinstated him and he was given a promotion later. He was a colonel by the end of the war. We were there for several weeks. The Americans and the Allies took thousands of prisoners at the Falaise Gap.

Then we started moving faster. We were with General Patton at the time, and he ordered us to move so fast that whole Third Army ran out of gas and we had to stop. We were moving so fast that the supply trucks couldn't catch up, so all the tanks were without gas. We were close to towns named Dieulouard and Pont-a-Mousson, close to the Moselle River, and we had to stay there. I was in the recovery unit, but we didn't have anything to recover at the time. We stayed in a barn for a couple weeks before the gas caught up with us and we moved out again.

My unit was a recovery vehicle with a big boom on it and a .50-caliber machine gun, actually an aircraft gun, for shooting at planes. If we were going to ford a stream or ravine, it might be narrow, but deep, and tanks couldn't go through. So we would put in a treadway, like a bridge. It could have been ten or fifteen feet long and was strong enough to hold the tanks. We'd span the ravine with it so the tanks could go over it. We did that many times over ravines that were not passable by the tanks.

Our job was also to go and retrieve tanks, and when we retrieved tanks they were always in no-man's land. Nine times out of ten, the Germans were afraid to go up to those tanks, for fear we had booby-trapped them. One time in particular I was told to retrieve a tank that was between the two lines. They said it would start, that it was only bogged down in the mud, but by that time the mud had dried. It had been sitting there a couple days, but we hadn't gotten to it yet. Our reconnaissance said that the tank was still intact, but they didn't know if it had been booby-trapped by the Germans.

You only had two fellows in the recovery unit, for fear of losing more men, because these guys were all good mechanics, and we didn't want to lose good mechanics when we only had so many of them. So it was me and my buddy, the driver, who went up there. When I walked up to the tank I was hesitant, because they told me, "Look out for a booby trap because the Germans were around the tank." As soon as I stepped forward I tripped a wire that the Germans had put around there, and when I hit the wire, flares flew up. That's when the Germans, who were in the woods, started dropping mortar shells on the tank. They were dropping all around us, but didn't hit us. So I jumped into the tank and when I went to turn the ignition on, I was scared. I said, "If I turn this ignition, it's gonna blow up," because I thought they might have rigged it. But when I turned the ignition, that thing purred like a kitten. There was nothing wrong with it mechanically, and we used it right after that.

I retrieved a lot of tanks. One time it was raining and we were told to go up and retrieve a tank, but they told us to wait a little distance from the tank, because they were sending up a couple tanks for support because the Germans were in the area. So we waited in the recovery unit, me and my buddy. We were sitting there waiting for support from the other tanks, and I heard a cry, someone crying for help, real faint. I told my buddy, "Someone's hollering, 'help' and it's real faint." He said, "You're hearing things. Just listen for the tanks." I waited a little while longer and I heard it again, a holler for help. I said, "I'm going to see where it's coming from." I went over the little hill, and right at the bottom of the hill I saw an infantry guy laying there; he wouldn't get up. I said, "What's wrong?" He said, "I got hit. I don't know how long I was out." I said, "How long have you been here?" He said, "When the battle started." I said, "The battle started three days ago." He was in the rain, all soaked and wet. So I went to my buddy and said, "Help me carry this guy. He needs help bad. He's gonna die." My buddy said, "My orders are to retrieve this tank, and we can't leave a recovery unit wide-open. Germans are in that field. They might come up and drive this away." So I walked down the hill and saw a medic, and I asked him if he had a stretcher, if he would come up and help me carry this guy down. So the medic came with me. We had some small-arms fire, but it was a little distance away. You could hear them shooting at us, but they didn't hit us. We carried him down to the ambulance and they gave him blood plasma and I left. I never heard any more about him. We went up and retrieved the tank and everything went well, but I never reported it, and neither did my buddy, because he was afraid we would get heck about leaving our tank. But I don't know what happened to that fellow. I don't know if he's alive or not. But that's one time that, by refusing my buddy's opinion, I did something good for someone. I was proud of that.

In 1944, Roosevelt was still president, and he promised us a turkey dinner for Christmas day. We were in Luxembourg; this was during the Battle of the Bulge. We came with Patton's Third Army from the Saar Valley to help the 101st [Airborne] and the ones who were trapped in Bastogne. We got up there about December 19 or 20. I had my retriever parked right next to the kitchen. We were always welcome to eat with the infantry. They were making chicken in the kitchen, so I went to my recovery unit to get my mess kit. As I was stooping over to get my mess kit, three planes dove down.

Falaise Gap

The Battle of Falaise Gap, lasting from August 15 to August 22, 1944, marked the end of the Battle of Normandy, which opened with the massive Allied invasion of occupied France on D-Day, June 6, 1944. Although the Allies won this round, they lost the opportunity to end the war early when 100,000 German soldiers escaped across Western Europe, withdrawing into Germany and regrouping to fight another day.

Also known as the Falaise-Argentan Gap or Falaise-Argentan Pocket, the gap was a term describing the area outlined by four towns—Argentan, Chambois, Trun, and Vimoutiers—in the region east of the ancient medieval town of Falaise, France. The pocket was about forty miles long on an east-west axis, and ten to fifteen miles wide. Falaise lay about twenty-five miles south of the western reaches of the Normandy beaches and 125 miles west of Paris. Allied troops were advancing toward each other and beginning to encircle eastward-retreating German armored (Fifth Panzer) and infantry (Seventh Army) forces.

Because of a delay in closing the gap between Canadian and Polish troops from the north, British troops from the west, and American and French troops from the south, some 100,000 German soldiers escaped to the east. As they did, they left behind 150,000 prisoners and wounded, more than 10,000 dead, and thousands of wrecked trucks,

They were P-51 Mustangs, American planes, and they opened fire. They hit the kitchen and killed a couple guys. Someone hollered, "They're German pilots, but they're our planes." There were German markings on the planes, but they were American planes. These three P-51s fooled us and started strafing. We had a lot of antiaircraft set up around Luxembourg City, so they started firing at the planes. I was on top of my recovery unit, so I grabbed the .50 caliber and squeezed that trigger. I emptied the whole belt onto that plane. I could see by my tracers where to shoot. I hit it, and a little piece fell off the tail, but it was only a little piece of the tail. I heard the infantry holler "You got him," but I couldn't tell. A report came back that two of those planes were shot down by American planes that took off after them. Two or tanks, and artillery pieces. The fact that any troops at all escaped in a nearly surrounded situation frustrated the American commanders in the European theater—Gen. Dwight D. Eisenhower, Gen. Omar Bradley, and Gen. George S. Patton Jr. Accounts vary as to the reasons for the delay. Some military observers blamed Allied indecision on the part of Bradley, but at least some of it was due to the logistical difficulty of enveloping an enemy while coordinating firepower to avoid friendly fire casualties as the Allies neared each other to cut off the escape route. Uncertain communications caused by rapidly changing Allied lines also made it risky.

On August 15, Hitler ordered a counterattack, but in fact the Germans had already begun a general retreat the day before. As Allied ground forces advanced, British and American fighter-bombers attacked the retreating enemy column, using a tactic of destroying lead vehicles and then circling back to bomb and strafe the following vehicles that had been slowed and stopped by the attack on the leaders.

The Germans did not leave without a fight. They engaged and killed many Polish troops in a vicious battle as late as August 20. The Battle of Falaise Gap was over on August 22. Two days later, Allied soldiers, led by French loyalist troops, entered and liberated Paris. The escaped German Seventh Army indeed fought the Allies again, in the disastrous Operation Market-Garden and at the Battle of the Bulge. ★

three cooks in the kitchen were killed, and we never did get our turkey. I ended up eating cheese out of a can that day.

One time we came into town and infantry was already there. There was no shooting going on because the town was captured, so we walked. Someone told me, "You want some good wine? Go down in that basement." I walked into the basement and it turned out to be a winery. There was about six inches of wine on the floor. Infantry had come in and used their submachine guns to put holes in the big vats. I went up and grabbed my water can and dumped the water out and filled it up with wine. We ended up with two five-gallon cans of wine. Another time we came on a beer brewery. They didn't shoot up those vats. We just got in there and started opening up the spigot, putting beer in our cans. One time our outfit captured a train that was full of all kind of cheeses and whiskey. A lot of it was American whiskey and German schnapps. They passed it all out to the troops, so everybody was drunk for awhile. The officers were just as guilty as we were. A lot of things like that went on that you could get away with because it was wartime.

Our battalion lost fifty-six medium tanks out of about one hundred. We had sixty-three enlisted men killed in action, 201 wounded in action. When the war was over, our outfit was disbanded and we were sent to various units. I was sent to the 80th Division band because I was a trumpet player. I never got to play during the war, so they sent me to the war band. The rest of them went to another tank outfit or they were sent home based on points. Most of them beat me home by a couple weeks. But those fellows did get a lot of medals, a lot of Purple Hearts.

Our battalion came from northeast Pennsylvania—Tamaqua, Scranton, Wilkes-Barre area, and another portion of it came from Erie. Then another portion came from Uniontown, in southwestern Pennsylvania. The other quarter came from the Philadelphia area. So we were actually from the four corners, and most of them were coal miners and hard workers. We all had four or five battle stars. I ended up with five. In each campaign you get a battle star, and you had those things on your uniform. Our outfit, we weren't in the service too long, less than three years, and most of the guys came out ahead of people who were in four or five years because of the battle stars and citations they received, Purple Hearts and all.

AFTER THE WAR . . .

The coal mines were the destination for Pete Porreca two weeks after he was discharged from the service. He married in 1948 and fathered three children. Mr. Porreca was voted Secretary-Treasurer and Mine Committeeman for his local UMWA. He served forty years as a UMWA and USWA president. On top of it all, he still managed to play trumpet in a local orchestra four to six nights a week.

☆ Henry Moore ☆
Philadelphia, Pennsylvania

∙∙∙

Henry Moore was a crew chief in an all-black fighter squadron
that served in the Army Air Corps at Monte Cassino and
Anzio in Italy. He describes some of the frustrations of being
an African American soldier in a segregated army.

∙∙∙

I was born in a slave cabin on a dirt floor in Owen County, Georgia. I never knew my grandfather or grandmother on either side. They were slaves—that's how close we are to slavery now. I graduated from high school in 1940 in Osceola, Georgia. The great migration of black folks in those days was away from the South. There was really nothing to do down there except farm. I had registered for the draft, but I was on my way to Newark. I'm hesitant to say, I was on my way out of this country. I was subject to the draft at any time and I knew it, but it had nothing to do with running away from the war or running away from the draft; I want to make that clear. I was on my way out of this country because of the prevailing racial attitudes that I had encountered for twenty-one years. I was just on my way away from the South, and as far away from the South as I could get. I probably was on my way into Canada because I had heard from some friends in Canada at the time. This was just before the war.

When I got to Newark, where my sisters and brother had migrated, I was persuaded to stay there by my sister Violet. She was trying to keep me in this country and keep me near her because she and I were very close. I stayed there just about long enough to be drafted into the United States Army in 1942. I detested being drafted. I thought it was one of the worst things that could happen to me at that time. My brother Ben was in the Army. He and I had attempted to join the Army Air Corps after I graduated from high school and they told me that was no program for Negroes. I could join the Army, but I could not join the Army Air Corps where I really wanted to go. I had seen grasshopper pilots flying all over the little farm counties and landing in the exhibitions in this little town in Georgia and I had an ambition to fly.

I was drafted from the 22nd Precinct in Newark, New Jersey. I hadn't been there very long. All of the acquaintances I had made were Italians, because I was living in a predominately Italian neighborhood at the time. We were all called down to the precinct to get on buses to Fort Dix, New Jersey. When we got to Fort Dix and got off the buses—and as I said, all of my friends on the buses were Italians—I looked around and said, "I'm certain that we won't all be together, because this is a segregated army." A black corporal was called out and a white corporal was called out and they called the names of all of the recruits and asked them to join those corporals. I followed the black corporal and my friends followed the white corporal.

I had seen how black soldiers had been treated in the South. I had worked at a place near Camp Stewart, Georgia, and I had seen what they were there for; just labor, no matter what their aptitude. They were all put into some kind of labor group, moving of materials and things of that sort, not fighting. I thought this was so unfair and thought, maybe I'm heading for that, but I was fortunate. The group I joined at Fort Dix—there were about 250 of us—got on trains and headed for the West. We ended up at Buckley Field, Colorado. We formed the 86th Aviation Squadron, United States Army Air Corps.

Now I had the opportunity to fly, or at least be associated with airplanes somehow. But this is what they were doing with black people during those days; they were putting them into labor battalions called Aviation Squadrons. They were put in labor groups, but not fighting units, and not in a position where they could fly airplanes as fighter pilots. A typical day in the 86th Aviation Squadron was that we would be called every morning to go through exercises and calisthenics and march around the base. Of course we did learn how to sing the Air Force songs and Army songs, and we marched and marched and marched, and what for? It seemed there was nothing constructive that we were there for. A person would sometimes come into the barracks and say he wanted the squad to follow him and named the number of people to go to the commander's office and pick up trash. You were handed a stick with a nail in it to pick up debris and police the area. It was the most boring thing for a person to do who had graduated as high school valedictorian of their class in 1940—and that was me.

We did have officers who were kind; all white officers, and I believe they volunteered to be there, hence their kindness. They would permit us to be entertained by certain groups that would come onto the base, but it was all segregated entertainment. We were permitted to engage in such activities as boxing, and I became a boxer and I played trumpet. And as the opportunity arose, these officers were active in getting the word around that there was a way that you might advance yourself. There came some tests we could take; the Aviation Cadet Exams. I thought maybe now I'd have a chance.

I knew that I could finally take a test and if I passed I would become an aviation cadet and end up with the airmen at Tuskegee. So I took the test in December 1942, and I think I got a 94 on it.

My mother had been a schoolteacher and she had taught me such things as simultaneous equations up to quadratic equations, and I had studied calculus and chemistry and physics in high school, so the test was a snap. I was angry because I only made a 94. So I knew then that I had a chance, and the only bother might be my eyes. You had to have 20/20 vision to become a pilot. I waited and I waited and waited for a class to open up at Tuskegee, but no class opened up.

Another opportunity came up to take the test for aircraft mechanics, and I thought at least that would get me out of the labor battalion, so I took the test. It was a pass or fail test, and there were about ten of us in the organization that passed it. In January 1943 there was a call for those of us who had passed the aircraft mechanic test to go to Lincoln Air Force Training School in Lincoln, Nebraska. So they put the ten of us on a train from Denver, Colorado, to Lincoln, Nebraska. When we got there we were welcomed with open arms. This was a base for training aircraft mechanics, and it was one of the most sophisticated and highly technical airplane mechanic schools in the United States at the time, and there was one class for blacks. I was assigned to the 789th Technical Training Squadron; this was all black because they had to

Benjamin O. Davis

Benjamin O. Davis Jr., opened the door for abolishing segregation in the U.S. military by organizing and training the Tuskegee Airmen (see page 144), the all-black unit that defied conventional thinking about African Americans' ability to perform under combat conditions. He went on to distinguished service after World War II, becoming the Air Force's first black general, ultimately being elevated to the rank of four-star general.

A native of Washington and a 1936 graduate of the U.S. Military Academy at West Point, Davis was the son of another career military officer, Benjamin O. Davis Sr. The father instilled in his son the values of proving by doing and of maintaining dignity in the face of rampant racism in both society and the U.S. military. Deeply affected by a childhood ride with a barnstorming aviator, the younger Davis wanted to fly and secured an appointment from the only black congressman serving at the time, Rep. Oscar S. De Priest, R–Illinois.

At West Point, Davis faced extreme discrimination. Other cadets shunned him, not speaking to him except on official business; he had no roommate and he ate alone in silence. The adversity, which was intended to force him to quit, instead galvanized his resolve, and he graduated 35th in a class of 276. He was the first black to graduate from West Point in the twentieth century.

Although Davis was physically and academically qualified, he was turned down for flight training because of his race. He was assigned to Fort Benning, Georgia, as commander of the black service company and soon entered infantry school at Benning. The same treatment he had experienced at West Point followed him to Georgia. Also assigned to Benning were nine U.S. Military Academy classmates of his, who continued to speak to him only on business. Upon graduation from infantry school, he was sent to Tuskegee Institute in Alabama, where in 1940 he was assigned to start the program to train black military aviators. It was the exemplary record of these men, who fought in North Africa, Italy, and Western Europe, that

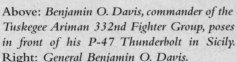

Above: *Benjamin O. Davis, commander of the Tuskegee Ariman 332nd Fighter Group, poses in front of his P-47 Thunderbolt in Sicily.*
Right: *General Benjamin O. Davis.*
BOTH WIKIMEDIA COMMONS

began to weaken the rationale for official segregation in the U.S. military.

After the war, Davis returned to the United States and embarked on a career that led him to become a base commander in Ohio. In 1947, the Air Force became a separate unit (previously it was the Army Air Corps), and an internal study of racial issues led to a recommendation that the Air Force be integrated. In 1949, it became the first of the U.S. services to do so. In 1950, Davis moved to Washington to serve at the Pentagon in the Air Force headquarters. During the Korean War, he was dispatched to that zone to command a unit of more than 1,000 airmen, most of whom were white. Later assignments took him to Japan, Taiwan, Germany, and back to Korea. He finished his thirty-three-year stint in the military back home in the United States.

(continued on page 192)

(continued from page 191)

As the most senior black officer in the U.S. armed forces, Davis retired from the Air Force in 1970 at the rank of lieutenant general with three stars. In 1998, President Bill Clinton awarded him a fourth star, meaning he was a full general.

After retirement, Davis served as public safety director for the city of Cleveland, Ohio, and later was appointed head of the anti-hijacking program that placed federal sky marshals on jetliners. He also served as an assistant secretary of transportation in the Richard Nixon administration. Davis died in July 2002 at the age of eighty-nine. ★

keep us separated. There was no black class before us and there was no black class after us. I was there for six months until June 1943 when I graduated.

I left the base two or three times. A couple of us went to Lincoln, Nebraska, to have a good meal. We found a little restaurant and had a meal, came back the next weekend, and we sat down in the booth and the manager came up and spoke with us. He asked us not to come back there again over the threat that they would spit in our food. We got up immediately and left. We found another place to eat and never went back to Lincoln, Nebraska, again.

I graduated in June 1943 as an aircraft mechanic with 250 others. Half of us went to Tuskegee to supplement their crew down there. They were trying to put together an all-black group; the mechanics, the crew chiefs, the specialists; all of them would have to be black. We were put on a train from Lincoln and we arrived in Detroit, Michigan in June 1943. They brought in some trucks and took us out to Selfridge Field, Michigan, where we formed the ground crew of the 332nd Fighter Group. Benjamin O. Davis had gone overseas with the 99th Fighter Squad that year and had come back to form the 332nd Fighter Group, and we formed the ground crew of the 332nd Fighter Group. We had a black commander over us for the first time. Before that there were two or three white racist commanders. They were racist because [during] our time in Selfridge Field, Michigan, we couldn't go into any of the service clubs, not the NCO club or the officer's club. We started breaking into the officer's club and Ben Davis heard about it and he clamped down on that one, because he knew that wasn't in our interest, and it really wasn't.

We had three fighter squadrons: the 302nd, the 100th, and the 301st. I became one of the crew chiefs in the 302nd. I was totally responsible for one aircraft. Sounds easy, and it was easy if you knew what you were doing. We had more pilots than aircraft, so each pilot was not fortunate enough to be assigned a crew chief and a specific plane all the time. But the crew chief, that was his plane. Period. We had P-40s and then after a while they gave us P-39s. A P-39 is not a real fighter plane. It was fast but not that maneuverable, so we suspected that wherever they were sending us, they weren't expecting us to run into too many enemy aircraft to fight. A class had opened up for Tuskegee, so I thought I was going there, but Ben Davis said, "I cannot spare a crew chief, soldier. We are heading overseas." We went overseas with him in December 1943.

We got on a Victory ship down in Virginia. We had some disturbances down there over the fact that they wouldn't permit us—we're on our way overseas now—they would not permit us to sit except in the last few back rows of the theater. So we got on Victory ships and headed out to sea, and twenty-seven days later we were at the Strait of Gibraltar after going over thirty-foot waves with the ship zigzagging to keep from being torpedoed by the German submarines.

We landed at Taranto, Italy, and we took a convoy of motor vehicles over the mountains to where the action was. A couple of days later we were near Saline. I have to say, once I got to Taranto, I kissed the ground and said that I felt free for the first time in my life as a black person and I said then that I might never come back to the United States.

I was not a combat pilot, but I flew as crew chief on B-25s all over the south of Italy. But sometimes my mission was to run and get away from the Germans who would come in at eleven o'clock at night and drop five-hundred pound bombs on us at Aviano Air Base. We were staying in tents on that base, and as the Germans dropped bombs, shrapnel came through the tents, so we would get out and try to dig foxholes. That was the first taste of war I had, and it seemed to be a continuous thing. I believe the Germans dropped some bombs over Mt. Vesuvius because it erupted at the same time. I don't know what happened, but that spewed hot lava on our tents and put holes in them, we were that close to Mt. Vesuvius.

Our assignment was up at Monte Cassino and the Anzio beachhead. Every day we were up at Anzio blasting trains and troop movements, everything of opportunity. By then we had gotten the P-47s, which had four .50-caliber machine guns in each wing, so you could do quite a bit of damage.

I spent most of my time in Italy at Ramitelli Air Base, and I stayed there until the end of the war.

We could tell when the war was dying down because after awhile we saw fewer and fewer enemy aircraft. We had destroyed the empire, really. Not that the soldiers on the ground didn't do a lot at the Battle of the Bulge and things of that sort, but air power really helped to destroy the axis.

Coming back, the war was over and they broke up my 99th Fighter Squadron. Some of us were sent to the 100th Air Squadron, so I ended up serving about thirty days with the 100th. I came back to New York on a boat with the group. I was home three days before I was a civilian, and there was no ticker-tape parade for us. We did go around the Statue of Liberty and stayed at Camp Kilmer overnight, then went to Fort Dix and stayed there one night, and the next day we walked out a civilian. When I got to Newark it was status quo, the same way it was before; I saw no black bus drivers. I saw no blacks doing anything at all. For blacks it was just as it was before.

AFTER THE WAR . . .

Henry Moore earned a masters degree in physics, and after twenty years of research and development with the Defense Department, the Army, and the Navy, he retired as a supervisory electronic engineer in 1973. After that he taught science and math in the School District of Philadelphia, retiring in 1983. Mr. Moore and his wife raised two daughters together. In his spare time, Mr. Moore enjoys lecturing about the Tuskegee Airmen.

☆ Joseph Bobby ☆
Port Carbon, Pennsylvania

••

Joseph Bobby was aboard the USS *Nelson* off Omaha
Beach when, just after D-Day, it was hit by a German
torpedo that killed twenty-four crewmembers.

••

I was a senior at St. Stephen's High School in Port Carbon, Pennsylvania,
and when I graduated the draft age was eighteen to forty-five. At that time
I was eighteen years old and I had to register at the draft board, so I went
and told them I would enlist in the Navy. I liked the water and the ships and
things like that. I went to boot camp in Sampson, New York, in March 1943.
It was mostly to get you indoctrinated into Navy life. It was six or eight
weeks of training, swimming, and abandon-ship drills. Then I was assigned
to the USS *Nelson* and sent to Boston, Massachusetts, to pick it up.

When I went aboard the *Nelson*, being a recruit, my battle station was in
a powder room down beneath the mess hall. We were feeding the Number
Two turret on the bow of the warship, so when general quarters came about,
that was my battle station. On that ship, we had abandon-ship drills, man-
overboard drills, and all different kind of drills to get us in unity. They even

timed us on how long it took to get from where we were to our battle station, because everybody's life depended on everybody else.

I made five trips convoying across the North Atlantic Ocean on the *Nelson*. We went out of Brooklyn, New York, and picked up sometimes as many as eighty to 120 ships; merchant ships, troop ships, ammunition ships, and they were always put in a row. Maybe there were ten rows, and one behind the other; ten ships in a row. Then the destroyers would circle all those ships like the hands on a clock to protect them. In the middle we had tankers to get our fuel and we had a cruiser or a battleship with us if you got sick or you had to get attended to. Then sometimes we went on scout duty, which meant a destroyer went east, about seven miles ahead; one was seven miles to the rear; another one went to the south, and to the north in a formation, like a cross. So if the destroyer in the front got in contact with submarines, they would notify by flashing lights and then the convoy would shift to a different direction. I was only nineteen at that point and I liked it. I really liked the ocean. I didn't see the danger. It didn't bother me at all.

We would always head for the North Atlantic because the waves were big, and it was safer to go that route. The submarines wouldn't get up in those

USS **Nelson.** NATIONAL ARCHIVES

high waves and if they did, they probably wouldn't get back down again. We would drop a lot of depth charges, and it got to the point where the *Nelson* was called "Depth-Charge Nelly" for all the depth charges she was dropping. I'm quite sure all the Nazi submarines didn't get away. I'm sure we got some of them, but we never saw any surface material come up. Our biggest trouble came leaving New York and coming into the coast of England and Ireland. We used to go into Northern Ireland to wait for the empties, and then we'd bring the empty ships back. Maybe after a week or ten days we'd come back again. We would make a round trip in six or seven weeks, over and back. I took at least five round trips, always on convoy duty.

We headed for Normandy in the beginning of May, 1944. We arrived in Ireland and went down the Irish Sea to Plymouth, England, to get some fuel. I don't know who made a mistake, but the *Nelson* backed over the anchor chain of the tanker. When they put us into dry dock they found out that the anchor chain was wrapped around the propeller. So the propeller and the shaft had to be removed. It looked like we weren't going to make the Normandy invasion, because this was the June 2 and Normandy was scheduled for the 6th. After they got us out of that dry dock they told us they needed every ship they could get, and that we would have to go to Normandy with one propeller. We were concerned about it, because with two propellers we could go maybe forty-two miles an hour, but when they took that one propeller off us, that took us down to half that speed. But we left anyway. We went over to Milford Haven and picked up a small convoy of ships, and took them over to Normandy with us. We arrived in Normandy on June 8. D-Day had been the 6th.

The first night we were there a German buzz bomb came from somewhere and flew into the water off our starboard quarter and exploded, but it didn't bother us. Then they told us we had to go out on the outer flank on a "Dixie Line," they called it, to protect the troopships from the German E-boats that came out at night. An E-boat was like John Kennedy's PT boat. The Germans used to call them "Fast Boats." They carried twin torpedoes and 20-millimeter guns and could do a speed of anywhere from forty to forty-five miles an hour. They would come out in bunches, maybe three or four at a time.

On this particular night, the German E-boats came out and it was pitch-black; you couldn't see a hand in front of you. We made the contact and they sounded general quarters. We were at our battle stations and the *Nelson* had to flash to challenge somebody, "Friend or foe?" When we flashed we didn't get any answer, so we opened fire, and all of a sudden, BOOM! We got hit so bad, you couldn't imagine the tremendous explosion. I was in the magazine loading powder for the five-inch gun. When it hit we flew against the bulkheads and the racks and powder cans came down; they had been held in place by straps on the side of the bulkhead. Everything came down. The torpedo that hit us went into the stern, where all of our three-hundred-pound depth charges were stored.

When it blew up, the ship rolled heavy to one side and came back to the other side, and then leveled off back and forth. When we came topside there was oil on everything and we couldn't see anything because it was pitch black. When daylight came we saw the damage to the warship; it was carnage. Guys we slept with and ate with, they were gone; there were twenty-four killed, and there were nine badly injured. The ship stayed afloat, and thank God it did because you couldn't see your hand in front of you. It was terrible! I couldn't believe that we were alive because of the damage that was done.

Then the USS *Maloy* came over and took the wounded and the bodies that could transfer over. The *Maloy* took us over to Plymouth, England, to a British barracks, and dumped us off there. In England they gave us clothes—we were filthy dirty—and they shipped us all the way up to Northern Ireland, outside of Londonderry, and I stayed there about three weeks. From Londonderry we took an empty transport ship back to Boston, and when I got back to Boston they sent me home for thirty days' leave.

Then they told me they were sending me to radio-communication school to learn the Morse Code, because I could type, so I was sent down to Newport, Rhode Island, to go to school there. Then I was assigned to a brand-new light cruiser, the USS *Little Rock*, so I stayed in Newport until June. A light cruiser has six-inch shells and forty-seven guns, and carries a crew of 1,200 people. It has a full captain for the command, and there is a Marine detachment aboard. It's real big.

We were sent down to Guantánamo Bay, Cuba, to take on crews, and while we were down there in July, the atom bomb was dropped on Japan. So they told us to bring the ship to Philadelphia. When the war was over they took all the war paint off and dressed it up as a peacetime warship.

The war made me remember to appreciate this country. I think when I look back at it, I didn't see the danger, but when that torpedo hit, my whole life changed. I couldn't believe what I saw. I couldn't believe how violent it was; that steel tore just like paper. I'm just fortunate I came out alive, and that'll be on my mind till the day I die.

AFTER THE WAR . . .

When Mr. Bobby returned home in 1946 after his service in the war, he entered the Fords Business School in Pottsville, Pennsylvania. From there he went on to work for the Lancaster Transportation Company until 1962. He later worked for Motor Freight Express until his retirement in 1985. Mr. Bobby married Anna Moran in 1952 and together they have three children and five grandchildren.

☆ Robert Long ☆

Greensburg, Pennsylvania

Robert Long was a B-17 bomber pilot in the European Theater, flying missions over Berlin and Munich and earning the Distinguished Flying Cross. He flew thirty-three missions, including two on D-Day.

I graduated from high school and got a job at Robertshaw Thermostat Company in Greensburg, Pennsylvania, as an inspector. I enlisted in October 1942 and went into the service in March 1943. I didn't want to be drafted. I wanted to go in the service in a unit that I wanted to be in, and I wanted the Air Force. I wanted to fly, that was the main reason. At night you always had a nice, comfortable bed. That's not like surviving in a foxhole. A lot of guys wanted to be pilots, but a lot of them didn't make it, they washed out. Seventy-one percent of our primary class in basic flying washed out, so the competition was pretty stiff. You just had to be efficient at flying. You had to pass all the exams they had. You got your eye exam, mental exam; they consider everything. And if you make it, you make it.

I went to indoctrination in Nashville and to Maxwell Field, Alabama, for basic training, then Ocala, Florida, for primary flight school, then Cochran

Field, Georgia, and Moody Field, Georgia, for advanced flying. I graduated at Moody Field.

Each section took about six weeks. They had a schedule set up that they knew exactly where you'd be on any day; where you should be if you don't fail anything. Like in primary, you had ten hours to do your solo flight. If you didn't complete the solo in ten hours they washed you out. Maybe you could solo in twelve, but they washed you out at ten. And you had to study radio communications, mathematics, weather; you had all those courses to take. Then they prepared you for combat. You knew where you were going. You knew that in the beginning. But it was worth it. I really enjoyed it.

In primary flight school, when you're underclassmen, you land on the grass. When you're upperclassmen, you land on the runway. That's a privilege you get when you turn upperclassman. So the day we turned upperclassmen, I went up, flew my training mission and came back down and landed. I was rolling down the runway, and all of a sudden, this big shadow came over me, and then kapow! That was it. And here Shorty Roberts forgot that he wasn't an underclassman any more. I was landing and he was coming at me at a 45-degree angle. I wasn't paying any attention to anything out the side; I was looking in my mirrors behind me. Nobody was supposed to be where he was. Anyway, we piled up. His plane went over and upside down, and mine was up in the air. I broke my nose, and there was blood all over me. I turned the ignition off and looked around and I heard someone down below me. I released my belt and crawled down through the wreckage, got down on the ground and crawled underneath, and saw Shorty hanging upside down. So I slid underneath and released his belt, and he dropped down, and we crawled out. We were standing on the runway when the fire truck and the ambulance pulled up. The ambulance driver said he couldn't believe that we were both standing there. I thought they'd wash us out right there, but they didn't, we just had meetings. Finally we went back to flying. No one said a word. But usually they would wash you out. One little accident and you're done. I graduated and got out of there.

I went to England with the 1st Division. We were in the 1st Bomb Wing. They had three groups to a wing and four squadrons to a group. They appointed your crew. As a new crew would come into the squadron, they would take you and break your crew up and put you on with older crews for about three missions to break you in. And oftentimes, maybe one of the crews would get shot down. So what happened with me was that this crew went down with a pilot, and they needed another pilot. So if you're experienced enough they'll advance you. So they put me on First Pilot with a crew, and I finished my tour with that same crew. You can advance very quickly in combat.

Our missions were all bombing missions. I think I flew two early-evening missions where we dropped supplies to the Free French, but the rest of them were all bombing missions. On a mission day we'd start off at four o'clock in the morning. You'd get up, go to breakfast, then they took you over to the headquarters into the pilots' briefing. The bombardiers and navigators all would have a separate briefing. After the briefing you'd go out to your aircraft. In the meantime the crew would get the aircraft ready. The armor men would put all their bombs in, then the gunners would put all the guns in, then they would pre-flight the aircraft; they'd warm the engines all up for you. Then you would go out and inspect it, and then get aboard. They would have a schedule for you to follow. You start the engines, say at seven o'clock. At 7:15 you start your taxiing. Everybody had a position. You get into your position, taxi out, and take off. Then you have a Buncher Beacon assigned to you. You form on that Buncher Beacon. The first, the lead plane takes off, makes a big circle, and the next plane takes off, he's inside of him. That's how you keep going until you all get formed. After you get formed, you go to another location where you line up in the formation of the flight. The squadron forms, and then the three squadrons form the group, and the group forms the wing. And you're on your way.

At first we had ten-man crews, and then they cut it to nine men. So any time an aircraft went down you lost nine men, plus the airplane. That was a lot of men. On some of those flights we'd have forty, fifty, seventy, or eighty airplanes. On certain missions you'd lose quite a few. Munich and Berlin were the bad ones. With Berlin, for example, we got thorough intelligence. They told us that any time you got in the defense area of Berlin, like thirty miles around Berlin, they could train 110 antiaircraft guns on you. That flak was so thick you could walk on it. I never minded a fighter attack. I'd sooner have a fighter attack than the antiaircraft. That was really bad.

We got hit over Berlin, and got a cockpit fire. The pilot got sprayed with hydraulic fluid and he caught on fire, and I got hydraulic fluid on me. My clothes were burning. I just kept brushing it off. I'd brush the fire down, and it'd come back up. I stood up in the seat and the pilot was laying on the seat on the deck, and the engineer came down to help him. In the meantime, the windshields all fogged up. This happened in just a second. I took my glove and wiped the window. When I did that, I looked down, and there was another B-17 right below us on fire, and we were sliding into it. I grabbed the controls and checked the engine and checked all the controls and straightened the airplane up and got out of there. We made it back.

Munich was a different story. We got hit between the number three engine and number four engine. When we got hit it took the airplane and it started down like an elevator. It went from 26,000 [feet] down to around 15,000 before it got leveled off. The number three engine was shot, number four was acting up, and we flew back with two engines on one side. Took one of the guns out of the top turret and used it for a brace between the rudder pedal and the seat to keep the plane straight, because you had two engines on one side and hardly anything on the other. All she wanted to do is turn to one side. You couldn't hold it. I stood with my feet on one pedal, both feet, standing up on the seat, to hold it, but I couldn't hold it very long. Too much pressure. So we used the gun for a brace, and it worked. Three days later they had a notice on the bulletin board, "You run into trouble and you need a brace, use a gun." So they took my advice, and it worked.

We would fly one or two missions a week. You didn't fly everyday. Now, when they were getting ready for D-Day, we had eleven missions in ten days. One day we flew two sorties, early in the morning and the evening. But on D-Day I saw so many ships in the English Channel, you couldn't believe it. Everywhere you looked there were ships. We flew only about 15,000 feet. Antiaircraft didn't bother us. There were so many airplanes and ships, you couldn't believe it. Everywhere. It was hard to believe.

We were early, just as they started in on the beaches. We went right ahead of them. We could see them forming in the Channel, getting ready. When we went over it was just getting daylight. We bombed the coastal road that runs from Saint-Lô to Cherbourg. Our target area was south of that road. We went through there, dropped the bombs, flew south, circled out to the east, the west, came up around Guernsey Island and Jersey Island and back to England, loaded up, and came back again. That day we had two runs. When we got back we got late chow and everybody was ready for the sack. We were ready to drop over.

A typical mission, from the time you got up in the morning until you finished up, was five or six hours, but a couple of them were ten hours of flying time. It was very exhausting. They gave the pilots two little white pills you put in your flight suit. The only time you ever took them was when you were coming back and getting ready to land. Right before you'd land, when you were in your flight pattern, you would take one of them. I don't know what it was, speed or what, I don't know. After you took it, you felt like you were a giant; wide awake and alert. After it wore off it felt like someone hit you in the back. But you wouldn't take them all the time. You had them just in case you thought you needed them. But on the long missions I would usually take one before I would land, but that was the only time I used them. I asked what they were but nobody ever told me.

One day a piece of shrapnel came through the plane. My co-pilot and I had an agreement. Each of us would fly at twenty-minute intervals. I watched the clock, and when it came to twenty minutes, right on the nose, I'd release the control and pull my seat back and say, "You got it." Then the co-pilot would take it over, and he'd do the same thing to me. One day we came off a target and they were tracking us with antiaircraft. They'd track you on the outside, and all of a sudden in front of you they'd concentrate on an area where they thought you'd be, and that's where they would hit. I had just said to the co-pilot, "You got it," because my twenty minutes was up. I pulled my seat back and crossed arms, and a shell burst, and a piece of shrapnel came up through the plane and took my right rudder pedal off. The piece of flak caught my jacket and it tore the whole thing off me. It left me with three little cat scratches. Then it hit the top turret and tore a hole in the side and went out. I don't know what kind of a piece it was, but it did a lot of damage. If I would have been on the controls it probably would have taken my leg and my arm. But I had just said to the co-pilot, "You got it," and I leaned back and it just missed me. Luck was with me.

We had sixty-seven holes in the aircraft one day. But that's just the way that shrapnel goes, it all breaks up into little pieces and flies everywhere. Some days you never got a scratch, other days you got a whole mess of them.

I had made up my mind before I got into combat what I was going to do to prepare. You had to fix yourself mentally, and when I did that I didn't have any problem. I saw quite a few fellas who had problems; they got shaky and whatnot. But I had made up my mind I wasn't going to do that, so I didn't have too much problem. But you can't just think of yourself. You got a lot more things to think about than just you. You got nine men on board. You got nine individuals depending on you. You can't let them die.

When I first got over there, I was writing home, telling them I was still training, that we weren't ready for combat. So it was after eleven or twelve missions we got shot up and they gave me the Air Medal. I was writing to my mother in Virginia, telling them that I'm still training, not in combat, then they picked up the paper and saw that I had my eleventh mission and

I was in combat. I was still writing, saying I was training, and they were reading about me in the paper.

You finished your tour, if you finished your tour, after thirty missions. Then they gave you the Distinguished Flying Cross. When I first went over it was twenty-five missions, then they raised it to thirty. Then I got to thirty and they said, "Fly until you get a replacement." So I flew three more missions before I got a replacement.

That last mission was scary. You didn't want to get shot down. You get pretty shaky. But I survived it.

AFTER THE WAR . . .

Returning home to Greensburg, Pennsylvania, after his discharge, Robert Long went back to work as an inspector at Robertshaw Thermostat Company, where he stayed for forty-three years. He and his brother Bill, a carpenter, did several home improvement projects over the years. Mr. Long married his wife, Virginia, in 1943. Together they raised four children. In addition to his love of hunting and family, Mr. Long was a volunteer fireman for the Southwest Greensburg Fire Department for fifty-nine years.

☆ Harold Brandt ☆

Hershey, Pennsylvania

• •

Harold Brandt experienced his first combat around Bastogne
during the Battle of the Bulge. He was involved in the
liberation of the Flossenburg concentration camp in Germany
and spent ten months as part of the postwar occupation force.

• •

I was a college student at Hershey Junior College in February of 1943.
Every branch of the service came to visit us, and their talk was not "If
you're going to be in," but, "When you're going to be in." They were saying, "If you enlist now we'll get you in the branch of the service you want
to be in." Needless to say, I didn't enlist and I did not get the branch of the
service I wanted to get. I was hoping for engineers or something in the Army
other than the infantry. And the infantry is where I ended up.

I took a test in Hershey Junior College and scored high enough to be in
the Navy V-12 program, so I went to Philadelphia to have a physical, and my
physical lasted exactly thirty seconds. My eyesight was 20/30, and they wanted
20/20 vision. So when I went into the service they put me in the A-12 program, which was comparable to the Navy V-12.

I ended up in college, but first they sent me to the infantry for basic training at Camp Roberts, California, in August 1943. I could do everything they asked me. The worst thing was a twenty-five-mile march at the end of the program. Most of us did it, with very few people falling out. In the program at Camp Roberts, we were all ASTP (Army Specialized Training Program) students. Every one of us went to college after basic training. I think 1,000 of us were in the area that trained for infantry.

After basic training they sent us to College of Puget Sound in the state of Washington. We got there around Thanksgiving Day and were there until March 10. We studied English, history, biology, chemistry, and they gave us majors. I think we had about six majors. They kept us busy; we didn't have much free time. Then they sent us back to the infantry in Camp Cooke, California. That is where Vandenberg Air Force Base is right now. There were 235 of us that came from the College of Puget Sound to Camp Cooke, and almost all of us went in the infantry. I was put in the 11th Armored Division, which had about 150 tanks and 3,000 infantrymen. At our orientation, they let us know that the 11th Armored Division was going overseas.

On the trip overseas my berth where I slept was on the lowest part of the ship, and when I got down there I had to lie down or I'd be seasick, so I was up on deck the whole time. They had a great dance band that performed for us every afternoon. It was a fantastic voyage. An aircraft carrier followed us across, and it took us fourteen days to cross the ocean because we zigzagged across. We only ate two meals a day; breakfast and the afternoon meal. At evening meal time we went to the mess hall to listen to the ballgame on radio. What shocked me was when we got to the mess hall it looked like Monte Carlo. Everybody was gambling. Every mess hall table had lights down over them, and had the guys with the hats like in Las Vegas. There was gambling all over the ship.

We got to England at the end of October 1944 and we were there until December 16, 1944. England was just an island full of United States soldiers. I imagine it was fuller up until D-Day, but there were plenty of soldiers on the British Islands at that time. We got off at Southampton and went to Warminster, which is pretty much in the middle of England; about a two-hour train trip from London. I got to see London two or three times. We also went to Bath and Bristol for a weekend. In fact, I was in a dance hall in London and we could hear the bombs. On the train the next day going back to Warminster we had three soldiers and three British women in our compartment with us. To make a conversation, I said, "Where did those bombs hit last night?" I was quickly told by one of the women, "We don't talk about that." They kept it quiet so the Germans would not know where the bombs hit, which was a learning experience for me. I thought, "Well, keep your mouth shut, Harold."

We crossed the English Channel to Cherbourg and after we climbed down a cargo net with all our equipment, trucks took us out to a field outside of Cherbourg where we saw our half-tracks for the first time. The organization was phenomenal. At one point we thought we were going to Saint-Lazare because there were a couple thousand Germans surrounded there. We left on December 16, which is when the Germans made the attack of the Battle of the Bulge. So we changed from Saint-Lazare to go to the Bastogne area.

We arrived were there on December 24 on our half-tracks, but no tanks were with us at that point. It was noontime, and we saw all these airplanes above us in the sky. One guy said, "Boy, the Germans are going to get it today." Well, the airplanes went in, and three minutes later they're coming back out. They weren't bombing anybody. They were delivering ammunition, guns, food, and supplies for the soldiers surrounded in Bastogne. We were about twenty miles from Bastogne at that point. That night, Christmas Eve, was when we heard our first airplane strafe. They called it "Bed-Check Charlie." So Bed-Check Charlie came over and shot his machine gun. I had dug a slit trench, and I rolled out into the slit trench, got my foot caught, and had to be helped up to get out of the trench. That was my first experience of enemy fire.

On December 28 we got into combat and had shells landing on us for the first time. We ended up hitting the side of a Panzer division, Panzer Lehr, going toward Bastogne, and were able to stop that division. It was cold. That was our baptism of fire. My best friend Cook and I were lying together along a road and shells were exploding over our heads. We didn't get hit, but we spent the first day there and I dug three different holes for protection. At about eleven o'clock at night they came and said, "Mount up. We're going." I don't know where we went, but I have talked to officers in the sixty years since then, and nobody knew where we were going, but we left that area. I think we just made a big circle and came back to almost the same place. You talk about bitter cold; it was maybe five degrees. Every time the half-tracks stopped we'd get out and jump on our feet to keep them from freezing.

We were in the Bastogne area from December 28 until about January 16, when we went to the Siegfried Line. We were back and forth on the Siegfried

Line for a couple weeks, but then we made an attack around February 15. Our company commander, his name was Dale Howard, he got us up at two o'clock in the morning. We had breakfast, and he took us on a march along a road that lasted about two hours. We were attacking with about thirty-five or forty men. When we went came to a fence we used clippers with a cloth so the Germans wouldn't hear us cut through it. When we went through the fence it was so dark that we had to put our hand on the shoulder of the man in front of us. When it started getting light we could see the "dragon's teeth" fortifications. We were at the exact spot we were supposed to be, and we could see three pillboxes ahead of us. As we were laying there a German opened up with a machine gun, and I thought, "Oh, boy. We've had it. This is it." Here he was just clearing out his machine gun, and he hadn't seen us. So in another ten or fifteen minutes Dale said, "Let's go." The first pillbox was taken by another squad. We took the second one. At the dragon's teeth there was a trip wire, and the first man across yelled to the second man, "Trip wire, trip wire." We all crossed without setting it off.

At the pillbox we went up to, nobody was inside, but the third pillbox had seventeen German soldiers in it, and they were throwing potato mashers at us. That's a hand grenade, and it looked like a potato masher. I have to admit,

Troops of the 82nd Airborne Division march through a snowstorm during the push towards Belgium during the Battle of the Bulge. WIKIMEDIA COMMONS

Dragon's Teeth Fortifications

As Allied forces pushed toward Nazi Germany after the June 6, 1944, D-Day invasion of Normandy, they encountered massive fields of defensive obstacles that were intended to hamper and delay their attack.

These included minefields, trenches (antitank ditches), pillboxes (enemy-occupied bunkers), and multiple rows of "dragon's teeth." These were three- to four-foot-high reinforced concrete pyramids that were emplaced in a pattern, four to five rows deep, that were designed to stop tanks. Between the dragon's teeth, which were spaced about four feet apart, the Germans often buried land mines and strung barbed wire to impede the advance of infantry troops.

They were lined up in such a way either to stop tanks and troops or to funnel them into "killing zones," where artillery and small-arms

Grounds-eye view of dragon's teeth fortifications. NATIONAL ARCHIVES

An Allied tank advances through a track cleared of dragon's teeth fortifications.
NATIONAL ARCHIVES

weapons could easily be aimed. These fortifications were part of Hitler's Siegfried Line (so named by the Allies because of its similarity to the World War I fortification of the same name) defense that had been built in anticipation of an Allied invasion from England. Stretching about four hundred miles from the Netherlands to Switzerland, the Siegfried Line was part of the West Wall (also called *Atlantikwall* or Atlantic Wall) that stretched across the whole of Western Europe.

Dragon's teeth were most prominently placed in France, Belgium, and Germany, but also along the East Wall, on the Eastern Front. Russian Red Army troops who were driving toward Berlin and Nazi-held Poland from the east found them in the Baltics as they pushed through Latvia.

Advancing Allied troops "pulled the dragon's teeth" in a number of ways. One method was planting charges of TNT to blow up the concrete obstacles, often just minutes before a tank attack was set to

(continued on page 212)

(continued from page 211)

begin. Another tactic was to remove just enough of the dragon's teeth to allow a line of tanks to pour through.

As the war continued, combat experience taught the Nazis that fortified villages, with small garrisons of mobile soldiers trained in street fighting, proved to be a more effective deterrent than permanent, dug-in installations of antitank defenses and pillboxes. As a result, toward the end of the war, the Germans moved their more experienced officers and troops to this assignment and left less-experienced soldiers at the actual front. When Allies broke through the dragon's teeth and captured or destroyed pillboxes, they frequently found demoralized troops, many of them ready to surrender.

As Allied combat troops advanced, engineers behind them destroyed the networks of dragon's teeth, pillboxes, and other emplacements. One captain and engineer with the U.S. Third Army explained to a United Press reporter the rationale for doing so: "First, in case the Germans try another breakthrough (as in the offensive German "bulge" made famous by the Battle of the Bulge) they won't have any fortifications; second, to leave the enemy nothing to start with if he tries to arm for another war; and third, 'the terrific psychological effect it has on the Germans to see their famous defenses blown to hell.'"

Not all of the dragon's teeth were destroyed, however, and some are still visible today. ★

every one of them looked like they were coming down on our heads, but they all missed us. Then we got shot at by troops in the town below us, and somebody said, "That's an American machine gun." So we yelled down to them, "Hey, we're Americans," and the guy yelled back to us, "Well, prove it." So our platoon leader ran down and proved that we were Americans, so they would stop shooting at us.

There was a lot of friendly fire. We had men killed by friendly fire. I had my closest call with friendly fire near Bastogne, at Longchamps. We had been in combat for two weeks by this time. We were the last to come out of Longchamps; our whole battalion was in front of us. I was lying down, facing Bastogne. I was supposed to be laying the other way, but my head was facing Bastogne. I heard an artillery piece in Bastogne go off and something told me, "This is coming for me." When an artillery piece goes off, you can hear it for the first ten or fifteen seconds, and then the sound disappears, then you can hear it for the last ten seconds before it comes in. So I had the choice of getting up and running, but I was afraid if I got up and ran I'd miss my timing, and just as I would get up and run the shell would land and get me. So I stayed lying down and the shell landed just a few feet behind me. A man next to me did get hit in the legs from it. It missed me completely. It wasn't the only shell that they fired. They fired four or five other ones, and, one man, Tojo Walsh, was killed.

I took my first prisoner in Reichwalde. The guy next to me, Matthew Schultz, had yelled, "Heinies." Germans were called Heinies or Jerries. And we saw a machine gun set up at the opening of a foxhole, and in the foxhole were two German soldiers. I was lying on the ground and I thought, "Maybe I'm lying on top of a German foxhole," so I look around and saw a German foxhole just a few feet away. I decide to retreat. This was the first time I was going to shoot my rifle, and I shot it at the foxhole. I got out of there, and shot two or three more times and then all the guys around me saw what I was shooting at. Then everybody started shooting at the foxhole and out came a German soldier. I looked at that German soldier and thought to myself, "He's no different than I am. He doesn't want to be here any more than I do." But when he came over somebody said, "Make him take his shoes off." Now, I don't know why that was. I mean, here it was a winter day, January 1, and they took his shoes off. I wish I could meet that German soldier today. I hope he lived. I'm not sure what happened to him, but I guess what I learned is that he is no different than I am, except I was in the American army, and he was in the German army.

I got sent back with frozen feet for about a month, and then I came back in April, at a place called Hildburghausen. A jeep with a lieutenant colonel in it led the attack with five tanks and five half-tracks. The whole line might go for five, ten, or fifteen miles, and that's the way we were attacking the last part of the war.

Of course, it's no good talking about it, but if they had let us get in Berlin, we could have taken it. But because they divided Germany up, Berlin was supposed to be taken by the Russians. So we went close to Leipzig, made a right turn and went down along the Czech border into Austria, and we ended up in Linz. We took three concentration camps: Mauthausen, Flossenburg, and Guesen. At Mauthausen, they were still taking people to be killed in the gas chambers when our tanks drove up. I wasn't there; I was twenty or thirty miles north of Mauthausen, but the 11th Armored tanks did take it. We took Flossenburg, and I was right there. When we got to Flossenburg the prisoners were lined up outside the gate, and some of the guards were getting beaten up by the prisoners. We had no idea what was going on. The only thing I knew was, here's my half-track, and there's the gate, and there are the prisoners. We didn't know we were coming to a concentration camp. They talk about the big picture; well we didn't know about the big picture. We just knew about the little picture. The only thing that concerned us was whatever was one hundred yards in front of us. So I had no idea we were coming to a concentration camp.

The war was over in May 1945, but I didn't get home until March 1946. I was part of the Occupation troops. It was the finest ten months I ever had. At Christmastime I stood guard at the POW cage in Landshut, Germany. I think they were White Russians. These guys were dignitaries of the Russian

The ruins of the Reichstag Building in Berlin following the city's capture in 1945.
NATIONAL ARCHIVES

army that were captured by the German army. We had them in our POW cage, but at Christmastime people were escaping from our POW cage. There were five of us; all my friends. Our job was to go out there in the woods, lay there with M1 rifles, and if anybody escaped, we were supposed to shoot them. So we had to go out there for three days and three nights, and thank goodness nobody escaped those three nights. So we were out there all night for three nights at Christmastime. Basically, Occupation was a pretty nice ten months. What I did most of all is go to the Red Cross place and drink coffee, play Ping-Pong, and have food. And the Red Cross women were there.

The German people were wonderful, we were buddies. Right after the war in August we were in a little town called Eschenbach, and we were moved from Eschenbach to Landshut, about a hundred miles away. But we had found this woman in Eschenbach who was doing our laundry, so we would hitchhike to Landshut with our laundry every Saturday, and then when it came Christmastime we emptied our lockers and gave her everything we had in payment

I was in Europe eighteen months, and every city was practically destroyed. One thing intrigued me most of all; I thought it was amazing to get on the train at Fort Dix and come to Harrisburg, Pennsylvania, and see the United States untouched. That was wonderful. It just didn't seem right, but it was wonderful that the United States was untouched as far as being bombed or shelled or having anything happen to it.

AFTER THE WAR . . .

Harold Brandt received an undergraduate degree from Ursinus College in 1949. He went on to finish his masters degree from Temple University in 1952 and did additional graduate work at various colleges in Pennsylvania and Delaware. Mr. Brandt taught school and coached basketball in Annville, Pennsylvania, and was a counselor and principal in Hershey, Pennsylvania. He retired from Hershey in 1986. Mr. Brandt and his wife of more than sixty years, Jane, are the parents of three sons.

☆ Lloyd Kern ☆

Harrisburg, Pennsylvania

• •

**Lloyd Kern's bomber was shot down near Berlin on what
was scheduled to be his last mission. He was captured and
held in a German POW camp for thirteen months.**

• •

The draft came along when I was twenty and I was called up to the service. They put us through a series of tests because you had to have a certain IQ before they put you in the Air Force. Then I was assigned to a bomber crew. There were ten of us; four officers and six enlisted men. We then went through training in Pyote, Texas, and Miami Beach. Eventually we went overseas to Molesworth, England. We went over on the *Queen Mary*. I had a pass before I went overseas; I was home four or five days. I told my mother, "Mom, don't worry. I'll be back." Honest to God, I said that. She said, "Well, I'll still worry." I said, "I know you're worried, but I'll be back. You watch."

I remember the first time I was really under fire. We were flying along, and in the back of us, the tail, I saw these bright lights blinking. I thought, "What the hell is that?" I had no idea. Then I said, "Jesus Christ, that's a German fighter shooting at us." So I fired at him with two .50-caliber machine guns,

216

and they make a hell of fire going back, and that drove him off. That was the first time I was in combat, and I thought, "Boy isn't this something?"

Because there were such a high percentage of the fliers being shot down, they said, "You have to fly twenty-five missions. When you finish your twenty-five missions over enemy territory, then you can go home." So, would you believe it? We got up to twenty-five missions in April 1944, and they said, "You're going to have to fly three more, because the invasion is coming up soon."

Part of our job was to help destroy German fighters, and the strange thing about that is, some people might say, "You don't use a bomber to destroy fighters." But what they had told us is, "We want the German fighters to come up. When they come up, we'll shoot them down, but we can't get them if they don't get up in the air. We're using you as targets." They also said, "What we're going to do is, you will fly in on one route, and fly back the same route." We used to always come back on a different route, so the Germans wouldn't be waiting for us. They said, "We want them to be waiting for you. You're going to be targets. Let them work on you, and we'll try to shoot them down with the Allied fighters." It didn't make us too happy, but that's what we had to do.

So we did the extra three missions. We were on our last mission and everything was going well. We went over the targets outside of Berlin and dropped our bombs. We were coming off the target, and all of a sudden, there was a hell of an explosion, and it blew off our right wing, with the two engines on it. Well, it wasn't as scary as you'd think. I say that not to be brash about it, but I'll tell you what we tried to do. As we were going down, we had eight or ten .50-caliber machine guns on the plane. They were heavy as hell and very sturdy. We said, "Throw out everything you can." We had a waist gunner and big openings on both sides, so we picked up everything we could. The ammunition was .50-caliber rounds, which are big. We threw those overboard, and everything else lying around, we picked up and threw out.

Our pilot said, "We have to bail out! I can't hold it up here!" so everybody was getting ready to bail out. There were nine guys that had parachutes on, getting ready to jump out the door, and I said, "Wait a minute fellows, I don't have a parachute." The reason for that was that in a ball turret, you're sitting down in a tight spot and you can't have a parachute on, because it's too big, too bulky. I said, "Wait a minute fellows, I have to go with somebody." One guy said, "We're right at treetop!" I said, "Holy hell. We're at treetop? No time to bail out." So I ran and jumped headfirst and hit the deck and put my head down on it. The next thing I knew, there was a hell of a crash and things flying everywhere. All the ten guys got out, which is a miracle in itself. We must've had a hell of a good pilot.

Obviously we would try to get back to England, but we were deep in Germany and don't know where the devil we were. We came across railroad tracks, and we did have an escape map, so we said, "Let's try to get up on the railroad." Because you could see all the railroad tracks around there and there's always stuff on either side clear. We had been told that, if we got captured, "Don't tell them anything," which is nice to say when you're back home. That's great to be brave when you're back in London.

Our radio operator and I started walking around a bunch of trees we found. Over in Germany they keep them trim and looking nice like Christmas trees. So when it got toward evening we burrowed into them to hide. We were buried pretty much under the trees, when along came these German soldiers. I said, "It doesn't look too good for all of us." One guy poked into the trees with his rifle like you've seen in motion pictures. We were being very careful not to move. But they went on by us, and we slept there that night. You know, it's surprising we could sleep.

We were out a couple days and we didn't get any food. The only thing we had was the rations. It was a box with some type of carbohydrates or protein. They were on the plane, and we were supposed to pick them up and take them with us. Well, I grabbed a box of them and all we had was some of those for four or five days. As I said, we saw railroad tracks. At least on railroad tracks you can move. We went through a damn swamp one night, and one time we were walking out on a road and it was dark as the devil, and all of a sudden we heard people singing. I'm pretty sure they were Hitler Youth. Remember reading about them? Some of them were nasty SOBs. So we dove into the bushes real quick and laid there while they marched on by. All those guys were walking by and we were thinking what would happen if one of them went to take a piss in the bushes, and he found us. But anyway, they didn't.

We marched at night, but one night we started out a little too early. The next thing we knew, four or five German soldiers were after us, and we were stuck. They picked us up and took us to a police station where we were going to go up against trained interrogators. I was twenty-three years old, what the heck did I know about dealing with some expert? So it got a little shaky. He said, "Why do you fight the fatherland?" I said, "I'm not fighting the fatherland." He said, "Well, don't you think your mother would rather have you home alive?" I said, bravo me, "I'm sure she would rather have me dead than a traitor to my country." But I always felt, if they got me up in front of a firing squad, I was going to say, "Wait a minute! What do you want to know?"

I was there three or four days. You lose track of time, because they didn't let you know the time and didn't give you anything to eat. It is a little scary when you're in an interrogation center with trained interrogators. It was war and they were killing people left and right. Was I going to be one of those? They said they were going to take us to Stalag 17, and they put us on the train, in a forty-and-eight boxcar. They mainly used them in World War I. Each boxcar had room for forty men or eight horses. They shoved us in tight; you couldn't even sit down, couldn't lie down, and had no bathroom facilities. There being all guys, though, you could piss out the door. But it got to be a hell of a mess in there, if you know what I mean. Funny how quickly you adapt to a situation like that.

I was in the prison camp for thirteen months. In all fairness to the Germans, they tried to get us food, but there wasn't any food across Germany. As you might expect in Germany, there was a lot of cabbage, and Jesus, the worms. Little, white worms got in the cabbage. When they cooked it, obviously it killed them, but they'd be scattered all over the soup. That's what you got; soup and all you got were these damn white worms all over your soup. You might say you got used to it after a while, honest to God. We did nothing there all day long. We were all staff sergeants, and they couldn't make us work, so we'd sit around and talk.

A month or two before the war ended the Germans said, "We're going to move you out, back to your line." We could hear the Russian artillery coming in over Vienna. We said, "Leave us here. We'll just wait until the American troops come." They said, "No, we can't do that." They could have said, "The hell with you," and left us there, but they said, "We don't know what will happen to you." So we marched for about thirty days toward the American lines. Russians were coming up on one side, Americans were coming up on the other side, and there were a couple thousand of us all standing around. And nobody could tell us what to do because the Germans all left. We ran into some American troops while we were wandering around, and we said, "Hey, we're POWs, help us out," And the American soldier said, "Tell you what, I saw a Mercedes back there in the garage. Do you guys want it?" We said, "Hell, yeah, we want it." So we got a Mercedes and we just wandered around like a bunch of dopes, because we didn't know what to do. We were on the loose for three or four days. Finally, the American troops caught us and took the car away.

We were put in some sort of holding camp, Camp Lucky Strike, and my buddy and I decided we wanted to go to Paris. So we stole a pass book, and we borrowed some money and went to Paris. I can't tell you the rest, but we did catch on to a couple girls; Paris hookers. We were just wandering around Paris and I heard that there were planes leaving for England for people who might want to go. I said, "Hell, I'll go over." When I got there I looked up a girl I'd met on an earlier date in London. Next thing you know we got married, and we've been married fifty-nine years. We have three kids. One daughter is a lawyer, one is a registered nurse, and my boy has three masters degrees. So my wife and I feel pretty good. I never went to college, but we put three kids through school.

Anyway, I wouldn't take a million dollars for my experience in the war. It was the best time of my life. I had always wanted to be a soldier of fortune, and boy, I got into it. When our plane was going down, I thought to myself, "You dumb son of a bitch. You wanted an experience like this? You got it now, buddy." But honest to God, when I was shot down I looked at it as one big adventure. It was fun.

AFTER THE WAR . . .

When Lloyd Kern returned from the service he went back to his position at the Middletown Army Depot. He married his wife in London and they are the parents of three children. Mr. Kern has attended most of the POW reunions. At this time there are only three men still living who were in Barracks 29A.

✯ Harold Sargent ✯

Hermitage, Pennsylvania

••

Harold Sargent joined the Army at age eighteen. He saw
his first combat on the island of Cebu in the Philippines,
where he operated a Browning automatic rifle.

••

The only thing I did before the war was go to school. I graduated in June
1944, but I didn't want to go into the service until September. They
accepted me because that was after the Normandy invasion and they needed
bodies. And they wanted young bodies, because once a man gets to be
twenty-five or twenty-six years old he realizes that life can end, but when
you are eighteen that doesn't occur to you. So I volunteered.

I lived out in the country in Riceville, Pennsylvania, and I got on a bus
and went up to the armory in Erie. I went through the regular routine,
which was always the same; you go through different stations and they said
to me, "What do you want to go into?" I said, "I'll try the Marines." So I
went through the Marines and they told me I didn't qualify because they
said I had high blood pressure. So they asked if I wanted to try for something else and I said, "How about the Air Corps?" So I went through the
Air Corps and they didn't want me, and they asked me if there was anything

else I would like and I said, "How about the Navy?" I went through the naval routine, and I was not acceptable. But I had to get into the service, because I was the only one left at home; everyone else had gone into the service and it was lonely. So they asked me about the Army and I said, "Okay, I'll go in the Army." So I went through that routine and the doctor shook his head and told me I didn't pass and I said, "Well what am I going to do, I don't even have a way to get home?" I was twenty-five miles from home and came in on a bus. He said, "I'll tell you what, you lay there for a little while longer and I'll come back." He came back and tested my wrist and listened to my heart and said, "You're in the Army now." So that's how I got into the service.

I went to Camp Wheeler, Georgia, for fourteen weeks, then to Fort Ord, California, where I got on the USS *Butler*. We went out under the Golden Gate Bridge and all the way to New Guinea without stopping. In those days, in order to avoid subs, they zigzagged. When we got to Hillandia, New Guinea, we stopped for the first time, but we did not get off. Then we took off for the Philippines. They never told us anything. All I knew was that I was on a boat and heading for trouble.

We went to Leyte, which had already been invaded and secured, and we stopped in Tacloban. I got off there and went to a Repo Depot, they called them; a replacement depot. That's where they fanned everybody out to different units. After about six days there they put me on an LCT—Landing Craft, Tank, but there was no tank in the hold, it was supplies. It was a beautiful trip on the Visayan Sea. It was 90 to 100 degrees, but we were moving, and it was beautiful.

We then went to Cebu and had to unload the boat. The next morning a man came along in a jeep and he asked if there was a guy by the name of Sargent, and said, "Get in here, I'm going to take you up on the hill." The 132nd Regiment had invaded Cebu three days before I got there, and they were on top of this hill. I went up, and there were a lot of soldiers around. No one had any identification on, because the enemy snipers would kill any officer. On the first night, we were attacked. We were not attacked there again, except they would shoot at us in the morning. The Japanese had a guy beyond the hill 250 or 300 yards, and he would open up with a machine gun. We called him "Chow-time Charlie" because he always opened up at breakfast, and we all knew it was going to happen.

One time Lieutenant Goss was our platoon leader, and just an unusual guy, he was so thin. He had been over there a long time, through Guadalcanal and Bougainville and then Leyte. He came along and said, "Sargent, I'm going to take your squad and we're going down the hill and search around back to make sure there are no enemies in the huts that we bypassed." So we went down and started going around, and I came to this hut and we walked around it, and out back was a very old man sitting on a stool maybe a foot high, and his foot was on the stool, and his foot was bigger than his body. He had elephantiasis. It is a sight that, once you see it, you never forget. There were flies buzzing around and there were two or three children, from two to five years of age. I had my weapon on him and I looked in his eyes and I thought, "He's afraid I won't shoot." Isn't that odd?

A day or two later we decided to leave the hill because we had secured it, and we marched down to the ocean. One night this guy from Philadelphia, Scardizio was his name, was talking about his sweetheart in Philadelphia. He called her Polish, and she was the love of his life. He said, "You know, when we go into battle tomorrow I'm going to get killed. How do you feel?" I told him, "I made up my mind a long time ago that there is no bullet made with my name on it." He said, "Well, I'm going to be killed, and I want you to do me a favor afterwards. I want you to write my mother and tell her how it happened." Then it started raining. Over there, when it got to noon it started raining everyday. I got in one foxhole and the water was really deep. That's when the lieutenant came back and said, "Sargent, I want you to help Scardizio. An enemy mortar has landed right on top of him and we have to carry him out." When someone died they would carry you back and put you in one pile, and then someone would come along and take care of it. So they asked me to help them carry him back. I told him that I couldn't do it, and he knew exactly what I meant. About ten minutes later they walked past with a poncho filled with Scardizio. I remember that day clearly, because that was the day that President Roosevelt died. He had been president for so long, he was the only president that we had ever known. Well, about six months later I did write to Scardizio's mother. She wrote back and wanted me to continue writing, but I didn't.

That night we had to dig in because the Japanese were up on this hill. It was maybe 2,000 feet high, but it rose right from the sea, so it looked high. They told me I had to get in the foxhole with this guy from Kentucky. Usually these hillbillies were the best fighters that we had, but this guy was crazy. He was illiterate, and he had just married this girl before he left and she had written a Dear John letter to him, which had to be read to him. He was the kind of person that never should have been taken into the Army. That hap-

Browning Automatic Rifle

Born in Utah of Mormon parents, John Moses Browning (1855–1926) was one of the most successful firearms designers of all time. In Allied military circles, his name came to be associated with one of the most widely used field weapons of World War II, the Browning automatic rifle.

Although it was designed and first produced in the closing years of World War I, the rifle saw much more widespread action in World War II. It was an in-between firearm, being neither a standard single-shot rifle nor a true machine gun. And that was the niche it was intended to fill—a weapon that offered greater firepower than a regular rifle, but with more mobility than a machine gun.

The BAR was air-cooled, gas-operated, and magazine-fed—each detachable magazine held twenty rounds of .30-caliber ammunition. So while it could fire rapidly (a rate of 550 rounds per minute), it could not deliver extended bursts as would a machine gun. When the magazine was emptied, it had to be changed out for a fresh one, a switch that took six to eight seconds to accomplish.

While the BAR was designed in such a way that it could be held and fired by one man, it weighed about twenty pounds and measured four feet long. With that much weight, it could not be fired from the shoulder in automatic (repeating) mode with much accuracy. Thus, most were equipped with a bipod (two-footed stand) for steadying the barrel when firing from the ground. An ensemble consisting of the BAR, bipod, and a loaded bandoleer (belt holding twelve fresh ammunition magazines) weighed about forty pounds.

Early versions could be fired in either single-shot or repeating mode. The single-shot option was dropped in later models (those

pened during the war; there were people taken into the service who never should have been taken in, they just couldn't take it.

At night the Japanese would roll out the Howitzers. They would point them straight down at us and fire. About every fourth bullet was a tracer, so you could see them going over your head, and they were no more than three

Browning Automatic Rifle. WIKIMEDIA COMMONS

manufactured from 1940 on) and the operator could choose between two rates—350 rounds per minute or 550 rounds per minute. The BAR was complicated to manufacture, but reliable in trench conditions so long as it was regularly cleaned and serviced in the field. That its original design was sound is proven by the fact that it served in four wars—World War I, World War II, Korea, and Vietnam—with few modifications.

Typically, one BAR (later changed to two) was issued to each nine-man Army infantry squad and assigned to the squad's best marksman. The gunner was aided by an assistant who carried extra ammunition and helped with reloading. As used by the Marines, a thirteen-man squad consisted of three fire teams, each assigned to a BAR.

All men in each squad were trained to fire the BAR in the event that the designated gunner was killed or wounded. Multiple BARs were assigned to each squad because of the weapon's short, twenty-round firing cycle. One group fired until its magazine was empty, and then the second or third group would open fire while the first reloaded.

While the Army replaced the BAR as its main automatic weapon in 1954, the rifle later gained wide public exposure when it appeared in the 1998 film *Saving Private Ryan.* Fifteen BARs were used in the making of that picture. ★

or four feet over your head. If you couldn't see any of them it wouldn't matter so much, but the fact that you could see them took something out of you.

We got through that night and we were going to go up and take the hill that I talked about. The Japanese had been there maybe a year, digging fortifications. We were walking along those fortifications and one guy said,

"Sargent, come up here, I want to show you something." And there were I don't know how many dead Japanese; they had laid in the sun for two or three days. And what happens when the body lays like that in the sun in 100 degree temperatures, the body expands, and it had broken through their belts and their suits and everything. You always had what you would call social outlaws in an outfit like ours, and one guy came along and opened up the Japanese uniforms and used his bayonet to get their wallets and trinkets, anything to save. We always said our first duty was to collect souvenirs, and these guys collected souvenirs to take back home.

The next day we went up to the top of the hill. I think that our platoon was given the honor of taking the hill because of what we had done previously. One of our "social outlaws" went into the caves where the Japanese kept those guns and he brought out propaganda leaflets, flags, money, everything. He threw the Japanese money up in the air and let the breeze carry it on down. He was the only one who would go into the caves. None of us would go in because we thought they were booby trapped. Then we saw someone, and we assumed he was Japanese, but he was so far away. Someone started shooting at him and he just kept walking, but eventually he toppled over and we asked, "Why shoot someone like that?" And they said, "If you don't shoot them today they will be shooting at you tomorrow." Well, that made a lot of sense didn't it? Those things happened, and you don't think about the morality of it when you are fighting for your life.

We were up there two days and we started back down. There was a road that went along the ocean and there were twenty or thirty of us who rode in trucks. We got to a spot and stopped and waited until the officers came with their maps, and they were pointing up at this hill. When we started up they had placed rope around trees so that we could hold onto the rope and pull ourselves up, because it was so steep and there was so much underbrush. When we got to this opening we saw ten or twenty dead Japanese there. Of course, as far as we were concerned, we saw an enemy and we were going to shoot them. But one of our guys said, "Don't shoot anymore lead into them, they already weigh a ton!"

Then we ran into this blazing brush fire. Over there all the grass is dry. Even if it rained the day before, that grass would be dry like tinder. So we had to run through the fire, and it was all around us. An officer named Goss said to me, "Sargent, we can't be flanked, I want you to go down there to the left," and he pointed down to where there was elephant grass, maybe five foot tall, and he told me to go down there and be their guard. So I went down there and after awhile I looked up and here was this Japanese squad coming up, maybe one hundred yards away, and there were six or seven of them. They were carrying a machine gun, and some of them were carrying carbines. I had been given a Browning automatic rifle, and that was the greatest thing since mother's milk. One BAR man is worth twenty soldiers because you can shoot twenty bullets within seconds, so I aimed at them and emptied the twenty bullets and then I jumped back down. I waited a little while and looked back up and they were still coming, so I stuck another round in and shot twenty more, and then I looked down and little bullets were hitting all around me. It was like in the summertime when you're in the dust and raindrops fall, that's the way it was all around me. And I said to myself, "Those guys are shooting at me!" Well, I knew I had to move, so I went over about ten feet, and they were still shooting, so I shot some more at them. Then I moved over another five feet, and that's what I kept doing; moving back and forth. Then I unloaded another round of twenty shots at them and I discovered that there were no more bullets. I knew that up on the hill, maybe two hundred feet away, was this brush fire, and Goss was up there. He had sent me down there all alone, which was a mistake, I think, but in the heat of battle you make mistakes. On the other hand, I was the only guy dumb enough to go down. I don't think he could have gotten any-one else to go down, but my attitude at that time had been that nothing was going to kill me. So I looked up, and the Japanese were going the other way. They had admitted defeat, and apparently I killed some of them, but I don't know, because I wasn't going to go chase after them. I thought, "I'm a nine-teen-year-old kid, and I'm alive and I didn't expect to be, and they're run-ning away, so I'm going to let them go." So I did.

Well, five minutes later Goss came over and said, "Go over there and help those guys." We had on the side of the hill what you would call a placement of troops. I didn't know any of them, except one guy, and he was Portuguese; five foot two and had arms like a leg, and he lifted his hand up and yelled "I got four of them, I got four of them!" And just like that a piece of shrapnel hit his bicep and took a piece of it out, and he yelled "I'm hit, I'm hit!" Then I looked up and saw a hand come up from behind a bush and I screamed "Grenade, grenade!" I pointed at it and everybody rolled away, and it didn't hurt anybody. Then I threw a grenade and started firing my BAR at where I saw the arm. I was looking around and it felt like a horse hit me. I didn't know what it was, so I waited and felt a tingle and put my arm down and there was blood, and I said, "I'm hit, I'm hit!" The medic came up and said,

"Well, you and everyone else." He told me to go on back, so I got up and I left my weapon. I went back to the battalion aide station and they hooked up a plasma bag, and I started crying.

Finally a truck came and this African American guy came over and said, "Hop up on that truck and let's get the hell out of here." He got behind that wheel and took off and I was holding on for dear life. We went down to Cebu City and they took me into a church, and in there was a big table. They put me on the table and started to examine me. They shook their heads and told me I was very lucky. I was still alive and I was happy.

There were nurses there, and that's the greatest thing, you go three or four months and never see a woman, and here's a nurse all pretty and in white, and that was the biggest morale booster. The next morning they put me on a boat and took me out to Macan Island, which was our airstrip, and flew me to Leyte. I was there about two months, then I went back. I kept trying to find where my outfit was, because for a soldier the strongest urge is to get back to your outfit.

They said my outfit was up this hill, so I started up the hill and saw all these familiar faces that were coming down the hill. They said, "This is our last day of combat." The oddest thing is, in the Pacific the Japanese never surrendered, and we knew that. But I was sitting there with my BAR, looking out two hundred yards and saw a guy walking toward us in a black uniform, very formal dress and it's a Japanese soldier, and he's a high officer. He came up and he stood in front of us and he had his hands out indicating that he wanted to surrender, and in his hands was his pistol.

We kept busy after that, training for the invasion of Japan. We spent about two weeks practicing going off boats into landing craft. By now it was the middle of August, 1945, and I was coming down a hill and I heard an incredible roar, like the entire island shook. They had announced that the Japanese had surrendered.

The next day we learned that they had dropped the bomb and that the Japanese indicated that they would surrender. Our troop ship was out in the bay and we were the only outfit that was ready to leave, so we got on that troop ship and went through Tokyo Bay, right past the USS *Missouri* a day or two before the surrender signing. There must have been two dozen aircraft carriers, two dozen battle ships, and all of the other troop ships there. It was a forest of ships in Tokyo Bay. The day they surrendered they flew bombers overhead for about an hour, one after another while they were signing the document.

AFTER THE WAR...

Mr. Sargent took advantage of the GI Bill after the Army and received his bachelor's degree from Edinboro University, a master's degree from the University of Pittsburgh, and a doctorate from Penn State. He married Mary Conner, and together they raised three sons and a daughter. After teaching for fourteen years, Mr. Sargent helped create the Shenango campus of Penn State. Upon retirement, he became a stockbroker and spent much of his time writing.

☆ George Harker ☆
State College, Pennsylvania

• •

George Harker was a math and science teacher when he went into the Army. He attended Officer Candidate School and was assigned to the Army Signal Company amphibious operations. He landed at Omaha Beach on D-Day.

• •

I graduated from Temple University as a teacher of math and science and saw a chance to go to the University of Pennsylvania and take 350 hours of engineering defense training through a government program. Supposedly there was a shortage of electrical engineers. When I got done with that I got a job with the Philadelphia Electric Company as a screwdriver-and-pliers mechanic in the shop. That got me a year's experience in electrical engineering.

When I went into the Army I was in the 8th Division at Fort Monmouth. It was newly activated and they had a lot of slots for Officer Candidate School, so I filled out application forms and submitted them. Of course, the commanding officer, the general of the 8th Division, denied all the applications because his whole cadre had applied. When my denial was sent to OCS, they crossed it out and said, "You will." So I was in and was automatically made a corporal.

I had gone to college for a while, so I had no problem with OCS because it was just classes and work. They told me, "You qualified for OCS because you are a math and science teacher, and we like to get them for the infantry." I didn't want to go to the infantry, but I did. I went into the 80th, but as part of the signal company. Because I had that one year's experience in electrical engineering they shifted me from the line companies to the Headquarters Company and trained me on teletype, instead of having me crawl through the mud and being a GI.

But they got back at me. When I graduated from OCS my first assignment was to amphibious operations, getting ready for D-Day. When they announced it, everybody wanted out. "I can't swim." "Doesn't matter." Well, the only way you could get out was to go to paratroopers or airborne, and a couple guys went. So I did my basic training with the amphibious down at Fort Pierce, Florida, on the Indian River Delta. They had cut a pathway out to the ocean, and the LCVP's, those are the Higgins boats, would come in, we would climb down a rope ladder into the LCVP, go out in the ocean and circle around, and then come down to the beach and land. Then we would have to dig a hole and set up a switchboard. We did that eight hours on, eight hours off.

When D-Day came, I went in on an APA, that's a Navy-operated ship for personnel. I had radio operators and I had signal people: a radio operator, switchboard operators, and linemen. The message came over the radio that Omaha Beach was in trouble. My radio operators were up there at the radio room listening, and they heard a message come over, saying, "All unnecessary personnel will be held aboard ship." They all thought, "No way." We were seven miles out and the sea was rough. When the back end of the ship went up you could see the whole beach. When the front went up you see the bottom of the ship. I had two seasick men and I had been permitted to offer them the opportunity to not come in. They could've stayed in the ship, but they wanted to come in. My first master sergeant was over forty-five years old and he didn't have to come. He said, "You think I've been in the Army all this time and I don't want to see what combat is?" So, there we go; we all came in together.

We came in near the back end of a destroyer that was over on our left. We weren't too far from the beach but there was sand shooting up two or three feet above the water, coming off the destroyer's propellers. Turned out he was sitting on the bottom, parallel to the beach. He had a front gun and a rear gun with optical sights. So when the ramp went down and we came in onto the beach, there were German machine-gun bullets bouncing off the side of our boat. The first few of my men go off and that machine gun just stopped. Period. What had happened? Did he run out of ammunition? Baloney, I think a five-inch shell from the destroyer got him.

So we landed and the first thing we saw was somebody's barracks bags. Barracks bags! Who in the hell's making an invasion carrying barracks bags? They were thirty inches wide and six inches high. You could hide behind them, but that's about it. Our barracks bags were back on the ship, but somebody's barracks bags were there on the beach. So we started.

There's a thing called shingle. You know how, many times when you go to the beach, you have to walk through this very coarse sand before you get into the water? That's shingle. The Germans had raked it, so it was six to eight feet high. And there were stones three or four inches in diameter, and they were piled up, too. If you'd try to drive a jeep over that, your wheels would spin and you'd be bellied up there, stuck. If you tried to drive a tank over it, your wheels would spin, spit all the stones out the back side, and you'd be bellied. The shingle was very effective in keeping motorized stuff from getting off the beach. You had to clear it, first of all with a bulldozer, and then you could go off.

There were men lying on that shingle, shaking so hard that the stones rattled. They had no control over their arms or their legs or their head. They were just scared stiff, only not stiff; just scared. You could kick them, do whatever you wanted; yell at them, and they'd lie there and shake. We went past them and came up to the back end of a mounted twin .50-caliber machine gun. Well, there was a gunner right there and he was strapped in place. The top of his head was gone, and his helmet was gone. Not a very effective gunner. We just kept going.

Before we left England, we had been given some practice putting this launcher on the end of your rifle and putting a grenade over the launcher. You'd put a special cartridge in your gun and shoot it and the grenade would launch. We had fired two or three dummies in practice. That day two guys had them on their rifles and they were carrying three live rounds. Well, the first round they fired went way over somewhere, so they corrected it. The second one went right down a hole that had some Germans in it, but it didn't explode. Two Germans came out, laid down flat and it still didn't explode. Then the two Germans came back and threw the grenade out of the hole. It turned out you had to take this damn wire off before you fired it, and they were so excited they didn't take the damn wire off and so it was a dummy.

We had landed almost in the middle of the beach and then went east, which is where we were supposed to be. There were wounded and dead lying on either side of my path, and you had to duck under barbed wire as you went. I was supposed to report to the group which came in the first wave, with the 37th Engineers. I went to the senior, and they had just had a round hit. The lieutenant was talking to the sergeant, and this piece of ammunition landed on his shoulders and vaporized him. Vaporized him all over the lieutenant and all over the surrounding area, and the shrapnel had gone off to the side and the junior signal lieutenant had been injured. They evacuated him later in the day. Well, there was no point trying to talk to this guy, he was in total shock, so I spoke to the sergeant in charge of the switchboard and told him we had landed and we were supposed to set up a lateral from his switchboard to our lateral switchboard.

I went back down the path and heard this fellow over in the minefield calling, "Medic!" I met a medical officer I knew who was checking wounded soldiers to see if they were dead. If the fellow was dead, he'd put a tag on him, "Dead." If he was injured he'd go with morphine, and so forth. I said to him, "What about that guy out in the field?" He said, "If he's got enough energy to call for a medic, he doesn't need attention now. These guys who are quiet need attention."

I went on down and joined my men and we went several hundred feet and decided to take a rest. The tide had begun to recede and there was room between the shingle and the water where most of the ground was flat. As I was going I saw a tank up on top of the shingle, towing a trailer, and the stupid guy bellied, and couldn't go anywhere. Well, I think there was a spotter up on a hill because not too long after that, in came some ammunition. When it came down it landed in the sand. The sand was relatively soft, and it went down about eighteen inches into the ground before it exploded. But one of the rounds landed on the shingle and exploded immediately, and all the shrapnel came out just six or eight inches above the sand. One man who was closest to the shingle caught the whole bit. My master sergeant, who was thirty-two years old and had been the manager of an A&P store in St. Louis, came over and said, "Lieutenant, I think we've lost a man." Then he showed me that a piece of shrapnel had just hit his wristwatch so the watch caught the shrapnel, not his wrist. If the shrapnel had hit his wrist, he might have lost his hand. I went back with him to see this fellow who had been hit. We took a peek, saw who he was, and I turned to go back to say, "Let's go on." I think I just had about enough at that point because I blacked out.

I left the beach in December. When I got home I had a thirty-day leave, and then I went back to Fort Monmouth to get ready to go to Japan. But then they dropped the atomic bombs, and it was an unconditional surrender. I was living in Camp Edison, just south of Fort Monmouth. Camp Edison was a designated discharge center. I had the points, so I got discharged. I got paid for my terminal leave and I was out and on my way on the October 10, 1945. My father had died while I was overseas, and my mother had taken off. My aunt and uncle down on the farm wanted to see me so I went home to Laconia, New Hampshire.

When I look back on it, I think that war is not the great thing that Patton made it out to be. He loved it, however. He had a purpose and he served that purpose. But you don't settle a damn thing with a gun, all you do is kill people.

AFTER THE WAR . . .

Just after enlisting in 1942, George Harker married Janet Collins. Following his service, he completed his Ph.D in experimental psychology at the University of Iowa. He then worked for the Department of Defense at the U.S. Army Medical Research Laboratory at Fort Knox, Kentucky, for twenty-three years designing improved equipment and training practices. Dr. Harker retired in 1973 as director of the laboratory's Psychology Division and then taught psychology at the University of Louisville. The Harkers raised three children. Dr. Harker passed away in 2006.

☆ Francis Miller ☆

Lancaster, Pennsylvania

••

Francis Miller served as a gunner on B-17 bombing missions over Germany, which included several near-misses. On one occasion, his damaged plane was forced to land by German fighters and he and his crew were taken prisoner.

••

When the war broke out I was working in civil service in Washington, DC, and I thought, "Darn, I want to be a pilot, and the best way to do that is to take some exams." So I took the tests for the four different branches of the service: the Air Corps, the Navy, the Marines, and the Coast Guard, and I passed everything with flying colors with one exception. I had a spot on my lung which would not permit me to fly at high altitude.

I went on a troop train to Miami Beach for basic training. On the way down it was Thanksgiving and we were to have a big turkey dinner. Well, someone goofed and there wasn't any food on board, so we had to stop at the nearest place, and the sergeant in charge went off and came back with crates of oranges. So that's what we had for Thanksgiving.

I wanted to enter flight school and had my first airplane ride. I learned how to operate a machine gun and how to parachute out of a plane and so forth. I also went to radio school and learned things about the radio which I didn't know before. From Miami Beach we took a troop train to Sioux Falls, South Dakota. It was 80 degrees in Miami and 35 below when we got to Sioux Falls. We were put into barracks there and I went to radio school. That was for three or four months. There were approximately three hundred people in that school. I was in the top twenty of the graduates of the school, and those people became eligible for commissions. I was sent into the room for an interview and I was chewing gum, and I'm sure that's a no-no, so I flunked out.

While we were at Sioux Falls a sergeant came to the barracks and said we needed recruits to go to flight school . . . you, you, and you. Well, the whole barracks went to Tyndall Field, Florida, for training in gunnery. After gunnery school we went off to Pyote, Texas, to meet our new crew. That's where we got together and flew short missions; flights over Texas. We went from Pyote to Dalhart, Texas, and learned all the basic things about flying and shooting machine guns.

I got airsick every time I went up, but I didn't get airsick flying in combat because I was flying at a high altitude and it didn't affect me. But after our flights we had to go to the shack and get a bucket and mop and clean up the plane. On one occasion I was lying on a radio floor, just so sick that I wanted to die, and a tail gunner came up and stooped over. He had a bologna sandwich with mayonnaise on it, and he asked me if I'd like to have a bite. Well, later on in our journey through life we went across the seas in a boat and Joe, the tail gunner, got seasick; I didn't. You can imagine what I asked him if he wanted.

When it was time to go overseas we went to the Jersey Shore and took off from there on the *Queen Elizabeth*. We were unescorted, but it was a fast ship, so we did evasive action the whole way over. It was a stormy trip and a lot of times the boat was rolling, and a lot of people got seasick. It was not a trip you'd want to take every day, that's for sure. We landed in Southampton, then we took a troop train to our base at Kimbolton in the southern part of England.

Our first mission was to Osnabruck, Germany. We were all apprehensive, but everything went just fine. We had some enemy fire and some flak came up, but it didn't harm us. On the way back we were talking about the milk run we had just been on. We were over the English Channel and all of a sudden two engines on the one side went out, for whatever reason I don't know, so we had to seek the nearest base. We were too far away to get back to our home base, so we headed for the nearest airbase, but unfortunately we were dropping in altitude too fast, and up ahead the pilot saw a plowed field and we headed for that. As he banked the B-17 he came down in a little too low and hit the chimney of a house and knocked part of his wing off. That pushed him over into a telephone pole, and he knocked part of the other wing off. So we landed at kind of an angle, going I'd say, 130 miles an hour. It was quite a trip. And we didn't know what would happen because when it did stop several of the engines were smoking. We got out of there in a hurry. The next day they sent a plane down for us and we went back to the base. The morning after that we were flying our second mission.

Outside of the crash-landing on our first flight we had several other incidents. Around the fifth mission we took off and it was dark. Usually it was daylight, but we had a long way to go; we were going to Berlin. In the formation of the B-17s over the airport three of the planes crashed together, landed on the runway and hit another plane taking off. We were to be the next plane to take off. That mission was aborted for that day.

I had another near-miss around January 5, 1944. I was called from the barracks and asked if I wanted to be an operator on another crew because the radio operator was in the hospital with frostbite. I said, "Sure," because you wanted to finish as many missions as you could as soon as possible and get home. So I got my gear, got into a jeep, went out to the plane, got my radio equipment all ready and was all set to take off, and up came a jeep from the hospital with the regular radioman on board. Well, naturally he would bump me because that was his crew. I was a little disgusted because I had gotten out of bed so early, but I went back to the barracks. I no sooner strolled into my bunk and covered up that I heard this terrific boom. The plane that I was to be in took off and it banked too hard and hit a gun emplacement. It had a full bomb load and it exploded, and everyone on board was killed. That was pretty close, I would say.

Another time we were on our way to Braunschweig and it was 10/10ths cloud, which means that it was really cloudy. In other words, you couldn't see your face in front of you. We were into the bomb run, ready to drop the bombs, when suddenly a bomb from one of the planes above us dropped down and hit our plane. It hit the winch bar at the fuselage and weakened the wing. It knocked out number three engine and it crippled us, so we dropped our bomb load and dropped out of formation and headed for home. We were losing altitude at about the rate of forty feet a minute, so we kept dropping our ammunition and whatever else we could. It was about one o'clock in the afternoon. The clouds had cleared, it was sunny, and there were six German FW190s all around us. We fought with them—we had ammunition left—and we got one of the planes, but then we signaled that we would land. We were only at about four hundred feet at the time, and the international signal for surrendering is you drop your wheels to indicate you're going to land. As soon as they drew back the pilot pulled up the wheels and headed for Belgium because he thought it was only about ten miles away. Well, we didn't make it. They swarmed back over us and we landed in a plowed field on a beautiful day. As soon as we landed the planes that were pursuing us started to strafe us. They were upset because we said we would land and we didn't. So all of us were wounded at that time. A piece of 20-millimeter hit me in the head and I had a wound in my knee and one in my finger. As we got out of the plane there were German farmers around with shotguns which they held to our heads. They were asking us to surrender, which we did. My wounds were not bad enough to send me to the hospital, but four of the troops did have to go to the hospital. Then the regular German Army showed up and they took control. Otherwise, we might have been shot.

Then the Red Cross nurses showed up and were working on our wounds. The right tail gunner had—they counted them—fifty-four holes in him, and one was through his penis, so he was not in good shape. The soldiers rounded us up, put us on a truck, and took us to the nearest town, which was Borthen, and put us into jail. I'm not sure how long we were there, but I know we didn't get much to eat. We found some raw potatoes in the jail and we ate them. Then we were put on a train to go to Frankfurt, which was the interrogation center. That's where we were questioned and of course, all we gave was our name, rank, and serial number. They said they didn't need that since they had all the information they needed from the plane.

As prisoners we all had the same experience; we'd have some lieutenant question us and he'd say, "Well, that's not good enough." Then he'd send me back to the jail and someone else would show up. That continued for several days, but we got used to it. We knew that was going to happen, and we just told him the same story, that we didn't know anything. They took our pictures and gave us our prison tickets; a piece of metal with our prison number on it. We were at the interrogation center for two or three days, then they loaded us into a forty-and-eight, we call them; the boxcars. They were named after World War I, for the forty men who were in one end of the thing, and eight horses in the other end. We were stuffed in there and sent to a camp in East Prussia. On our trip we stopped overnight in Berlin, and that night the English came over to bomb Berlin, so it wasn't much fun. We continued from there to Camp Number 4, called Gross Tychow, in Poland. It was pretty cold all the time.

One of our crew, Tom Stapleton, a ball-turret operator, was assigned as one of four men to escape. The only part I played was that I was called a "lookout man." When his name was called at roll call, which they had every morning and every evening, I was supposed to get to his place and say "Here," when his name was called, and rush back to my unit and say "Here," when my name was called. That continued for about two days, and then they discovered that these four men had escaped. The story on them is that they were out for about three days and they were captured and put in jail.

The prison camp held about 6,400 men and it had four different compounds. We were in barracks that held twenty men to a room, and those rooms were about twenty feet by twenty feet. There were five rooms on each side of the barracks and there was a long hallway in the center where we sat and read, or whatever. There was a table in the middle of the room where we sat to eat, and there was a small potbellied stove near the door where we would toast our German bread.

While I was there I had a Christmas I'll never forget. Christmas Eve they let us out of the barracks. Usually the lights would go out in the barracks at nine o'clock. But on Christmas Eve they let us out at about nine at night, and we walked around the perimeter of the prison camp arm in arm, singing carols. The Germans in the towers even waved to us and it was really nice, and they let us stay out till midnight. So we were outside from nine to midnight in the snow singing Christmas carols. It was very nice.

I was there for seven months and then they loaded us into boxcars again and sent us south to near Nuremberg, where they put us into Camp Number 13D. The food there was terrible, and it was the Red Cross parcels that kept us going. They were wonderful. If we hadn't had those we would have starved. The bad part about that camp was that it was near Nuremberg, and the British would come over almost every night and make raids. Some of their bombs would be pretty close to our camp, so it was very upsetting.

In March 1945 we left there to get on the road once again. We had a twelve-day hike to our next camp at Mooseburg on the southern border of Germany. That was a huge camp. They had thousands of prisoners there; a lot of Russians, a lot of English, and a lot of Americans. I was there only about a month when we were liberated by General Patton. I remember him standing on the back of a tank, and he was swearing at the jeep in front of him. I got to see his pearl-handled pistols. I was within six feet of him at one time. We were very happy to see our liberators arrive.

Then it was a matter of getting us back to civilization. We took trucks to the nearest airport where there they put us on a plane and flew us to France to a recuperation camp called Lucky Strike. We stayed there for a month in the open air in tents, and it was really nice. I gained back the forty pounds I had lost in the prison camps. We were at Camp Lucky Strike for at least a month. They didn't let us out of that camp because they wanted to make sure we got the proper nourishment.

From there we went to La Havre, where they loaded us on the USS *Argentina*, which was a hospital ship, for the trip back to the states. After we got back to the States we were given sixty-day leave and of course, I went home and met my family again and rejoiced with them.

Today the war is so far behind us that young people have forgotten about it. I don't blame them for that, because there were other wars; the Vietnam War and so forth. I do think though, that every man should be in the service for at least a year. The discipline he receives there is invaluable whether he goes into the service or goes on and makes another career for himself. I learned to be cooperative and be nice to other people.

AFTER THE WAR . . .

After the war, Francis Miller went to work for RCA for thirty-three years before retiring in 1981. He and his wife, Bertie, have been married for forty-seven years. They have three children and six grandchildren. Mr. Miller likes to spend time with his family, attending plays, playing bridge, and squeezing in a little golf every now and then.

☆ MAPS ☆

THE EUROPEAN THEATER
1942–1945

NORWAY • Oslo
SWEDEN • Stockholm
FINLAND • Helsinki

Baltic Sea
ESTONIA
Riga • LATVIA
LITHUANIA
E. PRUSSIA
Moscow ★
SOVIET UNION

North Sea
DENMARK • Copenhagen
GREAT BRITAIN
NETH.
Amsterdam
Berlin ★
GERMANY
Cologne
Warsaw ★
POLAND

IRELAND
London ★

BELGIUM
Normandy • Bastogne
English Channel
Paris
FRANCE
SWITZ.
Munich
Pilsen
CZECHOSLOVAKIA
Vienna ★
AUSTRIA
Budapest ★
HUNGARY
ROMANIA
Bucharest ★

Atlantic Ocean
Bay of Biscay
ITALY
YUGOSLAVIA
Adriatic Sea
Black Sea

PORTUGAL
Madrid ★
SPAIN
Rome ★
Anzio
ALBANIA
BULGARIA
GREECE
TURKEY

Bizerte
Algiers • Tunis
Tripoli
Mediterranean Sea
CYPRUS

MOROCCO
TUNISIA
ALGERIA
LIBYA
Cairo ★
EGYPT

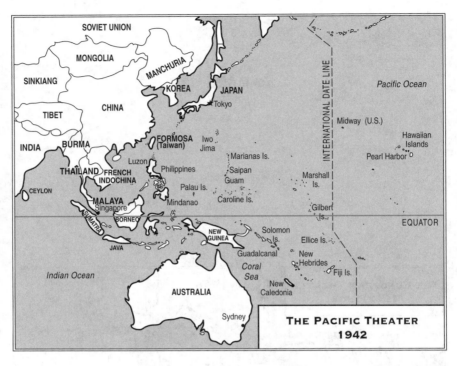

THE PACIFIC THEATER
1942

SOVIET UNION

MONGOLIA

MANCHURIA

SINKIANG

KOREA

JAPAN

Tokyo

CHINA

TIBET

INDIA

BURMA

FORMOSA
(Taiwan)

Iwo
Jima

THAILAND

FRENCH
INDOCHINA

Luzon

Philippines

Marianas Is.

Saipan

Guam

CEYLON

MALAYA

Palau Is.

Singapore

Mindanao

Caroline Is.

SUMATRA

BORNEO

JAVA

NEW
GUINEA

Solomon
Is.

Guadalcanal

Coral
Sea

AUSTRALIA

New
Caledonia

Sydney

Indian Ocean

INTERNATIONAL DATE LINE

Pacific Ocean

Midway (U.S.)

Hawaiian
Islands

Pearl Harbor

Marshall
Is.

Gilbert
Is.

EQUATOR

Ellice Is.

New
Hebrides

Fiji Is.

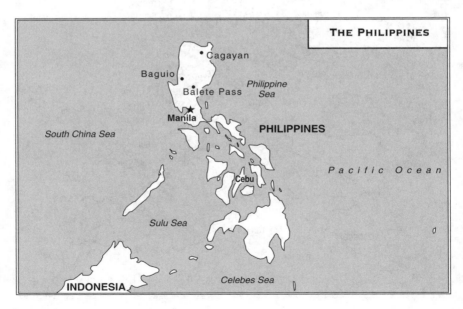

THE PHILIPPINES

Cagayan

Baguio

Philippine
Sea

Balete Pass

Manila

PHILIPPINES

South China Sea

Pacific Ocean

Cebu

Sulu Sea

INDONESIA

Celebes Sea

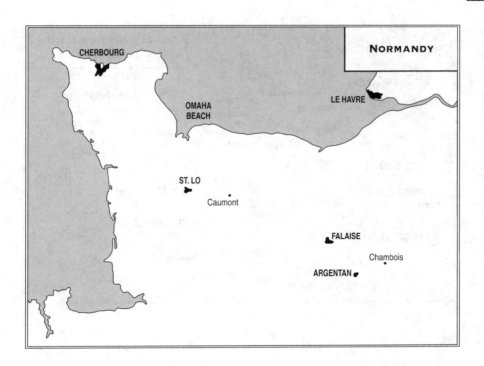

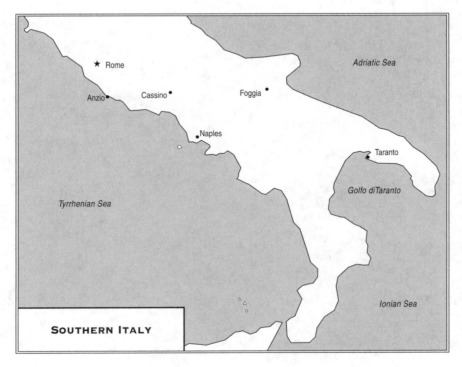

☆ BIBLIOGRAPHY ☆

BALETE PASS

Bell, Walter F., compr. *The Philippines in World War II, 1941–1945: A Chronology and Select Annotated Bibliography of Books and Articles in English (Bibliographies and Indexes in Military Studies)*. Westport, CT: Greenwood Press, 1999.

Salazar, Generoso P. *World War II in North Luzon, Philippines, 1941–1945*. Quezon City: University of the Philippines Printery, 1992.

On-line transcript of official U.S. Army history. *The War in the Pacific: Triumph in the Philippines*, by Robert Ross Smith, Chapter XXVII: The Bambang Front—II; The 25th Division on Route 5: www.ibiblio.org/hyperwar /USA/USA-P-Triumph/USA-P-Triumph-27.html

BED-CHECK CHARLIE

Brewer, James F. *China Airlift: The Hump, China's Aerial Lifeline*. Nashville: Turner Publishing, 1992.

Nickl, Ferdinand. Peragimus: *"We Accomplish": A Brief History of the 358th Infantry* [Regiment of the 9th Infantry Division]. Weiden, Germany: U.S. Army, 1945.

Schrivers, Peter. *The Crash of Ruin: American Combat Soldiers in Europe During World War II*. New York: New York University Press, 1998.

Zaslow, Harry. *A Teenager's Journey in War and Peace*. Bloomington, IN: Authorhouse, 2006.

BENJAMIN O. DAVIS

Davis, Benjamin O., Jr. *Benjamin O. Davis Jr., American: An Autobiography*. Washington, DC: Smithsonian Institution Press, 1991, 2000.

BLACK SHEEP SQUADRON

Walton, Frank E. *Once They Were Eagles: The Men of the Black Sheep Squadron* (paperback). Lexington: The University Press of Kentucky, 1996
"'Pappy' Boyington a black sheep no longer" [Associated Press article], *San Francisco Chronicle*, Sunday, February 10, 2008, page A-2.

BOUGAINVILLE ISLAND

Ramsdell, Lorraine, JO1, USNR. *Bougainville*. Washington, DC: Navy & Marine Corps World War II Commemorative Committee, Navy Office of Information (CHINFO), The Pentagon, Room 2E352, Washington, DC 20350–1200, n.d.
Gailey, Harry A. *Bougainville*. Lexington, KY: The University Press of Kentucky, 1991.

BROWNING AUTOMATIC RIFLE

Browning, John, and Curt Gentry. *John M. Browning: American Gunmaker*. Morgan, UT: Browning, 1994.
Hogg, Ian V., and John Weeks. *Military Small Arms of the 20th Century*. 7th ed. Iola, WI: KP Books, 2000.
Smith, Joseph E., and W. H. B. Smith. *Small Arms of the World*. Harrisburg, PA: The Stackpole Co., 1943 and 1945. (Also note: 11th edition published 1977)

DRAGON'S TEETH FORTIFICATIONS

"Dragon's Teeth in Siegfried Line Easily Visible," International News Service article by Larry Newman, published in *New Castle (Pa.) News*, Wednesday, December 20, 1944, page 12
"Push Through Siegfried Line Dragon's Teeth," International News Service photo published in *Uniontown (Pa.) Morning Herald*, Saturday, February 24, 1945, page 2.

"Russ Drive Will Reveal if Eastwall is Real Thing," International News Service article by Pierre J. Huss, published in *Connellsville (Pa.) Courier*, Thursday, January 25, 1945, page 5.

"Dragon's Teeth in Nazi Defense Pulled With TNT" [Associated Press article] *Muscatine* (Iowa) *Journal and News-Tribune*, Wednesday, March 28, 1945, page 7

"EIGHTY-EIGHTS" GERMAN ARTILLERY

Hogg, Ian V. *German Artillery of World War Two*. 2nd corrected edition. Mechanicsburg, PA: Stackpole Books, 1997.

"The New 88 and Its Carriages," article published in *Intelligence Bulletin*, January 1945, Vol. 3 No. 5. Text available at http://www.lonesentry.com new88mm/index.html

U.S. military intelligence report of February 1943: http://efour4ever.com 88.htm

EXERCISE TIGER

Ambrose, Stephen E. *D-Day, June 6, 1944: The Climactic Battle of World War II*. New York: Simon & Schuster, 1994.

Lewis, Nigel. *Exercise Tiger: The Dramatic True Story of a Hidden Tragedy of World War II*. Upper Saddle River, N.J.: Prentice-Hall Professional Technical Reference, 1990.

Small, Ken, and Mark Rogerson. *The Forgotten Dead: Why 946 American Servicemen Died Off The Coast of Devon in 1944 & The Man Who Discovered Their True Story*. London: Bloomsbury, 1988.

"The Tragedy of Exercise Tiger," *Navy Medicine* 85, No. 3 (May–June 1994): 5–7.

www.exercisetiger.org

www.mikekemble.com/ww2/tiger1.html

FALAISE GAP

Parrish, Thomas, ed. *Encyclopedia of World War II*. New York: Simon & Schuster, 1978. www.americainwwii.com/stories/trap.html

GUADALCANAL

Coggins, Jack. *The Campaign for Guadalcanal: A Battle That Made History*. New York: Doubleday, 1972.

Griffith, Samuel B., II. *The Battle for Guadalcanal*. Philadelphia: J. B. Lippincott, 1963.

Hammel, Eric. *Guadalcanal: Decision at Sea*. New York: Crown Publishers, 1988.

HALF-TRACKS

Mesko, Jim. *M3 Half-track in Action Armor*. No. 34. Carrollton, TX: Squadron/Signal Publications, 1996.

Georgano, G.N. *World War II Military Vehicles: Transport & Halftracks*. London: Osprey Publishing, 1994.

INVASION OF TULAGI

Griffith, Brig. Gen. Samuel B. *The Battle for Guadalcanal*. Philadelphia: Lippincott, 1963.

Rottman, Gordon L. *World War II Pacific Island Guide: A Geo-Military Study*. Westport, CT: Greenwood Press, 2002.

www.history.army.mil/brochures/72-8/72-8.htm

www.history.Navy.mil/photos/events/wwii-pac/guadlcnl/guad-1c.htm

LSTS

Parrish, Thomas, ed. *Encyclopedia of World War II*. New York: Simon & Schuster, 1978.

Rottman, Gordon L. *Landing Ship, Tank (LST): 1942–2002*. London: Osprey Publishing, 2005.

LCI(L)S

Rottman, Gordon L. *U.S. World War II Amphibious Tactics: Army and Marine Corps, Pacific Theater*. London: Osprey Publishing, 2004.

———. *USS LCI—Landing Craft Infantry*. Paducah, KY: Turner Publishing, 1995.

USS Landing Craft Infantry Association (Navy veterans)
http://www.usslci.com/index.html

MONTE CASSINO

Ellis, John. *Cassino: The Hollow Victory*. New York: McGraw-Hill, 1984.
Hapgood, David, and David Richardson. *Monte Cassino*. New York: Congdon & Weed, 1984.

NURSES

Brayley, Martin J. *World War II Allied Nursing Services*. London: Osprey Publishing, 2002.
"Nurses Speeding Enrollments in the Red Cross: Need 50,000 in First Reserve; Response is 'Magnificent'." Article in *Piqua (Ohio) Daily Call*, Wednesday, February 11, 1942, p. 4

TBF AVENGERS

Parrish, Thomas, ed. *Encyclopedia of World War II*. New York: Simon & Schuster, 1978.
Swanborough, Gordon, and Peter M. Bowers. *United States Navy Aircraft since 1911*. London: Naval Institute Press, 1990.
www.acepilots.com/planes/avenger.html

TUSKEGEE AIRMEN

Blum, John M. *V Was for Victory: Politics and American Culture During World War II*. New York: Harcourt Brace Jovanovich, 1976.
Sandler, Stanley. *Segregated Skies: All-Black Combat Squadrons of WWII*. Washington, DC: Smithsonian History of Aviation Series, 1998
www.geocities.com/wmaxwell/racism1.html#N_8_
www.nationalmuseum.af.mil/factsheets/factsheet.asp?id=1356
"On Freedom's Wings: Bound for Glory, The Legacy of the Tuskegee Airmen," documentary commissioned by the Pennsylvania Veterans' Museum, Media Armory, 12 East State St., Media, PA 19063; 610-566-0788; info@paveteransmuseum.org

☆ INDEX ☆

☆ ABOUT THE AUTHORS ☆

Brian Lockman, president and chief executive officer of PCN—the Pennsylvania Cable Network, is the host of the weekly television series, *PA Books*, as well as host of the PCN Call-in Program. He joined the network in 1994 after fifteen years at C-SPAN, where he served as vice president of operations. A native of Norwood, Pennsylvania, he is the son of Felix Lockman, who served in Burma with the First Air Commandos during the Second World War. He is the author of three previous books, including *World War II: In Their Own Words*, published in 2005 by Stackpole Books.

Dan Cupper, a railroader who is also a historian and author, has written ten books on railroad, highway, and Pennsylvania history topics. A native of Lewistown, Pennsylvania, he is the son of Ralph C. Cupper, a World War II combat-decorated veteran, who as an eighteen-year-old with the Army's Seventh Division, 32nd Infantry Regiment, won a Purple Heart after taking a bullet during the invasion of Okinawa in the spring of 1945. Dan and his wife Shirley live in suburban Harrisburg.

Ken Wolensky is a historian, author, and frequent speaker on industrial, labor, political, and social history. He has published numerous articles and books on these topics, serves as a historian for the Pennsylvania Historical and Museum Commission and is on the faculty of Penn State University.